MW00587574

To:

_____

From:

_____

Message:

_____

_____

_____

_____

Published by Christian Art Publishers
PO Box 1599, Vereeniging, 1930, RSA

© 2023
First edition 2023

Designed by Christian Art Publishers
Cover designed by Christian Art Publishers

Images used under license from Shutterstock.com

Scripture quotations marked NLT are taken from the Holy Bible, New Living Translation,
copyright © 1996, 2004, 2015 by Tyndale House Foundation.
Used by permission of Tyndale House Publishers, Carol Stream, Illinois 60188.
All rights reserved.

Scripture quotations marked NIV are taken from the Holy Bible,
New International Version®, NIV® Copyright © 1973, 1978, 1984, 2011 by Biblica, Inc.®
Used by permission. All rights reserved worldwide.

Scripture quotations marked ESV are taken from the Holy Bible, English Standard Version®.
ESV® Text Edition: 2016. Copyright © 2001 by Crossway, a publishing ministry
of Good News Publishers. Used by permission. All rights reserved.

Scripture quotations marked AMP are taken from the Amplified® Bible (AMP),
Copyright © 2015 by The Lockman Foundation. Used by permission. www.Lockman.org

Scripture quotations marked NASB are taken from the New American Standard Bible®
(NASB), Copyright © 1960, 1962, 1963, 1968, 1971, 1972, 1973, 1975, 1977, 1995 by
The Lockman Foundation. Used by permission. www.Lockman.org

Scripture quotations marked MSG are taken from The Message,
copyright © 1993, 1994, 1995, 1996, 2000, 2001, 2002 by Eugene H. Peterson.
Used by permission of NavPress. All rights reserved.

Scripture quotations marked NKJV are taken from the New King James Version®.
Copyright © 1979, 1980, 1982 by Thomas Nelson, Inc. Used by permission.
All rights reserved.

Scripture quotations marked KJV are taken from the Holy Bible, King James Version,
and are in the public domain.

Printed in China

ISBN 978-0-638-00044-3 Faux Leather
ISBN 978-0-638-00045-0 Hardcover

23 24 25 26 27 28 29 30 31 32 – 10 9 8 7 6 5 4 3 2 1

LIVE
free

Dalene Reyburn

CHRISTIAN ART
PUBLISHERS

Contents

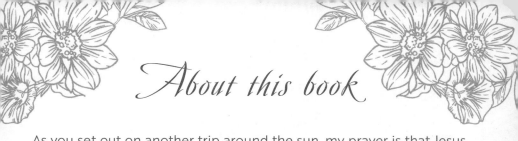

About this book

As you set out on another trip around the sun, my prayer is that Jesus would use the truth of His Word and the ideas on these pages to lead you into a deeper understanding of the life He died to secure for you. Whatever your season or circumstances, may these daily devotions, questions, prayers, and journaling prompts challenge, inspire and encourage you as you discover more of the boundless freedom of the God who breaks chains.

Over the course of the year, we'll consider twelve different kinds of freedom. You can check the Contents to see all twelve themes.

Each week, we'll keep to a rhythm I hope you'll find accessible and effective. Days one through five include a Scripture and related devotional thought. Day six offers questions drawn from the themes covered in the five preceding devotions. These can be used for personal or group study. Day seven focuses on applying the comfort or conviction found in the devotions, to prayer and journaling.

At the back of the book is a handy Bible reading plan. If you want to read the Bible in a year, then this will help you achieve your goal.

May the truth set you free, and may you be free indeed.

In His grace-grip,

Dalene

DAY 1

Free indeed

'So if the Son sets you free, you will be free indeed.'
John 8:36, NIV

When the gospel of Jesus Christ arrests our hearts and we surrender to the truth of it, the immediate and glorious consequence is freedom.

We're set free from sin. We're set free from the cruel whip of impossible law-keeping. We're set free from fear of the past, present and future – which can hold us captive with regret, stress, and uncertainty. We're set free to become who God created us to be. We're set free to enter a love relationship with our King and Savior, to flourish in our gifting and follow Him into His purposes for us and the world at large. We're set free to love others, giving our time, talents, and treasures to see God's Kingdom come. We're set free to learn and to fail and to learn some more, secure in who our Father says we are. We're free to rest. We're free to dream.

As we journey together through a new year iridescent with possibility, we'll explore all these marvelous freedoms. May you be galvanized to emulate Jesus in action and attitude. May you catch a glimpse of the way forward through whatever you face, even if all you can see is the very next step. May your hope be replenished. May your joy be unleashed.

I pray that from the spacious place of freedom in Christ, you would step into your full potential, so those coming after you might find the world different – and better – for the glory of God.

Freedom foundation

Fear of the LORD is the foundation of wisdom.
Knowledge of the Holy One results in good judgment.
Proverbs 9:10, NLT

The quest for greater freedom starts with the fear of the Lord. To choose freedom over captivity – to choose to live liberated from the slavery of self, sin and all the trappings of society – we need the extraordinary wisdom and good judgment of God. Our tiny brains simply don't have what it takes to choose wisely and well. And wisdom begins with fearing God: coming before Him in awe and reverently surrendering to Him every influence and opportunity, every part of ourselves and our psyches.

Put another way: if we want to *rock* at life, we need to go to the *source* of all life: Yahweh. Fearing Him leads to wisdom. Wisdom will teach us how to live well. And living well will set us free.

But it doesn't end there. Fear of the Lord also defeats every other fear. Fear of the Lord is the answer to our fear of the future, fear of our own inadequacies, and fear of what others have done or might do to us. When we fear God first and foremost – when we give Him rightful place in our lives as Lord (not just Savior) and when we're happy to embrace the King (not just the Kingdom) – we gain perspective. We see life the way our perfectly wise, loving, and powerful God sees it. Fear dissipates. Faith develops. Today, may God begin to increase your faith and your fearlessness, by teaching you how to fear Him.

DAY 3

Real deal free

For you have been called to live in freedom,
my brothers and sisters. But don't use
your freedom to satisfy your sinful nature. Instead,
use your freedom to serve one another in love.
Galatians 5:13, NLT

The word *freedom* conjures up fantastic images for me. Usually there's a beach and a big sky, and I've got all day. This fits the dictionary definition of freedom ('the power to act, speak, or think without externally imposed restraints; immunity from obligation'), because in Western culture being *free* has nothing to do with communal responsibility. Quite the opposite. It's about aspiring to absolute individuality and self-determination. It's about doing what we like, when and where and how we like, and with whom we like doing it. It means not feeling forced to do anything we *don't* like doing. It means being free to sleep late. Or sleep around. It means being free to spend as much money as we like, on whatever we like.

We tend to be entitled when it comes to this kind of freedom, believing we deserve it, and indignantly complaining when it's withheld. One commentator writes, 'Freedom has come to represent the individual's right to determine his or her own destiny with little or no regard for the corresponding destinies of those around them.'

The good news is that God calls us to a deeper, wider, *better* freedom, because freedom without purpose is really just slavery to self. The freedom God calls us to is all about what's best for those around us, and ultimately best for us too. May God set you free to reach beyond yourself to unlock others with His love.

Chain-free choice

'Go back to Pharaoh,' the Lord commanded Moses.
'Tell him, "This is what the Lord, the God of the Hebrews, says:
Let My people go, so they can worship Me."'
Exodus 9:1, NLT

God's miraculous rescue of the Hebrews from Egypt is humankind's archetype of freedom. The Hebrew word for Egypt is *mitzrayim*. It means *constriction*. Egypt represented extreme bondage to God's people, and their eventual escape represented ultimate freedom.

But the marvelous freedom God granted them was more than just a sigh of relief. It wasn't a vacation. Their newfound freedom was indivisibly linked to their purpose and responsibility.

There are two words for *freedom* in Hebrew: *chofesh* (the freedom to do what you like) and *cherut* (the freedom to do what you should). *Chofesh* is the slave-turned-free-spirit, unaccountable and unrestrained by anything and anyone. *Cherut* is the covenant freedom the Israelites were given at the time of the Exodus. A commentator writes, 'God's message to Pharaoh was clearly one of *cherut*: "Let My people go *that they might worship Me.*" However, He did not desire that His people simply transfer their slavish obedience from Pharaoh to Him. Service to God would be much different than service to the Egyptian king. Deliverance from slavery in Egypt meant the opportunity to choose to be in covenant with the God of the universe. *Cherut* would allow the Israelites to freely bind themselves to God and to His commandments.'

Here's to a life of chain-free, *cherut* freedom: the true freedom we find tethered to the One who created us to live free.

Empty freedom

That's the whole story. Here now is my final conclusion:
Fear God, and obey His commandments ...
Ecclesiastes 12:13, NLT

These words come at the end of a book written by Solomon, a man looking for liberty. He's the *original*, original gangster. He tries to party his way to meaning, purpose and freedom, then realizes disappointedly and with the sobriety of hindsight, 'Wow. That *really* didn't work.' He puts in countless hours of hard graft and reads whole libraries of books but still: no freedom.

Reading Solomon's detailed (meaningless) escapades reminds us that everything we live eventually becomes a story we'll tell. And Solomon seems bent on saving us some valuable time by telling us the stories he's lived, and how he wishes he'd lived them differently. Hence, these closing words: 'That's the whole story. Here now is my final conclusion: Fear God and obey His commands ...' It's dawned on him: he's been searching for the wrong kind of freedom. He found things that *looked* like freedom, but they left him dissatisfied and hungry for more. He was looking for *chofesh* freedom. He wanted to be free to do anything and everything, with anyone, anywhere. He thought freedom would come with euphoric experiences, wealth, and power – the dangerous trifactor of pleasure, possessions, and prestige (1 John 2:16).

But after trying it all, he comes up empty, and with renewed understanding and appreciation that true freedom – *cherut* freedom, and the peace and satisfaction it brings – is found in fearing God. May we learn from his mistakes and misfortunes in this new year, remembering that the fullness of God's presence ushers in freedom enough, and more.

Free to ask yourself:

**These questions are drawn from
themes covered over the past five days.**

- What do you long to be free from, this year?

- What are you most afraid of? How might fearing God eradicate that fear?

- Can you think of a time when you chased after something that promised you freedom, and when you found it, you realized it hadn't set you free at all?

- Read Exodus 14. The Israelites are afraid, and Moses encourages them: 'Don't be afraid. Just stand still and watch the LORD rescue you today. The Egyptians you see today will never be seen again. The LORD Himself will fight for you. Just stay calm.' (Exodus 14:13-14) How can you apply this ancient reassurance to your current situation?

Free to ask God:

FATHER GOD,

I commit this year to You. Have Your way, in me and through me. Teach me about real freedom, and remind me every day: in You, I'm truly free! Please evaporate the fears threatening to drown my joy and resolve, as I seek to fear You in all ways, for all my days. I want to chase lasting freedom that satisfies — not the fake freedom full of promises that leave me hollow and hurting. I freely choose to obey You, living the free life that draws others to You too.

AMEN.

Cosmic giveaway

For the wages of sin is death, but the free gift of God
is eternal life through Christ Jesus our Lord.
Romans 6:23, NLT

Life experience can make us naturally suspicious. We know there's never really a free lunch. There are always strings attached. And most giveaways arm-twist us into giving away our time or money or something else we'd much rather hang onto.

Because of all this, the gospel seems too good to be true. Paul writes to assure us that what God offers – eternal life – is absolutely free to us, even though it was unspeakably expensive to Him, costing Him the life of His Son. A few chapters earlier, Paul writes, 'Don't you see how wonderfully kind, tolerant, and patient God is with you? Does this mean nothing to you? Can't you see that His kindness is intended to turn you from your sin?' (Romans 2:4)

Not only are we suspicious when free stuff is promised, we're also excellent at religion. If we feel bad enough about our sin, we tend to want to work ourselves into a frenzy, to make amends. We invent self-flagellating penances. And yet God's ways are not our ways (Isaiah 55:9). They're deeper, wider, higher, *better*. Instead of punishing us for our sins, or demanding we punish ourselves, He took the punishment for us. Instead of exacting from us impossible, crippling compensation, He sets us completely free from our sin. Free of charge. No strings attached.

Take a moment – and a deep breath – to let the truth of all this settle your soul today. We're the recipients of indescribable, cosmic generosity, and unfathomable love.

Beyond mudpies

All of us used to live that way, following the
passionate desires and inclinations of our sinful nature …
But God is so rich in mercy, and He loved us so much,
that even though we were dead because of our sins,
He gave us life when He raised Christ from the dead.
(It is only by God's grace that you have been saved!)
Ephesians 2:3-5, NLT

Earthside, it's safe to say we'll never fully grasp how glorious God's offer of freedom from sin really is. C. S. Lewis described our inability to recognize or value God's astonishing invitation as being like someone offering a beach holiday – endless summer days of sunshine and sandcastle building – to children who have never left the slum in which they're eking out an existence. The children barely look up at their beach-holiday benefactor. They scarcely acknowledge the generous offer. They decline, saying they'd prefer to keep on making mudpies in filthy alleyways.

If we're honest, this is our story too. We were trapped, making mudpies in slum streets running slick with sin, not knowing that a better life – a freer life – even existed. We didn't know we were trapped and needed rescuing from our poverty of spirit. We weren't looking for an escape. We were quite comfortable with the squelch of sludge between our toes, having grown used to the dull ache of dissatisfaction and disillusionment because, well, *this is life, and this is all there is.*

How incredible that Jesus interrupted our self-centered, sin-bent lives, lovingly leading us into ultimate freedom. His death, resurrection, and relentless pursuit of us drags us from the slums and onto the shores of freedom.

Quench

> Jesus replied, 'Anyone who drinks this water will soon
> become thirsty again. But those who drink the water I give
> will never be thirsty again. It becomes a fresh, bubbling
> spring within them, giving them eternal life.' 'Please, sir,'
> the woman said, 'give me this water! Then I'll never be
> thirsty again, and I won't have to come here to get water.' ...
> Many Samaritans from the village believed in Jesus because
> the woman had said, 'He told me everything I ever did!'
> John 4:13-14, 39, NLT

Imagine you're this woman, wearing shame like a straitjacket you can't get out of. You meet a stranger at the well. He's kind and gentle but He tells it like it is, which startles you. He knows everything you've done, and everything that's been done to you because your culture has made you an object to be used and abused, then tossed. And the stranger offers you *life* – the kind that doesn't leave you wanting. How astonishing that it's exactly because He knows all about your past, that He also knows how desperately you need His living, loving, thirst-slaking sustenance in your future. And it's exactly because He knows all about your past – bringing your pain and your shame into the light – that others are drawn to Him too.

Don't be scared of God's loving exposure of your personal history. He was there as each saga or surprise unfolded. He knows your story by heart. He also knows that perhaps you're tired of living the story you're in, and He longs to offer you a tall glass of freedom.

DAY 11

Freedom news

'The Spirit of the Sovereign LORD is upon Me, for the LORD
has anointed Me to bring good news to the poor. He has
sent Me to comfort the brokenhearted and to proclaim that
captives will be released and prisoners will be freed.'
Isaiah 61:1, NLT

FREE FROM FEAR

In the eighth century BC, the prophet Isaiah announced these good-news words about the coming Messiah. Jesus read this prophecy – *about Himself* – in the synagogue of Nazareth (Luke 4:14-21) when He was on earth, bound in a human body and experiencing human heart-ache firsthand. And this same Jesus, in your twenty-first-century reality, comes in power and love to proclaim freedom over your life and all that your poor, broken, or captive heart has suffered.

You've likely experienced some kind of poverty – if not financial, then spiritual, relational, emotional, or social. You've probably had your heart broken. I'd hazard a guess you know what it is to feel trapped – held captive by something or someone.

Whatever kind of poverty you face, the good news of the Messiah is enough. His presence and provision surround you this very moment. He is mighty to save. He is measurelessly rich, and He does not let His children go begging (Psalm 37:25).

Regardless of who or what has broken your heart, the Messiah was broken for you, so that ultimately you could be healed, whole, and free. Let the psalmist's words soothe you today: 'He heals the broken-hearted and bandages their wounds.' (Psalm 147:3)

And if you feel trapped by your circumstances, know that the Messiah – breaker of chains – fought for your freedom, and won.

Light and easy

> 'Take My yoke upon you. Let Me teach you, because I am
> humble and gentle at heart, and you will find rest for your souls.
> For My yoke is easy to bear, and the burden I give you is light.'
> Matthew 11:29-30, NLT

In his book, *Soundtracks*, Jon Acuff describes how most of us are overthinkers. We're consumed by negative loops blaring on repeat through the corridors of our minds. These broken soundtracks discourage us and even convince us of imminent failure.

For many years, Jon believed and *lived out* an over-and-over soundtrack stuck in his head. It told him the work he did as a writer was painstaking and costly. So whenever he sat down to tackle a chapter, he felt like a martyr and a victim. That is, until he switched off the broken soundtrack and replaced it with a new song, the lyrics of which were, 'light and easy.' He would repeat those words to himself when he set about his tasks for the day – *light and easy* – and they transformed his writing from drudgery to delight.

The bonus good news is that we can play the 'light and easy' soundtrack in every area of our lives, because the phrase describes the life Jesus has freely invited us into. That's not to say all of life is light and easy. Sometimes the way is treacherous, and we're overloaded with responsibility or grief. But when we trust Jesus to shoulder our burdens, and when we take His hand on steep or slippery byways, we can walk lightly, and easily, and *freely* through our days, knowing we're yoked to Him, and we never walk alone.

Free to ask yourself:

These questions are drawn from themes covered over the past five days.

- What kind of freedom are you trusting God for, in the season you find yourself?

- When you think about the audacious, extravagant freedom of God's gospel giveaway, what strikes you most, or stops you in your tracks?

- How might you explain the good news of freedom in Jesus to someone struggling to break free from a habit or addiction, or perhaps someone desperate to be free from anger, jealousy or a bent towards gossip and slander?

- Read John 4. When Jesus' disciples return from finding food in the village, they're shocked to find Him talking to a woman. Do you ever find yourself expecting Jesus' acceptance, forgiveness, and freedom for yourself, yet feeling indignant when others get to enjoy it too?

Free to write it out:

If you've never accepted the forgiveness of Jesus, take time to write out a prayer of repentance and celebration as you step into the freedom of new life.

If you've known Jesus for years and have somehow lost your sense of wonder at all He's done to set you free, take time to write out a prayer of repentance and celebration as you step back into the unentangled, abundant life you've been given.

_____

_____

_____

_____

_____

_____

_____

_____

FREE FROM FEAR

Lawless, but in a good way

*So Christ has truly set us free. Now make sure that you stay free,
and don't get tied up again in slavery to the law.*
Galatians 5:1, NLT

People have walked away from Christianity in droves because of a grossly incorrect understanding of the place law occupies in the life of believers. The good news that Jesus came to fulfil the law, not enforce it, too often gets swallowed up by misguided religion.

The truth is that obedience to God's commands is our beautiful, joy-filled, win-win response to God's love and grace. His commands are always to keep us safe and to set us free – to protect us from ourselves and others, and to keep us clear of the entanglements of sin, which get us stuck. God's laws also point to His holiness and the standard of perfection His spotless character demands of those entering His presence – a standard you and I have never been able to live up to, and never will. In that sense, the law points out our desperate need of a Savior because, left to our own devices, we'd be doomed. No matter how hard any of us tries, we just don't have it in us to keep the law.

Jesus is the only person *ever* to have kept every one of God's laws flawlessly. He died to save us from our sin, but also to save us from relentlessly, impossibly, trying to keep the laws we can't. He fulfilled the law on our behalf, so we don't have to. Our attempts to live up to the law don't make us righteous. Jesus alone makes us righteous. That's very good news indeed.

Covenant not contract

Then the LORD took Abram outside and said to him,
'Look up into the sky and count the stars if you can.
That's how many descendants you will have!' And Abram
believed the LORD, and the LORD counted him as righteous
because of his faith ... So the LORD made a covenant with Abram
that day and said, 'I have given this land to your descendants,
all the way from the border of Egypt to the great Euphrates River ...'
Genesis 15:5-6, 18, NLT

Salvation has always been by grace, through faith. Even in Old Testament times – before Jesus came – God's people, like Abram (later Abraham), didn't *do stuff* to get a nod of God's approval. They didn't have to tick tasks off a list to be counted as good enough by God. They *believed* God, and He gifted them with righteousness.

God has always related to humanity through covenant, not contract. That's been His rescue plan from the start, and it results in indescribable freedom. I mean, think about how genuinely terrifying it would be to be tied into some kind of contract with God. Imagine He said to us, 'If you mess up – if you break your side of the bargain – the deal's off.' It's an enormous relief that God has enfolded us in a covenant.

He has *chosen* to be in relationship with us, and He promises to *stay* in relationship with us, no matter how weak and fickle we turn out to be (2 Timothy 2:13). His unblemished character and unblinking love hold us in the grace embrace of an unbreakable bond. And we can live – *really live!* – fear free.

FREE FROM FEAR

Free from scarcity

'And why worry about your clothing? Look at the lilies of the field
and how they grow. They don't work or make their clothing,
yet Solomon in all his glory was not dressed as beautifully as they are.
And if God cares so wonderfully for wildflowers that are here today
and thrown into the fire tomorrow, He will certainly care for you.
Why do you have so little faith? So don't worry about these things,
saying, "What will we eat? What will we drink? What will we wear?"
These things dominate the thoughts of unbelievers, but your heavenly
Father already knows all your needs. Seek the Kingdom of God above
all else, and live righteously, and He will give you everything you need.'
Matthew 6:28-33, NLT

I doubt I'll ever reach the point of sublime spiritual maturity where I no longer need reminding that God is my provider. Most of us (or is it just me?) tend to look to ourselves (our qualifications, jobs, and opportunities) or to others (our spouse, parents, or government) to deliver our wants and needs. We have a goldfish-like memory and attention span when it comes to God as our first-and-foremost provider.

We also default quickly to a poverty mindset, sliding self-pityingly into scarcity thinking. We behave more like slaves reaching for scraps, than children invited to feast with the Father.

Friend, Jesus didn't come to make you rich. He came to set you free. And part of that freedom is resting in the knowledge that He will never leave or forsake you (Hebrews 13:5), and He will generously meet your needs (Philippians 4:19), in His way, time and strength, and for His glory.

Chillax

Don't be obsessed with getting more material things. Be relaxed with what you have. Since God assured us, 'I'll never let you down, never walk off and leave you,' we can boldly quote, 'God is there, ready to help; I'm fearless no matter what. Who or what can get to me?'
Hebrews 13:5-6, MSG

*B*e relaxed with what you have. Maybe this is a soundtrack we need to play through our mental headphones when we're wandering through malls and carparks, or at opulent dinner parties, or whenever what others have and what's available for us to buy lead us straight into the pits of discontent and coveting.

Poverty is a battle worth fighting and as God's people we absolutely need to be leading the charge, because He has charged us to be generous, and to be champions of social justice (2 Corinthians 9:11, James 1:27). And of course, each of us has at some point legitimately *needed* something. Perhaps you've needed expensive but indispensable medical care. Maybe your kids have outgrown their shoes and justifiably need new ones. But I'm guessing there's food enough in your fridge, at least for today. (If there isn't, it's likely just because a crowded schedule has kept you from getting to the store.) Yet we're so quick to convince ourselves we need-need-*need* certain things to make us happy.

The remedy? *Be relaxed with what you have.* And even take it a step further by giving some of it away. Hoarding fuels fear and a poverty mindset. Generosity sets us free by highlighting the happy truth that we have so much.

DAY 19

Kick rocks, punk

For God has not given us the spirit of fear;
but of power, and of love, and of a sound mind.
2 Timothy 1:7, KJV

I always remind my kids to speak kindly. Except when they're speaking to their fear. Then I encourage them to say, 'Kick rocks, punk.' Because when they're churning out negative thoughts, their brains are unable to think creatively. Fear shuts down the hippocampus, the part of your brain that regulates emotional responses, stores memories, and plays a role in spatial processing and navigation. So, fear effectively locks your ability to come up with out-of-the-box, imaginative solutions.

If fear is keeping you up at night, and keeping you from consistently healthy thought patterns, start by writing down exactly *what* it is that terrifies you. Next, try to write down *why* those things scare you. Then take those raw and real feelings to Jesus and ask Him to set your brain free from the negative loops that wear down your resolve and your powers of reckoning. (And then say to your fear, 'Kick rocks, punk.')

Just before Paul tells Timothy that fear is not from God, and that He's called us to live with power, love, and clear thoughts, he writes, 'This is why I remind you to fan into flames the spiritual gift God gave you when I laid my hands on you.' (2 Timothy 1:6) To live out your gifting – fulfilling your God-given potential to make Him known to the world around you – you'll need your mind free from the crippling effects of fear. Today may you trust your powerful, loving Father to set you free by eradicating fear from your thoughts.

Free to ask yourself:

**These questions are drawn from
themes covered over the past five days.**

- If a friend said to you, 'I'm just afraid I'll never be *enough* of a Christian ...', how might you explain to her the remarkable news that Jesus has set her free forever from trying to do enough good things to measure up to God's standard of perfection?

- When have you knowingly disobeyed God by committing an act that would've broken a contract with Him, but which didn't break His covenant with you? How did He lead you to repentance?

- In which area of your life (finances, relationships, career?) do you struggle most to rest in the truth that God is your provider? Is there a lie you've believed – about yourself or God – which makes you doubt His faithfulness in this area?

- Read Philippians 4:6-8. Paul is concerned about our brains! He's addressing anxiety and urging us to seek out God's peace which protects our minds. He's exhorting us to choose God-centered, God-honoring thoughts. How might this way of living and thinking defeat fear, which damages our creative thought processes?

Free to ask God:

FREE FROM FEAR

JESUS,

Your death and resurrection set me free from sin, and from the fear that I'll never do or be enough to please You. You paid the price I should've paid – and I want the rest of my life to be my thanks to You! I want to follow close behind You, doing as You do and doing what You say, in joyful obedience (not joyless obligation). Thank You for entering an unbreakable covenant with me. You're not just holding up Your side of the bargain. You're holding up me, and all things, for Your Kingdom and glory. You are kind and faithful. Except, some days I forget all this. I get scared that I won't have enough. Please show me again today in ways that make sense in my reality that You are and always will be my Provider of all things. And God, set me free from the fear that cripples my creativity. I want to use the mind You gave me to imagine ways of making You known.

AMEN.

Still, small signals

My heart is not proud, LORD, my eyes are not haughty;
I do not concern myself with great matters
or things too wonderful for me. But I have calmed
and quieted myself, I am like a weaned child
with its mother; like a weaned child I am content.
Psalm 131:1-2, NIV

In the cutthroat cancel culture we inhabit, one way to cancel fear is to discern between *noise* and *signals*.

Noise is the cacophony of real things happening all around you – things you can do nothing about. Noise doesn't truly influence or affect your direction or purpose. Noise is the din of alarming newsfeeds bent on widening your circle of concern and distracting you from your circle of influence. Noise deafens you with what you think others are thinking about you. Shush it. Noise takes up space and muddles the signals.

Signals are worth listening to. Discern their pure note above the clatter and clamor, the blares and blasts that sidetrack you. A signal sounds like wisdom. A signal will align with the fruit of the Spirit: love, joy, peace, patience, kindness, goodness, faithfulness, gentleness, and self-control (Galatians 5:22-23). A signal will sink and settle with comforting heaviness and clarity into your swirling heart and mind. Factor the signals into your thinking, planning, and moving. Signals are the prompting of the Holy Spirit to act boldly or hold back humbly. Cognitive alertness and creative clarity dawn when we disallow noise and respond to signals. And it's only in the quiet place of resting in the presence of God that the noise fades, we're able to rest and surrender, and hear the signals of His still, small voice.

Free from confusion

But I am afraid that just as Eve was deceived by
the serpent's cunning, your minds may somehow be
led astray from your sincere and pure devotion to Christ.
2 Corinthians 11:3, NIV

In his first interaction with people, Satan muddled them with misperceptions and misunderstandings (Genesis 3:1). That's been his tactic with humankind ever since. The Greek word for devil – *diabolos* – means to *throw across* – to slander, accuse and confuse. Where God brings clarity and comprehension, the enemy will seek to destroy with chaos and uncertainty. And you can be pretty sure he'll heap on shiploads of guilt and shame as well.

One commentator notes that the devil is relentless about throwing things across your path – and thereby penetrating your mind and emotions – to drive a wedge between you and other people. His objective is to separate people from one another with his railing, accusing, slanderous accusations. He's relentless in his pursuit to render you powerless and fearful, and so prevent you from stepping confidently into your God-given authority.

But the enemy doesn't have the Holy Spirit, and so he doesn't have the fruit (Galatians 5:22-23). He's not patient or self-controlled. He will always overplay his hand. He spoils his chances of success through excessive confidence in his position because he doesn't have wisdom and discernment and patience and perseverance. If you're a follower of Jesus, *you do*. Pray for the good judgment and insight to spot Satan's fear-mongering tactics. James says it best: 'So humble yourselves before God. Resist the devil, and he will flee from you.' (James 4:7)

How many roads ...

Put on all of God's armor so that you will be able
to stand firm against all strategies of the devil.
Ephesians 6:11, NLT

The word translated 'strategies' in this verse (or in other Bible translations, 'schemes' or 'wiles') is the Greek word *methodeias* – from the root word for 'way', 'road' or 'travel'. Bible scholars observe that the devil is sly and devious and yet, all things considered, somewhat predictable. He travels roads – the *same* roads – and his intended destination is your destruction. He will pave the roads leading into different situations in your life to attack you in the same ways, in the same weak spots. Also, he knows how to turn God's statements into questions – like he did with Eve so long ago ('Did God really say ...?') – making you wonder if you're on the right road at all. He's determined to make you believe that God's intentions towards you are *not* good.

But you know better. In Jeremiah 29:11 God says, 'I know the plans I have for you ... They are plans for good and not for disaster, to give you a future and a hope.' The Hebrew word translated 'plans' can also be translated 'thoughts', 'purposes' or 'intentions.' God's heart toward you is only ever for your good, and His glory. Before you are anything or anyone, you are His beloved.

Ask God to help you recognize Satan's movements as he travels down the same roads, attempting to attack you and undermine your effectiveness for the Kingdom. And don't for a moment let the lie settle over your soul that God doesn't see you, love you and intend His great goodness for your life.

Worrier or warrior?

Don't worry about anything; instead, pray about everything.
Tell God what you need, and thank Him for all He has done.
Then you will experience God's peace, which exceeds
anything we can understand. His peace will guard your
hearts and minds as you live in Christ Jesus.
Philippians 4:6-7, NLT

I met a woman once whose son was hitchhiking across Africa. He regularly encountered danger – like, child-soldiers-with-guns kind of danger. Weeks would go by during which she and her husband wouldn't know where he was. She's one of the most beautiful, poised, serene people I've ever met. I asked her how on earth she did it. She said, 'I'm not a worrier.' She stated a fact. An unshakeable part of her identity in Christ was that she did not worry. It was a choice she had made because, she said, 'You can't grow an inch by worrying. Also, it's a sin.'

I'm prone to worry, which gives way to fear, which traps me. So, I'm trying to break free from that toxic cycle by taking a leaf from this brave lady's book, making a daily choice to surrender my fear and fretfulness to the God who already knows my present and future needs, and has done so much for me in the past.

Let's flip the script in our minds. We needn't be *worriers*. We can be *warriors*, wielding the Word as our weapon, and remembering that our wide-awake, tireless, mighty Savior fights with us and for us, even when we're asleep. We're in strong, safe hands, today and always.

DAY 26

What if?

'Be strong and very courageous. Be careful to obey all the law
my servant Moses gave you; do not turn from it to the right or to
the left, that you may be successful wherever you go. Keep this
Book of the Law always on your lips; meditate on it day and night,
so that you may be careful to do everything written in it. Then you
will be prosperous and successful. Have I not commanded you?
Be strong and courageous. Do not be afraid; do not be discouraged,
for the LORD your God will be with you wherever you go.'
Joshua 1:7-9, NIV

Some people are more prone to fear, depending on their temperaments and natural inclinations. This *can* be a strength, because every organization needs someone who is farsighted with excellent peripheral vision: someone who can spot trouble on the horizon without being blindsided by imminent threats. Sometimes, asking *What if?* is a way of predicting and preventing disaster. It's when fear overrides rational thought, distorting reality and clouding judgment, that it becomes destructive.

If you're a *What if?* person, it may help to picture the *very* worst-case scenario of the situation confronting you – and *solve it*. Talk yourself through exactly what you'd do if such a situation arose. What's at your disposal? What agency do you have? Who would you call? What decisions would you make?

Thankfully, our worst-case-scenario predictions seldom materialize. But acknowledging the possibility of something awful going down, and then preparing your mind with a host of responses, goes a long way towards dispelling your restless fears. You're free to get busy living the situation by faith.

Free to ask yourself:

**These questions are drawn from
themes covered over the past five days.**

- Where is the noise in your life coming from? How can you intentionally dial it down this week?

- Who or what is God signaling for you to take note of? What response is required from you?

- Looking back over your past, can you trace the paths worn smooth by the enemy in his attempt to take you out in the areas of your greatest weakness or vulnerability?

- Read John 14:27. Then think about how might you explain to someone you love that God's peace can sustain them despite the cares they carry?

Free to write it out:

**Take some time to write down your worries and fears.
Any you can think of. Massive and miniscule.
Prayerfully picture yourself leaving all that anxiety
and stress and disquiet before the throne of grace,
from which Jesus, the Prince of Peace, rules and
reigns with perfect love, wisdom, and power.**

_____

_____

_____

_____

_____

_____

_____

_____

FREE FROM FEAR

DAY 29

Fearless love

Do not be afraid or discouraged, for the Lᴏʀᴅ will personally go ahead
of you. He will be with you; He will neither fail you nor abandon you.
Deuteronomy 31:8, NLT

My darkest fears often swirl sickeningly around the lives of my children. It's a mom thing. I don't mind too much what happens to me. I mind *a lot* what happens to my kids. If you're not a parent, you've surely experienced a sense of helplessness, too, as you've watched the lives, decisions, or directions of those you love and worried about their faith or their future.

When our family faced an enormous transition that would profoundly, irrevocably affect our lives and shake our stability to the core (moving countries), a friend advised me not to feel too sorry for my kids. She reminded me that God's grace for them (and me) is enough, that resilience is the gift of preparing our kids for the road (not the road for our kids), and that faith doesn't mean an absence of uncertainty but rather our tenacious obedience. What's more, change and challenges reinforce that faith muscle like nothing else, strengthening it for even greater deference to God's perfect ways.

If you're concerned about a loved one today, may the Father give you the grace to place that precious person in His hands – and let go. He goes ahead of them. He's with them. He will never fail them or abandon them. John tells us, 'There is no fear in love. But perfect love drives out fear …' (1 John 4:18). God loves you perfectly, and He perfectly loves those you love too. Do not be afraid.

FREE FROM FEAR

Need to know

And this same God who takes care of me will supply all your needs
from His glorious riches, which have been given to us in Christ Jesus.
Philippians 4:19, NLT

We're good at telling God exactly what we need, and even what others need – as if He needs our advice and direction. He's a kind, patient Father, and we're allowed to tell Him and talk to Him about anything. But let's be real. He always knows better. He knows *best*.

For example, you might think a beloved friend needs healing more than anything else. You might think life should just cut your cousin or your co-worker some slack. But God sees that person's whole life, from beginning to end. He knows where they've been. He knows what's coming. And perhaps He knows they don't need healing – or a job or a husband or a vacation – because these aren't the things that make a success of our lives. Character is what makes us a success, or not, in the eyes of heaven. And character is developed through perseverance.

That might all sound a little hardcore – like God is some kind of boot-camp instructor who is only into tough love – but fear not. Paul's encouragement to the Philippian believers brings such reassurance to us too. God's fathomless wealth of grace is poured out on us because of what Jesus did for us on the cross. He's a loving God who promises to supply our needs and the needs of those we care about because He alone truly knows what our needs are.

FREE FROM FEAR

Fighting free

> But Moses told the people, 'Don't be afraid.
> Just stand still and watch the LORD rescue you today.
> The Egyptians you see today will never be seen again.
> The LORD Himself will fight for you. Just stay calm.'
> Exodus 14:13-14, NLT

Total freedom from fear is found in total surrender to God, as we trust Him to fight for us. Even if you're not entirely sure who or what you're fighting, and why, you can confidently cast yourself on God's kindness and pray: *Fight for me!* Even if you know you don't have the sharpest or the shiniest weapons, you can be sure He does, and you can pray: *Fight for me!*

Right after Moses' instruction of 'Don't be afraid,' he expands and explains with, 'Just stand still.' I don't know the fights you face, but if you're anything like me, the biggest fight is sometimes to get ourselves just to stand still and watch in awe as our warrior Savior fights on the frontlines, for us. On days when the battle is fierce and I'm all but convinced it's already lost, I wish I could tell you I never run around in wild panic trying to fix everything and fathom every terrifying depth in my own strength. I need constant reminding to *just stand still*. Be silent. Stay calm. And watch as God fights for me and rescues me.

In our fight for freedom from the fear of sin and death and law and fear itself, let's allow God's war cry of truth to resound in our souls: 'The Lord Himself will fight for you. Just stay calm.'

Just be

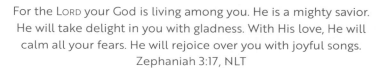

For the Lord your God is living among you. He is a mighty savior.
He will take delight in you with gladness. With His love, He will
calm all your fears. He will rejoice over you with joyful songs.
Zephaniah 3:17, NLT

Zephaniah speaks here of God's presence and power, but also of the tremendous pleasure He takes in us. In Him, not only can we live free from fear; we can live free to be who He has created and called us to be, knowing we delight Him.

In the readings for the next few weeks, we'll explore the freedom of being truly content in the continual becoming of who we were born to be. We'll talk about character and values, and the freedom intentionality brings in those crucial areas. We'll learn how to be free from FOMO, people-pleasing and unhealthy ambition, and what it looks like to be free to step into our gifting and God-given authority, changing the atmosphere in our spheres of influence.

For now, I pray you'd realize fully you don't have to *be* anything or anyone other than who you are right now. No matter what state your life is in, God loves you immeasurably. Of course, He won't *leave* you just as you are. He's in the transformation game. He will meet you in your mess, and in your success, to change you, day by day and more and more, into the image of Jesus. You can rest completely in the marvelous knowledge that, even now, your mighty Savior sings expectantly, excitedly, and lovingly over you. In that wondrous place of being wholly cherished, you are free just to be.

FREE TO BE

Born to be

*Dear brothers and sisters, the longing of my heart
and my prayer to God is for the people of Israel to be saved.*
Romans 10:1, NLT

This is what got Paul up in the mornings. He was unashamedly, unabatingly passionate about seeing people come to a saving knowledge of Jesus. His logic and reasoning were excellent, and he was a great communicator: a winning combo.

That's all very well for Paul. But perhaps you've no idea who and what God created you to be. Maybe the concept of a calling freaks you out and you've wondered why it seems so obscure and elusive, and whether it's even discoverable.

It may be useful to answer, as fully and honestly as possible, questions like these:

What breaks your heart? What situations in your life, or the world at large, keep on pushing the boundaries of your circle of concern? What kind of world change do you long for? What are you good at? In which areas do you know you have the passion, power, aptitude, and capacity to add value or make a difference? What captivates and enthralls you so much that, while you're doing it, you forget about yourself? What makes you come alive? In which areas of your life are you keen to harness the support and expertise of others? What kind of people are you drawn to?

You may still need to make some big what-where-when-how decisions, to map out the details, but your raw, uninhibited answers to these kinds of questions may well begin to reveal the direction God is calling you to take.

Free to ask yourself:

**These questions are drawn from themes
covered over the past five days.**

- What three needs has God met in your life today?

- In which area of your life do you most need God to fight for you?

- How might you complete this sentence: *I was born to …* (You can answer with one word, or an essay. Don't just answer what you think the right answer is, or what you think others expect of you.)

- Read John 13:34-35. Can people tell you're a Christian? How? Can you think of someone whose transparent life makes it obvious that they love Jesus?

Free to ask God:

ALMIGHTY GOD,

Thank You that, through Your love and power in my life, I can overcome fear, and be free. Thank You that, though the enemy plants seeds of panic, dread and confusion, You deal in clarity, wisdom and understanding. Because of Your loving sacrifice, Jesus, You have called me righteous – I am in right standing with You! Thank You! Set me free from trying to be anything You never intended me to be. Take my life and lead me as I spend the rest of it becoming whom You have already declared me to be.

AMEN.

Be real

You do not desire a sacrifice, or I would offer one. You do not
want a burnt offering. The sacrifice You desire is a broken spirit.
You will not reject a broken and repentant heart, O God.
Psalm 51:16-17, NLT

Psalm 51 is an outpouring of repentance. And David's words in verses 16 and 17 reflect the truth that God is interested only in our *hearts*. He's not impressed by showy piousness. He's not even moved by external manifestations of the gifts He's given us. Scott Sauls writes, 'We are successful only when we have character that is greater than our gifts and abilities, and humility that is greater than our platforms and influence.' Being an Instagram influencer doesn't count for anything in God's books, unless your integrity outweighs your perfect pictures, and your humility runs deeper than your followers are spread wide.

In your quest to be free *to be* all God imagined you'd be in this one short life, what might it look like for you to be intentional about your character and values? Are you regularly accountable to someone who keeps your feet on the ground? Could you ask God to show you where pride has crept in, or where you've been willing to cut some corners on the roads of honesty or selflessness? Have you perhaps heard yourself talking the talk of a Jesus follower – and realized your heart's not in it?

The God of the universe isn't threatened by your candor, anger, doubt, or listlessness. He knows and names the thoughts and emotions that churn in your heart even before you do. Come real and raw before Him, ready to repent and to be restored.

FREE TO BE

No fear of missing out

... he went to the home of Mary, the mother of John Mark, where many were gathered for prayer. He knocked at the door in the gate, and a servant girl named Rhoda came to open it. When she recognized Peter's voice, she was so overjoyed that, instead of opening the door, she ran back inside and told everyone, 'Peter is standing at the door!' 'You're out of your mind!' they said. When she insisted, they decided, 'It must be his angel.' Meanwhile, Peter continued knocking. When they finally opened the door and saw him, they were amazed.

Acts 12:12-16, NLT

Rhoda was a servant, sent to open the door while a meeting she wasn't part of carried on without her. She was excluded and missing out.

Or was she? Because God saw fit to let Rhoda, not someone cooler or more important, be first to greet Peter after his supernatural prison-break. The people of the household didn't take her seriously. They called her crazy. And yet we know her name to this day.

Wanting to be on the list and in the limelight is part of the human condition, and social media has mushroomed FOMO into an unplayable force. But when you feel you're on the fringes of the main action: remember Rhoda, with happy relief. Because when we're following Jesus, we are *always* where important stuff is going on. We're not missing out on anything in life, because His *abundant* life flows in us and through us, right where we are. We needn't fear missing out on anything at all, because the center of God's will is the best place to be. Be *there*, and just be.

Free to be small

And He gives grace generously. As the Scriptures say,
'God opposes the proud but gives grace to the humble.'
James 4:6, NLT

To be all we were made to be in this life, we surely want more, and more, and *more* of God's changing, empowering favor to be poured out on us. We need His wisdom and strength and skill and pathfinding prowess, in order to take hold of our inheritance. We need His *grace*. And James gives us the gleaming key to attaining that grace: humility. The humbler we become, the more grace we receive. Ironically, the moment we start checking our humble-o-meter, it stops working. Humility asks us to forget about ourselves altogether and focus on God and others.

That doesn't mean we should stop brushing our teeth, or eating and sleeping, or monitoring our necessary progress in particular areas of life. Look after yourself and be the best version of you. But keep your thoughts about yourself *small*. Think *big* thoughts about serving God and the people you'll encounter today.

Beethoven began to lose his hearing in his late twenties, and by his mid-forties was completely deaf. He died at the age of 56. For decades, he composed in silence. He never heard orchestras play his pieces – all of which are still played around the world. He never heard the applause of audiences. For you and me to be truly free of unhealthy ambition – free to just *be* who God has called us to be – let's keep on composing our best and most beautiful work in silence, for the small audience of the one true and immeasurable God.

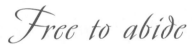

Free to abide

'Yes, I am the vine; you are the branches.
Those who remain in Me, and I in them, will produce
much fruit. For apart from Me you can do nothing.'
John 15:5, NLT

Paradoxically, it's in binding ourselves to God – abiding in Him or remaining in Him – that we're freed – let loose – to be all He created us to be.

Jesus explains that He's the metaphorical Vine, and we are the branches. One commentator notes that the Greek word translated *branch* carries the idea of tenderness and flexibility.

At times you may not be sure where you fit in the grand scheme of things. You may feel untethered and wonder, *Am I abiding in the true vine? Am I still deeply, irrevocably connected to the Source? Have I allowed something to become a tourniquet that's cut off the life supply to me, the branch?* It helps to simply ask yourself, *Am I still tender, and flexible?*

It's calming and clarifying, too, to remember that apart from Jesus, we can do nothing. Your temperament, talents, opportunities, instincts – all these come from God. Stay tender, flexible, and free. God will grow you and use you to make Him known.

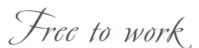

Free to work

It is the blessing of the Lord that makes rich,
and He adds no sorrow to it.
Proverbs 10:22, NASB

God made us to work. He set Adam and Eve meaningful tasks *before the fall*. Once they'd swallowed Satan's hook (Genesis 3:1), disobeyed God (Genesis 3:6), and plunged humanity into brokenness (Genesis 3:7), work became more drudgery, less delight (Genesis 3:17). And yet our Father and Creator, who redeems and restores us through the death and resurrection of Jesus, still calls us to meaningful work: to use our skills, gifts, passions, and aptitudes to glorify Him and leave the world better than we found it.

I don't know if you're delivering pizzas or chairing board meetings. Maybe you're working your dream job. Maybe you're not. Either way, if you're daily submitting your energy to God, adding value by responsibly filling your working hours, God will bless your efforts. Your work will bear fruit as you abide in Jesus. Your tenderness and flexibility will make Him irresistible to people impacted by your work.

Anne Lamott famously said, 'A hundred years from now? All new people.' No matter what work we're engaged in! Ecclesiastes 6:12 says, 'In the few days of our meaningless lives, who knows how our days can best be spent? Our lives are like a shadow. Who can tell what will happen on this earth after we are gone?' But don't for a moment let the briefness of your life depress you. Let it galvanize you into the good, hard, satisfying work of greater tenderness and flexibility as you live out your days deeply embedded in the vine and bearing all the fruit you can, while you can.

FREE TO BE

Free to ask yourself:

**These questions are drawn from themes
covered over the past five days.**

- Think of a time when you did something useful, valuable, or appropriate because it would make you look good, and not simply because it was the right thing to do. When a situation like that next arises, how might you reframe it so that God is glorified?

- What are you scared of missing out on? What's the real reason behind your fear?

- What kind or generous act, that no one but God will ever know about, could you plan to do today?

- Read 1 Peter 5:10. Have you suffered, or are you suffering, in your career, your homemaking, or your studies? Do you believe God is powerful enough, and loves you enough, to 'restore, confirm, strengthen, and establish you'?

Free to write it out:

**Think of an incident likely to arise this week —
with your kids, or a co-worker — that will require you
to abide in Jesus by being both tender and flexible.
Storyboard the moment. Write out how you'd love to live it.**

_____

_____

_____

_____

_____

_____

_____

_____

_____

Atmosphere

Live a life filled with love, following the example of Christ. He loved
us and offered Himself as a sacrifice for us, a pleasing aroma to God.
Ephesians 5:2, NLT

When we moved countries, I snipped off a twig from the *spekboom* growing in our garden in South Africa, wrapped it carefully in wet tissue paper, stowed it in a plastic bag inside my suitcase, and replanted it in a pot hanging in the kitchen window, in our new home in England. I did this because the succulent shrub known as a *spekboom* is a super plant. *Spekboom* means 'bacon tree', though it has nothing to do with bacon. The real power of the *spekboom* lies in the fact that, hectare for hectare, a thicket of *spekboom* is ten times more effective than the Amazon rainforest at removing carbon dioxide from the atmosphere. One hectare of *spekboom* can sequester between four and ten tons of carbon emissions per year. It literally changes the atmosphere, and a changed atmosphere can change the world.

God has set us free to change the atmosphere – to *be* the oxygen – in the spaces we inhabit. He's called us to be phenomenal, *spekboom*-like carbon sponges – absorbing offences and breathing them back into the air around us as forgiveness, love, peace, joy, and hope.

We're called and empowered by Jesus to breathe abundant-life oxygen into our homes, schools, workplaces, churches, and communities. And so long as our branches remain tender and flexible, we will flourish. So long as we abide in Jesus – a Person, not a place – we will breathe life into the world around us.

FREE TO BE

Six of the best

For as he thinks in his heart, so is he ...
Proverbs 23:7, NKJV

Our thoughts shape our lives. What we think determines what we feel, and what we feel determines how we behave.

I've no doubt you want to be free to be the best version of you. Me too. But to *be* that person we need to *think* like that person. Researchers in the fields of neuroplasticity and psychology have discovered it takes three positive thoughts to counterbalance one negative thought. And if you want a healthy, creative brain – able to solve problems and add lasting value wherever you have agency to do so – you need to up the positive thought count to *six*, every time a pessimistic, depressing, or destructive thought eats into your mind.

Of course, it's hard to think anything positive if you're exhausted, so if you're besieged by negative thoughts, make a good night's sleep your number one weapon. Snoozing isn't losing. Set a downtime alarm to remind you to wrap up the day. You need sleep. God doesn't. Give Him all the worries and get some shuteye. Next, choose the habit of gratitude. Think of three things a day for which you're thankful. That way, every time a negative thought invades your brainwaves, you'll be ready with an arsenal of three optimistic reflections. If three is too much? Think of one. Say it three times over – or better, six times over – when the negativity overwhelms you, or before you complain about the hard things in your life. Take a deep breath and think out your thanksgiving: *I'm grateful for coffee, coffee, coffee, coffee, coffee, coffee.* Negativity will begin to evaporate, leaving you free.

Safe in your skin

'Look at My servant, whom I strengthen. He is My chosen one, who pleases Me. I have put My Spirit upon Him. He will bring justice to the nations. He will not shout or raise His voice in public. He will not crush the weakest reed or put out a flickering candle. He will bring justice to all who have been wronged.'
Isaiah 42:1-3, NLT

Skin is both strong and soft. Your skin is a shield protecting you from so much harm. Like, a virus can't burrow into your body through your skin. But skin is also fragile – easily burnt or broken.

Maybe, because media storms have raged over the past few years around COVID-19, racial tension, and gender-based violence, you don't feel safe in the skin you're in. Perhaps you've felt overwhelmed, intimidated, and confused. God sees you and loves you in these threatening spaces. He's created more than enough space inside your skin for you to feel completely comfortable. The Holy Spirit dwells in you to console, protect and guide. You needn't be afraid. You can say with the psalmist, 'The LORD is for me, so I will have no fear. What can mere people do to me?' (Psalm 118:6)

God made your skin, and you can trust His promise that you will not be snapped like a twig or snuffed out like a cigarette. The God of justice – the lion of Judah – roars over your life. He will not be mocked. Rest in His strength to fight for you. You're held in the palm of His hand, safe and free in the skin you're in.

Free to be different

> O LORD, what a variety of things You have made! In wisdom You have made them all. The earth is full of Your creatures. Here is the ocean, vast and wide, teeming with life of every kind, both large and small.
> Psalm 104:24-25, NLT

Perhaps you feel impossibly different from those around you. Maybe you look in the mirror and hate what you see. Through the psalmist, God offers you a better perspective: you were custom designed. Your skin was sewn together to fit only you. There hasn't been another human ever who has fitted into it, and there never will be again. Please don't be tempted to squeeze yourself into someone else's skin. It's hard at first, but you *can* get into the habit of choosing to celebrate how God made you, and thank Him, like the psalmist did, for the wondrous diversity of His creation expressed through the kaleidoscope of people, places, and animals on this planet.

A skincare company has an ad that says, 'Love the skin you're in.' They're onto something. Genesis 1:31 tells us, 'God looked over all He had made, and He saw that it was very good!' God made *you*. And He called you *very good*. You can legitimately enjoy, appreciate, celebrate, and *love* the skin you're in.

Obviously, that doesn't mean boast and brag about it. Arrogance is never beautiful. But you can *totally* echo the psalmist yet again with these words: 'Thank You for making me so wonderfully complex! Your workmanship is marvelous – how well I know it.' (Psalm 139:14) You can hold those words close, lift your head high, and enjoy the favor of your Creator.

New skin

This means that anyone who belongs to Christ has become
a new person. The old life is gone; a new life has begun!
2 Corinthians 5:17, NLT

Every 28 days, the cells of your outer skin layer – the epidermis – are replaced, and you get a whole new skin. It's a beautiful picture of God's continual refreshing in our lives. He's always making all things new. The physical, external reality mirrors what's happening to our souls if we're following Jesus. As Paul reminds us, we're growing younger and younger on the inside: 'Though our bodies are dying, our spirits are being renewed every day.' (2 Corinthians 4:16)

Ridiculously, we're quick to overlook this happy, hopeful truth. We play the victim card, convincing ourselves we're hard done by, we've been shortchanged by life, and there's nothing we can do about it. The 'old life' has ruined us, and no 'new life' has begun.

Lousy stuff beyond our control happens to us all because the world and its systems and people are imperfect. But we're wrong to think we have no control over the script that's playing out in our lives. We needn't be victims of our own thoughts. We are free to choose true, noble, right, pure, lovely, admirable, excellent, and praiseworthy thoughts (Philippians 4:8). In fact, Paul *commands* that we 'think about such things', thereby choosing our responses, no matter what's going on around us.

In Christ, you are free to rewrite the regenerative story you're stepping into. Your past no longer holds the pen. In Christ, you can shed the skin of your old life. A new life has begun.

Free to ask yourself:

**These questions are drawn from themes
covered over the past five days.**

- Which people or situations tend to trigger your negativity?

- Which people or situations make you feel vulnerable or defenseless – unsafe in your own skin?

- No matter how much difficulty or negativity you may currently face, what is one true, positive thought you can dwell on, right now?

- Read Galatians 3:28 and 1 Corinthians 6:19-20. How might these truths change your internal narrative when you feel exposed or at risk?

FREE TO BE

Free to ask God:

FREE TO BE

JESUS,

Your skin was ripped open, for me. You came to earth to live and die and rise again, clothing Yourself in fragile skin, so I could always feel safe in mine. Let that be enough – just the truth of that – on days when I feel attacked or inadequate. Help me think on what is true. Help me see myself the way You do. Lift my thoughts to Yours, which are always higher and better than anything I could dream up.

AMEN.

Reshaped

'And yet, O Lord, You are our Father. We are the clay,
and You are the potter. We all are formed by Your hand.'
Isaiah 64:8, NLT

When we faced the life shift of moving our family across the world, I had to dig deep for increased capacity. I felt drained. Anything poured into me was quickly expended once again. I kept asking God to *re*-resource me – to strengthen me and fill me up. A friend said to me, 'What if God isn't just going to keep filling your glass? What if He's taking away the glass and replacing it with a bigger vessel – a vase or jug? What if He's *changing the container*?'

This rekindled my courage and stamina, as I clung to the idea that the great glassblower is willing and able to rework, reshape, or replace entirely the receptacle He's fashioning. He's into transformation, not just maintenance and sustenance, and He's able to shape His handiwork according to His perfect designs, which are always astounding because He is able, 'through His mighty power at work within us, to accomplish infinitely more than we might ask or think.' (Ephesians 3:20)

Maybe you find yourself in a season of change. Maybe suddenly more is required of you than ever before and it feels like your glass can't possibly get filled up quickly enough for all that's expected to pour forth from your life. Maybe God isn't going to fill your glass. Maybe He's going to change the container – growing you in ways you've never grown before. Perhaps you'll discover depths within yourself you've never fathomed – whole chambers never before filled with the joy, freedom, and purposes of God.

Seen and sent

The LORD gave me this message: 'I knew you before I formed you
in your mother's womb. Before you were born I set you apart
and appointed you as My prophet to the nations.' 'O Sovereign LORD,'
I said, 'I can't speak for You! I'm too young!' The LORD replied,
'Don't say, "I'm too young," for you must go wherever I send you
and say whatever I tell you. And don't be afraid of the people,
for I will be with you and will protect you. I, the LORD, have spoken!'
Jeremiah 1:4-8, NLT

God mentions fear – and the fact that we *shouldn't* fear anything or anyone other than Him – hundreds of times in the Bible. Certainly, we shouldn't fear stepping into His plans for us. He promises to equip and empower us for every situation into which He leads us. We needn't look to the world or ourselves for qualification. We *have* enough and we *are* enough to do and be what God's called us to do and be, because it's Him working in and through us, to accomplish His purposes in the world. While we endeavor to be our best selves, we can relax in the knowledge that 'the one who calls us is faithful, and He will do it.' (1 Thessalonians 5:24)

If you're not sure what it is you're supposed to step into, take just the next step. Do just the next right thing that ticks the box of being true, honorable, pure, lovely, admirable, excellent, and worthy of praise (Philippians 4:8). The God who longs to lead you sees you as you are, where you are, and He will send you.

Firm and flawless freedom

Purify me from my sins, and I will be clean; wash me, and I will
be whiter than snow. Oh, give me back my joy again; You have
broken me – now let me rejoice. Don't keep looking at my sins.
Remove the stain of my guilt. Create in me a clean heart, O God.
Renew a loyal spirit within me. Do not banish me from
Your presence, and don't take Your Holy Spirit from me.
Psalm 51:7-11, NLT

David's repentance expressed in this psalm brings on a simple, steadfast, single-minded resolve. He renews his devotion to worship wholeheartedly. In the same way, our quest for freedom to simply be who we were created to be begins with repentance. It begins with coming back to the simplest of ways: being single-mindedly fixed on God and His best for us. Another version renders Psalm 51:10 as, 'Create in me a pure heart, O God, and renew a *steadfast* spirit within me.'

David wrote Psalm 51 after committing adultery with Bathsheba. He gave into the promises of immediate pleasure and power, at the cost of his purity and another man's wife and life. He lost sight of what he valued most: his joy in the presence of the Holy Spirit (Psalm 51:8, 11). Living a pure and steadfast life – unwavering from the truth and stalwartly committed to living out God's ideals – requires asking ourselves what it is we value *most*, not just what we value *now*. It's being brave enough to be honest with ourselves and those around us about what we crave immediately, and what will ultimately deliver eternal results, bear fruit others can feast on, and set us free.

FREE TO BE

Nothing to prove

The LORD is for me, so I will have no fear.
What can mere people do to me?
Psalm 118:6, NLT

Auschwitz survivor Edith Eger wrote, 'If you've got something to prove, you're never free.' If, when you read that, you winced just a little (or a lot, like I did), it's likely you're a perfectionist, or you carry debilitating (or even subtle) insecurities, or you're desperate for the approval or affirmation of others.

I'm confident we all fall into one of these categories. We're constantly outrunning shame by forcing perfection, or we're trying anxiously to attract the attention and applause of a parent, a spouse, a boss, a friend, or total strangers on social media. We've believed the lie that we're not enough, and our life's ambition from there on out is to prove we are.

Jesus came to set you free. He came to set you free from yourself because you can be your own worst enemy. And He came to set you free from the opinions of others, which were never meant to define you. You have nothing to prove, because on the cross, Jesus proved His love and power were enough to cancel the curse over your life. He had the first say in your life when He imagined you in eternity past and then set your fetal heart beating, and He will have the final say in your life when your days are done. No one else gets to speak displeasure over you. You are sealed by the Holy Spirit (Ephesians 1:13-14) so the psalmist can preach it, 'What can mere people do to me?'

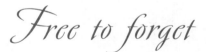

Free to forget

As for me, it matters very little how I might be evaluated by you
or by any human authority. I don't even trust my own judgment
on this point. My conscience is clear, but that doesn't prove
I'm right. It is the Lord Himself who will examine me and decide.
1 Corinthians 4:3-4, NLT

In his book, *The Freedom of Self-Forgetfulness*, Tim Keller writes that,
to be truly free from conceit and contempt and all other ego-driven
ugliness, we need to take on Paul's mindset as expressed in his letter
to the Corinthians. He said, in essence, 'I don't care what *you* think
of me. Equally, I don't care what *I* think of me. I care what *God* thinks
of me. He has gone to court over my identity. The verdict has been
passed. The court is adjourned. He has declared me innocent, and utterly loved.'

When we truly believe that it will change our thoughts, feelings, actions, and attitudes, and we'll be free. We won't be so easily offended. We'll have far more grace and compassion for others. We'll be
interested in their affairs and wish them well. We'll have nothing to
offer but kindness, because we won't constantly be trying to protect
our sensitive selves.

But let's not kid ourselves. Hearing this once won't be enough. We constantly forget to forget ourselves, so we need to preach to ourselves
several times a day. We need to coach and cajole ourselves, saying, 'I
will stop looking constantly inwards. I'll lift my head and look creatively outwards. I'll forget me. I'll focus on God and others.' Chances are,
we'll be happier, and freer.

DAY 55

Free to ask yourself:

**These questions are drawn from themes
covered over the past five days.**

- Do you fear God's power to remold and remodel you? What are you afraid of losing in that divine process?

- What do you value most? What are you willing to sacrifice today, to lay hold of that treasure tomorrow, or even in decades to come?

- Who are you frantically trying to please? Why do you suppose their opinion or approval is so important to you? What negative thing do you believe about yourself, that their approval will solve? And then, *will it really?*

- Read Philippians 2:1-7. What one thing could you do today to forget yourself? How could you lose yourself entirely in a moment, for the sake of someone else?

Free to write it out:

Take time to think about your purpose. If you're still breathing in and out, then you still have one. Write down your hopes and expectations. Which ideas or opportunities excite you? Are you hanging onto any misgivings that you don't have what it takes? Write down your fears. Give them to God.

_____

_____

_____

_____

_____

_____

_____

_____

_____

_____

FREE TO BE

Free to be bold

Some men came carrying a paralyzed man on a mat and tried
to take him into the house to lay him before Jesus. When they
could not find a way to do this because of the crowd,
they went up on the roof and lowered him on his mat through
the tiles into the middle of the crowd, right in front of Jesus.
When Jesus saw their faith, He said, 'Friend, your sins are forgiven.'
Luke 5:18-20, NIV

The focus of this story is often on the paralyzed man and *his* faith. But really, the faith Jesus notices and commends is that of his friends. How incredible that the paralyzed man had a band of brothers around him, willing to risk their necks (literally) by breaking into a house, through the roof, to get him an audience with Jesus. And how brave they were to risk the disapproval of the religious leaders who were watching it all go down (again, literally).

It seems these guys felt free to do whatever it would take to help a friend in need. They felt free to approach Jesus, no matter how unconventional the method. They weren't waiting for a door to open. They felt free to bash through the roof.

Do you feel hemmed in by tradition or the disapproval or expectations of others? What might it look like for you to be free to be bold enough to lean into the power and presence of Jesus – even if it means approaching a situation from an entirely surprising angle? God sees and rewards brave faith.

FREE TO BE

Free to be content

Yet true godliness with contentment is itself great wealth.
After all, we brought nothing with us when we came into
the world, and we can't take anything with us when we leave it.
So if we have enough food and clothing, let us be content.
1 Timothy 6:6-8, NLT

The advertising-slash-propaganda industry all over the globe sells us the lie that if we have more stuff, we'll be happier. We don't buy products or services anymore because we need them, or because they'll offer us a greater quality of life. We spend money in a bid for happiness and satisfaction – even as the truth gnaws that the happiness and satisfaction never last long. What's more, rafts of research indicate that retail therapy is counterproductive, resulting in disappointment and frustration, far higher levels of anxiety, and a pervasive sense of hopelessness.

Paul explains that enough to eat, something to wear, and a roof over our heads, is plenty for our souls to rest easy and content. Is there something in your fridge today? Are you currently wearing clothes? (I guess there's always a chance you're reading this devotional in the bath.) If you're choosing to be outdoors right now, chances are you'll have access to an indoor area, should a storm roll in.

None of this is to minimize any current trauma or confusion or dead-end direction you may face. But it does help to know serenity is possible, wherever you find yourself today. You can *just be* where you are, content to know you have access to the power, presence, and purposes of God.

FREE TO BE

Settle the day

Many people say, 'Who will show us better times?' Let Your face
shine on us, LORD. You have given me greater joy than those who
have abundant harvests of grain and new wine. In peace I will
lie down and sleep, for You alone, O LORD, will keep me safe.
Psalm 4:6-8, NLT

As you read this, life may have you entirely unsettled. You may be in
a season of flux or confusion or relocation or a looming decision.
You may have received news that's upturned your equilibrium. Content, settled, and steady are not even in your emotional vocabulary
right now.

But God. Whether you're afraid, uncertain, cash-strapped, disturbed
or disconcerted physically or emotionally, the joy of the Lord is your
strength (Nehemiah 8:10) and as counterintuitive as it sounds, the
psalmist is right: that gift of joy adds up to more than 'abundant harvests of grain and new wine', more than money and stuff can ever
provide for your soul. As unsettled as you may legitimately be, it's
possible to settle the day by asking yourself, 'Today, did I love someone? Laugh? Learn something? Can I reframe parts of today as adventure, rather than adversity? Did I pray?' If your day included food
and covering and any or all these other elements – even if in small,
snatched moments – then you can go ahead and call it a good day.

You can also settle the day knowing God watches you while you
sleep, and He can hold your hurry and your worries and your to-do
lists all night long, so you can rest before the dawn wakes you to
fresh, untasted mercies.

Everything always

And we know that God causes everything to work together
for the good of those who love God and are called according
to His purpose for them. For God knew His people in advance,
and He chose them to become like His Son, so that His Son
would be the firstborn among many brothers and sisters.
Romans 8:28-29, NLT

To curb negativity and fear, Jon Acuff coined a soundbite he repeats to himself in various situations throughout the day. He says, 'Everything is always working out for me!' This is not cute, feel-good, twenty-first century pop psychology. It's biblical truth. Paul said the same thing in his letter to the Romans in around 57CE.

No matter what you face today, you can be assured of the truth that *everything is always working out for you.* Like, fantastic situations that go according to plan and *save* you time, energy, and money. Opportunities to advance in your career or relationships. Great weather. Parking spots. All these things are examples of everything always working out for you. They're God's goodness in the land of the living (Psalm 27:13), drawing your thoughts to Him and invoking worship.

The same is true for unthinkable tragedy and loss. The frustrations of mundane daily life. Administrative obstacles that *cost* you time, energy, and money. Things breaking. Sports events rained out. Parties cancelled. All these things, too, are examples of everything always working out for you, because God will cause each of these situations to work out for your good, and His glory. He will use them to deepen your dependence on Him and chisel your character into greater Christlikeness. Everything really is, *always*, working out for you.

DAY 61

No one could distinguish the sound of the shouts of joy
from the sound of weeping, because the people made
so much noise. And the sound was heard far away.
Ezra 3:13, NIV

This is an emotional portion of Scripture. The foundations of the new temple have been laid, and God's people are feeling all the feels. Some are celebrating with singing, shouting and loud rejoicing. Some are weeping because they remember the previous temple. They've lived the history which has brought Israel to this point. There's pathos, nostalgia, reminiscing, and real grief at what they've lost.

We're created in God's image, and God is an emotional God. Jesus wept (John 11:35). He even wept so much His tears mingled with sweat and blood (Luke 22:44). He got angry (John 2:15). He celebrated with those who were celebrating (John 2:2). As the Creator of joy, and without sin to rob Him of it, He must surely have been the happiest person who ever lived. He felt all the feels too.

For the next few weeks we'll revel in our freedom to feel. Because how can we *not* get emotional when we think of what Jesus did for us? (Jesus got emotional when He thought of what He was doing for us. Take a look at Luke 22:42.) We'll look at measuring and managing our emotions: holding space for them while not allowing them to rule us. Put another way, we'll learn how to take our feelings along for the ride without letting them take the wheel. We'll come to understand our differing temperaments. We'll learn about grief and developing a robust theology of suffering. And here's hoping we'll laugh along the way.

Free to ask yourself:

**These questions are drawn from themes
covered over the past five days.**

- Do you face a situation in which going with your gut will result in the disapproval of people around you? Is God prompting you to throw a superhero cape of courage across your shoulders, and press into that situation anyway?

- Do you have something to eat and wear today? Are you content? If not, why not? What's chewing up your satisfaction?

- If all sorts of things in your life currently feel up-in-the-air and unsettled, could you thank God for a good day anyway, because the day held moments of learning, laughter, love, adventure, and prayer?

- Read through Psalm 138. How is *everything always working out for you*, even today?

FREE TO FEEL

Free to ask God:

FATHER,

You created my tears and laughter, adrenalin, excitement, grief and gratitude. I give You all my emotions – the good and beautiful feelings leading to actions that honor You, and the unhelpful – even toxic – feelings leading to destructive behavior. Please help me. I can seldom manage my emotions on my own. I need Your comfort and strength, Your wisdom, peace, guidance and perspective.

AMEN.

Liberating limits

A person without self-control is like a city with broken-down walls.
Proverbs 25:28, NLT

I don't know you, but I'm pretty sure you wouldn't want to be known as a *controlling* person. Controlling people are rigid, inflexible, uptight, strict, angry, domineering, manipulative – fill in the negative adjective blank. And yet, we're equally critical of people who have *no* control – people who act recklessly and irresponsibly and with zero restraint.

As ever, the best example we have of the perfect hybrid is Jesus. He was gentle, kind, compassionate and flexible, and yet never loose with His words or deeds, never careless, negligent, imprudent, or rash. What we see in the life of Jesus is how perfect self-control – that elusive fruit of the Spirit! – counterintuitively ushers in freedom. A life of self-control is not a restricted, hemmed-in, killjoy life. It's a kind, measured, sober life of well-timed, well-intentioned mercy. A life of self-control sets us free to love people well.

Think of it like this: Imagine you're sitting in a concert hall being transported by the exquisite, otherworldly music of an exceptional pianist or cellist. The musician is playing with passion, freedom, and abandon. She makes it look effortless. Yet choosing to play a musical instrument requires rigorous self-discipline. It's imperative and expected that you practice daily, for hours. It's having the discipline to stick with it and pursue excellence that ultimately frees you to play, *freely*. In the same way, the lives you admire most – lives lived with the passion, freedom and abandon of true compassion and humility – are built within the good, safe, indispensable parameters of self-control.

FREE TO FEEL

Free to laugh

'He will once again fill your mouth with laughter
and your lips with shouts of joy.'
Job 8:21, NLT

I often pray for laughter during stressful times. I always pray for it before a family holiday. I pray, 'God let us laugh a lot – loudly, uproariously, for a long time. Let there be tremendous silliness.' God created laughter. He called it good. And it's good to seek it out deliberately (though of course not at another's expense). It's good for our stomach muscles. It's good for our brains and their release of dopamine and endorphins. And it seems to shave off decades, leaving us feeling younger and freer.

Solomon may not have had all the science at his fingertips, but he knew all this to be true. 'A cheerful heart is good medicine, but a broken spirit saps a person's strength,' he wrote (Proverbs 17:22). Lawrence Robinson comments, 'It's true: laughter is strong medicine. It draws people together in ways that trigger healthy physical and emotional changes in the body. Laughter strengthens your immune system, boosts mood, diminishes pain, and protects you from the damaging effects of stress. Nothing works faster or more dependably to bring your mind and body back into balance than a good laugh. Humor lightens your burdens, inspires hope, connects you to others, and keeps you grounded, focused, and alert. It also helps you release anger and forgive sooner.'

Need a good laugh today? It's not ridiculous to bring that need before the throne of grace. It's not impossible that laughing may be the most spiritual thing you do all day. Trust God to come through for you with something hilarious, to heal.

Free to redefine

Yet God has made everything beautiful for its own time.
He has planted eternity in the human heart, but even so,
people cannot see the whole scope of God's work from beginning
to end. So I concluded there is nothing better than to be happy
and enjoy ourselves as long as we can. And people should eat and
drink and enjoy the fruits of their labor, for these are gifts from God.
Ecclesiastes 3:11-13, NLT

It's impossible to experience the ongoing bliss we imagine 'happiness' to be. While we're between Eden and eternity, we'll come up short if we continually anticipate perfect scenarios devoid of pain, conflict, and suffering.

Instead, it's freeing to redefine happiness within a now-and-not-yet framework. Happiness is found in this present moment – and the moments still to come in eternity. So, right now: what do you see, hear, taste, smell, or touch? What is good or beautiful about your immediate experience? If there really isn't much, focus on the not-yet, still-to-come aspect of happiness. Today is not the end of your story. When you get to the last page of your earthly account, you'll open the great volume of eternity.

We can also redefine happiness by holding lightly the hard and heavy things. Let them rest softly in your open hands. God gives and takes away. That doesn't change the small happy bits of today, and the splendid pleasures still to come. Don't clench your hands in fear or anger. Live palms up – nondefensively and expectantly, knowing God can and will (ultimately, if not today) deliver you from the severity you face. Until He removes it, He will use it, for your good and His glory.

73

Grief, fear, and love

That Sunday evening the disciples were meeting behind
locked doors because they were afraid of the Jewish leaders.
Suddenly, Jesus was standing there among them! 'Peace be with you,'
He said. As He spoke, He showed them the wounds in His hands
and His side. They were filled with joy when they saw the Lord!
John 20:19-20, NLT

W e can scarcely imagine the trauma the disciples would have
known in the days leading up to Jesus' crucifixion, and in the
days thereafter. They'd watched their only hope being mercilessly mur-
dered. Then they were left alone. What unspeakable grief – and *fear* –
must have flooded their senses and psyches. They feared the political
repercussions of His death. They feared what would become of them.
And they mourned the loss of His wondrous presence in their lives.

The thing about grief is that it's a kind of love. We grieve the loss of
someone when we've loved them and been loved by them. We even
grieve the loss of inanimate things because they've been part of a life
we've loved. What's more, grief and fear tend to show up as identical
twins. They run together, and often we mistake the one for the other.

If you're in a season of grief – if you've had to let go of something or
someone – take some time to list your losses. Whether you're numb
or angry, write out reams of thoughts and feelings. Write out all the
ways your heart is breaking. What do you miss most? What fills you
with fear? And know your Savior, who loves you more than you can
fathom, comes to your side and whispers, 'Peace be with you.'

Altered, not ended

'Don't be afraid, for I am with you. Don't be discouraged,
for I am your God. I will strengthen you and help you.
I will hold you up with My victorious right hand.'
Isaiah 41:10, NLT

Whether you've lost a precious person, or relocated far away from everything familiar, or gone through divorce or retrenchment or any other kind of loss: the grief is real. It can feel as if life has ceased to be worth the living. It may even feel as if life has stopped altogether.

But friend, hear the truth today: life hasn't ended. It's *changed*. It's different now and going forward it will always be different from the life you once knew. But if you're still breathing in and out as you read these words then there's purpose on the planet yet for you to fulfil. You're at a loss as to *how* to move forwards – or even *if* you should move forwards – but what God is asking of you in these grief-stricken days is to accept the loss. And unthinkable as it may seem now, even to embrace it and befriend it, because in time God will turn it into beauty (Ecclesiastes 3:11).

Allow the dramatic, painful change to take its course, taking you on a new course of growth and transformation. God hasn't taken His foot off the gas or His hands off the steering wheel of your life, leaving you stalling, faltering, broken down on the side of life's road, and alone. He is steering you through your grief, and if you let Him, He will bring you into the fresh and spacious places of new life.

FREE TO FEEL

Free to ask yourself:

These questions are drawn from themes covered over the past five days.

- Assuming you're not superhuman, in which areas of your life do you struggle most with a lack of self-control? (Food, finances, faith, friendships and relationships, sexuality, or some other area?) What one step could you take towards surrendering that stumbling block more fully to God?

- When last did you laugh so hard you felt ten years younger, and like everything was going to be ok? What's stopping you asking God to bring some of that laughter into your life today?

- Would you describe yourself as happy? Why or why not?

- Psalm 126 depicts pilgrims ascending to Jerusalem. They've experienced the grief of exile and the joy of deliverance. In the midst of whatever grief you currently face, how could you pray the sentiments of the psalmist, allowing yourself to feel what you feel, and yet also allowing hope to re-enter your heart as you thank God that your story isn't over?

FREE TO FEEL

Free to write it out:

Take some time to journal your own definition of happiness. What are the non-negotiables? What could you do without and still call yourself happy? Then write down a handful of things for which you're grateful, today.

_____

_____

_____

_____

_____

_____

_____

_____

_____

_____

FREE TO FEEL

Free to think

Above all else, guard your heart, for everything you do flows from it.
Proverbs 4:23, NIV

When life is particularly frenetic or demanding, it can feel as if your brain teems with a gazillion thoughts simultaneously. You may be thinking quickly and haphazardly and disconnectedly, but the truth is you can only think one thing at a time. Sometimes our thoughts are neutral. But mostly, we're either thinking something positive, or something negative. And of course, we know that our thinking influences our feeling, and our feeling influences our doing.

If you arrive at an event and your friend doesn't return your greeting from across the room, you may think, 'That was rude of her.' Her rudeness makes you feel angry, so you snap at the waiter taking your order. If she doesn't greet you and you think, 'She obviously didn't spot me waving at her in this crowd,' then that thought leads you to feel determined to head over to her because you're keen to chat. And that feeling propels you across the room in her direction.

Lately, what has consumed your thoughts? How has all that thinking made you feel? Have you found yourself behaving in a certain way – either negatively or positively – because of those thoughts and feelings? Jesus has set you free to live into the truth of Paul's words: 'Don't copy the behavior and customs of this world, but let God transform you into a new person by changing the way you think. Then you will learn to know God's will for you, which is good and pleasing and perfect.' (Romans 12:2) Slow down. Think one true thought at a time.

Free to hurt and hope

The faithful love of the LORD never ends! His mercies never cease.
Great is His faithfulness; His mercies begin afresh each morning.
Lamentations 3:22-23, NLT

The writer of Lamentations (Jeremiah) is realistic about allowing grief to run its course. Then he points us to the horizon of hope, and God's daily grace, urging us to lift our heads and look to the future. He also says, 'But LORD, You remain the same forever! Your throne continues from generation to generation.' (Lamentations 5:19) God's consistent character and reigning power are ultimately what steady us in our hardships.

Admiral James Stockdale was a prisoner of war in Vietnam for seven-and-a-half years. He wrote a memoir about the diabolical things he experienced there. And yet, his later life was happy. Jim Collins, who interviewed Stockdale, writes, 'If this memoir feels depressing for me, how on earth did he survive when he was actually there and *did not know the end of the story*?' Stockdale's response was, 'I never lost faith in the end of the story. I never doubted not only that I would get out, but also that I would prevail in the end and turn the experience into the defining event of my life ... You must never confuse faith that you will prevail in the end – which you can never afford to lose – with the discipline to confront the most brutal facts of your current reality, whatever they might be.'

We shouldn't be delusional about how hard life is. Yet we dare not lose faith in the glorious end of the story. And until we get there, we're promised, for the next twenty-four hours, grace enough for whatever we face.

Free to be crushed

'Father, if You are willing, please take this cup of suffering
away from Me. Yet I want Your will to be done, not Mine.'
Luke 22:42, NLT

Trials expose the authenticity of our confidence in God, and there's joy in discovering what's real about our faith, when faced with seemingly insurmountable opposition or sadness or disappointment or betrayal. That's not to say if we crumble or cry in the face of trouble, we're 'bad Christians'. But trials have a way of taking us to the very end of ourselves, and when we get there (kicking and screaming), we find Jesus and, marvelously, He's enough.

It's like, the scent of roses in full bloom is captivating. But even more powerful is the fragrant perfume released when rose petals are trampled. Similarly, there's a Christ-like aroma that rises from the lives of God's people when the world tries to stamp them out. The making of good wine requires a stripping of the fruit, a crushing, and a waiting. And for God to advance His Kingdom by bringing new wine from our lives – for new wineskins – we should expect to be stripped of people, places and things that detract from His purposes for us. We should expect to feel crushed by circumstances. We should expect to wait for the fulfilment of God's promises. We should expect the result to be sublime, and irresistible.

Trials take us to the place of desperation in which we're ok to pray (and to really mean it): 'God, do to me whatever will bring You the most glory.' It's perhaps in that sweet and strenuous space that we're most like our Savior.

Let the river run

Weeping may last through the night,
but joy comes with the morning.
Psalm 30:5, NLT

Thanksgiving is a magnet for miracles. But realistically, when we're in the thick of trauma or grief, it feels ludicrous, impossible, and inauthentic to look for rainbows and silver linings.

During one such season of hardship, I started a fresh thanksgiving journal, because I've done the experiment. I've lived habitually thankful and experienced how thanksgiving ushers in healing and happiness. I searched gratefully for small everyday gifts all around me. Like, driving past an incredibly beautiful tree, or finding there was a bit of leftover cream in the fridge I could pour in my coffee. I closed the curtains on my grief and cracked on, giving thanks instead.

But then a friend challenged me to open the curtains. Just a little. Every couple of days. Take a look. Feel the pain. Sit with it. Cry the tears. Then close the curtains to cope. I'd pour that cream into my coffee. Turn the music louder. Hold hands. Walk the dog by the river. Pick blackberries from hedges and revel in new and wondrous beauties as I discovered them. I began to understand that thanksgiving wasn't enough. I couldn't let the grief stagnate. I had to let its turbulent rapids course through me too. So I started writing down lists of my losses at the back of the thanksgiving journal. At the time of writing, I'm still using that journal. At some point, those parallel soul streams – the pages of gratitude and grief – will meet in the middle, and I think they'll meet me, healthier.

FREE TO FEEL

Feeling for others

Be happy with those who are happy, and weep with those who weep.
Romans 12:15, NLT

You may not find it easy to celebrate with someone as they revel in success, particularly when their accolade or breakthrough is something you've been working towards too. Rejoicing with those who rejoice involves putting aside your ego (and any jealousy or sulkiness it may spawn) and entering into an attitude of good-for-you. Fake it 'til you make it, if necessary. Be happy for the happy person, until you really are happy too.

Mostly, it's far easier to weep with those who weep. Sometimes the most acute pain we carry is the pain of other people. I've found this to be most true as it relates to my husband and kids. A mom is only ever as happy as her unhappiest child, and the one-flesh reality of marriage means we hold in our hearts one another's tensions and triumphs. I've also walked closely to friends who suffer with depression, or who have been victims of power imbalances, sexual abuse, or the narcissistic destructiveness of a parent or spouse. It's agonizing and frustrating to look on when there's nothing we can do or say to fix things, or even to comfort those we love.

It's ok to just sit with people in their pain. Allow yourself to feel that pain too. And know your hands are never tied. You can listen. You can love practically with acts of service like hot meals, mowed lawns, babysat children, and ironed laundry. Most of all, you can pray. Our Heavenly Father – who loves our people even more than we do – has every resource required to rescue them.

FREE TO FEEL

Free to ask yourself:

These questions are drawn from themes covered over the past five days.

- Is there a person in your life about whom you predominantly think negative thoughts? What positive thought could you choose, to replace this habitual pessimism?

- Where do you need to apply the Stockdale Paradox to your own life – the idea that you dare not lose sight of the end of the story because ultimately, in Christ, you will prevail and triumph, even as you enter the brutal battles, eyes wide open, of your current reality?

- Are you battling to let go of your will in a particular area of your life? What is it you so badly want? Are you scared God wants something different? What would surrender to Him look like in your life today?

- Read John 11:32-33. Jesus wept for Lazarus, and He wept for strangers and friends who were weeping for Lazarus too – even though He knew He was about to raise Lazarus from the dead. What does this say about His love for you, and the way He carries your pain? What does it teach us about our future in Him?

Free to ask God:

HEAVENLY FATHER,

Give me eyes to see the beauty all around me today. Make my heart soft and supple, so entitlement gives way immediately to quick and easy thanksgiving. Make me grateful for every good and perfect gift, every small mercy and surprise bonus and unexpected kindness. And yet, even as I give thanks, help me to acknowledge my griefs. Give me grace to see them too, to speak them aloud if necessary, to process my pain – transforming it, so I don't transmit it.

AMEN.

FREE TO FEEL

Free to be defenseless

He did not retaliate when He was insulted,
nor threaten revenge when He suffered. He left
His case in the hands of God, who always judges fairly.
1 Peter 2:23, NLT

The instinct to defend oneself at all costs is deeply embedded in the human psyche. It's a no-brainer. If you're pushed under water, you'll do anything to override your attacker, clawing your way to the surface with bursting lungs.

But in our interpersonal relationships, where the complexities of ego and reputation are often at play, Jesus shows us an astonishingly countercultural, more powerful way. He relaxes into the mercy-hold of His Heavenly Father, trusting Him to do all the defending.

Despite our different worship styles and church cultures, most believers would agree that holding out our hands, palms up, or lifting them in worship, isn't weird. It's a natural posture of praise and surrender. And there's no reason we shouldn't practice the habit beyond church walls. When negative or unhelpful emotions threaten to overwhelm us and drown out reason or objectivity, instead of fighting to the surface to issue a diatribe of self-defense, we might choose to rest in a palms-up posture. It's impossible to be defensive when you sit with the backs of your hands resting on your knees. Try it. It's true. It will keep you gentle. It will calm you down and help you breathe deeply, especially when you're in emotionally or relationally volatile situations, around people who are prone to annoy you or hurt you. It will help you to forgive quickly and easily, and it's a physical symbol of surrendering your case to the God who always judges fairly.

Knowing me, knowing you (and knowing Ones)

There are different kinds of gifts, but the same Spirit distributes them.
1 Corinthians 12:4, NIV

There are dozens of different personality profiling tests, each helpful in its own way. Self-awareness is tremendously freeing. Understanding the personality of your spouse, best friend, or colleague also sets you free to offer so much more grace and patience, because you'll appreciate their strengths, aversions, preferences, and tendencies.

The Enneagram is one such personality profiling tool. It's described as a nine-sided figure used in a particular system of analysis to represent nine broad personality types. Like any other of these tools, it's not perfect, but it's super helpful in fathoming what makes you, me and others feel what we feel. Enneagram Ones – Improvers or Perfectionists – place a high value on integrity and principles. They're described as 'driven by the motivational need to be good and right.' Quality, perfection, standards, structure, and self-control are important to them. An Enneagram expert says, 'At their best, Ones are tolerant, self-accepting and serene, offering dignity and discernment to themselves and the world around them. Less-healthy type Ones tend to be judgmental, uncompromising, and pedantic, driven by a critical gaze and an acute awareness of their own imperfections and sense of not being good enough.' Ones tell themselves they need to know right from wrong and work diligently to improve the world. They come across as responsible, organized, and conscientious, but at times critical, impatient, and even self-righteous. If you recognize yourself as a One, perhaps you might pray for gentleness in your dealings with others who may not share your clarity and passion for world change.

86

Knowing Twos

Do not neglect to do good and to share what
you have, for such sacrifices are pleasing to God.
Hebrews 13:16, ESV

Enneagram Twos are called the Considerate Helpers. They're motivated by the need to be appreciated and liked. Relationships are extremely important to them, so they're complimentary, generous, kind, and self-sacrificing. They want to fill the world with love, and they get to work offering care and attention to their nearest and dearest. An Enneagram expert says, 'At their best, Twos are unconditionally supportive, able to practice self-care and offer the gift of humility to themselves and the world around them. Less-healthy Twos may seem flattering and manipulative as they "give to get", motivated by a deep belief that they don't deserve to be loved for who they are.' It's not uncommon for a Two to believe they deserve love only because of all the help and support they offer to others.

Their empathy, other-centeredness, generosity, and warmth make Twos easy to like, though their anger may well flare up when they or someone they love is mistreated. They also tend to put their own needs and feelings second to others', stepping in to help whenever and wherever needed at a cost to their own wellbeing.

If you know and love a Two, be aware that he or she thrives on help and appreciation. And if you're a Two yourself, perhaps you might ask God to help you recognize your subconscious motivation for being generous or caring. Pray too for wisdom and resolve to set up appropriate boundaries so as not to neglect your own needs. You can't be helpful to others if you're falling apart yourself.

Knowing Threes

... as the Scriptures say, 'If you want to boast, boast only about the Lord.'
1 Corinthians 1:31, NLT

Enneagram Threes – the Performers or Competitive Achievers – are often maximizers. They want to be the best at whatever they do and place a high value on success and achievement. They're all about efficiency and results, and at their unhealthiest, they're too concerned about image and recognition, believing their worth comes from what they do, not who they are. Threes are generally flexible, hardworking, principled, and approachable. They're purveyors of hope and integrity.

While a Three is likely a 'doer' – driven, energetic, quick-thinking, adaptable, and results-focused – this natural ambition may go into win-at-all-costs overdrive, impatience, dismissiveness, or the habit of comparing themselves with others. An Enneagram expert writes, 'The adaptive Three is often referred to as the "chameleon" as they change their persona and adapt their role, behavior, communication and presentation to suit the audience they are trying to impress ... In a team environment, the Threes may find themselves drawn to leadership roles and others are likely to experience them as very energetic and confident. They dress for success and will make sure that the way they look serves their purpose, ambitions and audience.' A Three is prone to confirmation bias, believing their own PR, and framing failure as learning. Their feelings are also likely to be shaped by how others are responding to them.

If you recognize yourself as a Three, perhaps you might pray that God would grow in you a gentle authenticity. More and more, may you think of others before yourself, channeling your intellect and energy into the common Kingdom good.

Knowing Fours

Why am I discouraged? Why is my heart so sad? I will put my hope in God! I will praise Him again – my Savior and my God!
Psalm 43:5, NLT

Enneagram Fours – the Intense Creatives – are described as having 'the motivational need to express their uniqueness and be authentic. Fours value individualism and as a result, feelings, self-expression, and purpose will be important to them. They are quite romantic at heart and appreciate beauty and creating meaning for themselves and for others. At their best, Fours are experienced as sensitive yet content. They offer the gift of equanimity and authenticity to themselves and the world. A less healthy Four may feel misunderstood, while others experience them as melancholic and temperamental. This pattern stems from the Four's acute awareness of their own wounds and flaws.'

As with any of the Enneagram types, Fours have both gifts and blind spots. They're artistic, self-aware, sensitive, and understanding. They're inspired, brave and purposeful, unafraid to explore the full spectrum of human emotion. They can, however, be prone to negativity, envy, dissatisfaction, and self-absorption, and can be overly introspective, expressing an overdeveloped desire to be different or special.

If you recognize yourself as a Four, perhaps you could ask Jesus to heighten your sense of gratitude and contentment. In conversation, pray for ways to show an interest in others, and ask the Holy Spirit to nudge you when you're talking a little too much about yourself. If you're definitely not a Four, but there's a precious Four in your inner circle or an office cubicle near yours, ask God for the grace and wisdom to translate your intentions into his or her reality.

Free to ask yourself:

**These questions are drawn from themes
covered over the past five days.**

- Have you been maligned, mistreated, or misunderstood? Have you tried to defend yourself? What would it look like for you to trust God to do all the defending on your behalf?

- Do you recognize yourself as an Enneagram One, Two, Three or Four? (You're free to skip ahead and read about types Five through Nine!)

- Did you have any *aha*-moments as you read about the Enneagram types, suddenly identifying friends, family members, or co-workers who fit the descriptions?

- If you have time for extra reading today, have a look at Proverbs 18:2, Proverbs 14:29 and Colossians 4:6. How does understanding how you're wired, and how others are wired, change your relationships?

Free to write it out:

Ask God to reveal any personality blind spots you may have. Even just one! Take some time to write about it. Is there something you need to repent of? Do you need to ask a friend or family member's forgiveness? Is there a new pattern of behavior you could intentionally choose, to replace any toxic habits or natural reactions?

_____

_____

_____

_____

_____

_____

_____

_____

_____

_____

Knowing Fives

Intelligent people are always ready to learn.
Their ears are open for knowledge.
Proverbs 18:15, NLT

Enneagram Fives are the Quiet Specialists. They're objective and independent, driven by a need to understand the world. They're generally very private individuals, conserving energy and other resources so they won't have to depend on anyone in the future.

Unfortunately, Fives can come across as unhealthily self-sufficient, ungenerous, and intellectually snooty. And yet Fives have wonderful strengths. They're perceptive, curious, and ingenious. They're able to minimize their own needs and look at circumstances unsentimentally, making them effective visionaries. Fives will be chatty and engaging when conversation turns to their field of expertise but tend to come across as socially withdrawn.

An Enneagram expert comments, 'Fives may have a voracious appetite for information on certain topics ... They have the ability to categorize information, events, and people into partitions in their mind ... Fives tend to intellectualize feelings and trust their mind to make sense of what they are experiencing on an emotional level. Their preference for the objective may make it difficult for Fives to differentiate between thoughts and feelings. Fives are easily drained by emotionally charged situations ... Detachment is a way of protecting against the pain of emotions and Fives may become so detached that they disengage from life or appear cold to others.' If you reckon you're a Five, ask God to show up any changes you might make. Do others perhaps experience you as arrogant or patronizing? Do you opt for solitude over relational commitment, to spare yourself pain?

FREE TO FEEL

Knowing Sixes

'See, God has come to save me. I will trust in Him and not be afraid.
The LORD God is my strength and my song; He has given me victory.'
Isaiah 12:2, NLT

The Enneagram Six is the Loyal Skeptic. More than anything, Sixes want to feel safe, prepared, and as if they belong. Thus, they are loyal and responsible to a fault, and excellent at plotting worst-case scenarios. A healthy Six has overcome crippling fear and is able to offer clarity, steady devotion, and trust. An unhealthy Six worries unduly, and may appear anxious, cynical, or suspicious, carrying emotions ranging from mild unease to dread and panic. As an emotionally reactive style, Sixes are wonderfully consistent, cooperative, trustworthy, and dedicated, committed to causes and people they value, quick to bravely make a stand for what's right, regardless of the cost. Because they're risk-aware (and often risk-averse), Sixes are prepared, highly analytical, and ready to minimize risk.

Sixes are problem solvers but can be cynical when presented with solutions that seem too easy. You might hear a Six saying, 'Yes, but ...' Sixes are constantly aware of what might go wrong, and so tend to come across as pessimistic, stubborn, or overly cautious. They tend to overthink, and then give in to their fears.

If you're close to someone who is a Six, learn to listen to their intuition and scenario solutions, and ask God for ways to allay their fears and build trust. If you're a Six, may God set you free from every fear, empowering you to build strong relationships as you bring perceptiveness, spiritual acuity, trust, and rare loyalty to your circle of influence.

FREE TO FEEL

Knowing Sevens

This is the day the LORD has made. We will rejoice and be glad in it.
Psalm 118:24, NLT

Enneagram Sevens – the Enthusiastic Visionaries – are adventurous and spontaneous. They believe the future is full of incredible possibilities, all of which they want to experience to the max (while avoiding pain). They live *carpe diem* lives, prizing freedom, optimism, and inspiration, and always looking to create positive forward momentum. When they're not swept up in impulsive behaviors which make them seem unfocused, uncommitted, and unsatisfied, they're tranquil, content, flexible, practical, positive, upbeat, and future-oriented, able to bring themselves meaningfully to the present moment. Their bodies are usually as active as their minds. Sevens are quick to connect ideas and are always looking for mental stimulation, but this means they may get bored easily, may feel they're frustrated or trapped by limited choices, may not like their abilities to be questioned, and may leave projects unfinished as they jump to the next exciting thing.

Who are the Sevens in your life? How can you give them more space to be their enthusiastic selves? And if you're a Seven, would you ask God to show you parts of your makeup you need to surrender to Him? Like, do you tend to reframe failure to avoid taking responsibility, or gloss over important moments – moving on too quickly to more positive or lighthearted subjects? Might your energy and joviality be distracting to others? Ask God to use your irrepressible optimism to mobilize people to make a difference, for His glory and the good of all around you.

FREE TO FEEL

Knowing Eights

Therefore, since we have such a hope, we are very bold.
2 Corinthians 3:12, NIV

The Enneagram Eight – the Active Controller or Challenger – is driven by the need to be strong and avoid showing vulnerability. Eights like to be in control, directly impacting others. Caring and approachable, they don't shy away from challenges and are eager to do justice on behalf of others. If their strengths are out of balance and they feel the need to over-represent themselves in a larger-than-life way, they may come across as aggressive, domineering, intense and even lustful.

Still, the gifts of the Eight are beautiful to behold: they're assertive, direct, decisive, and protective. They go with their gut, and get things done. They're naturally influential. While they're irritated by the need to micromanage, they'll do it, to stay in control and get the outcome they want. Eights tend to size people up: strong or weak? They don't like incompetence or a victim mindset but will defend those in their circle of responsibility. Eights are prone to anger but are generally quick to get over it and move on. Fear and sadness render them extremely vulnerable, and they'll only show these softer emotions when they feel safe with others.

Eights don't always realize how intimidating they can be, and they don't always give others time to get on board as they take control and rapidly roll out decisions and actions. This can create relational tension.

Are you perhaps an Eight? When you feel trapped or controlled, remember you bear a beautiful freedom. Ask God to make you gentle and considerate of those who don't share your strengths or perspectives.

FREE TO FEEL

Knowing Nines

Do all that you can to live in peace with everyone.
Romans 12:18, NLT

Enneagram Nines are called the Adaptive Peacemakers. More than anything they want to feel settled and in harmony with the world, so, an expert explains, 'being accommodating and accepting will be important to them. They strive for a peaceful existence and appreciate stability, preferring to avoid conflict. At their best, Nines are experienced as self-aware and vibrant. They offer the gift of right, sustainable action to themselves and the world around them. Less-healthy Nines may be experienced as procrastinating, stubborn and self-denying. This stems from a pattern of going along to get along with others and the eventual discomfort that arises when this strategy is not satisfying.'

Nines are described as understanding, agreeable, patient, supportive and genuine, and you might hear them saying, 'Can't everyone just get along?' Nines will act (or remain passive and non-assertive) to maintain peace, easily adopting the habits, practices and feelings of people close to them, to blend or connect with them. Nines come across as serene and easygoing, but do experience, internally, intense emotions.

Do you struggle to say no to people? Do you sometimes set yourself up to be overlooked – then feel hurt when you're ignored, responding with passive aggression? Do you find others don't quite get it when you try to express what you truly need or want? If you recognize yourself as a Nine, pray for the courage and graciousness to assert your authentic feelings or opinions. If you're friends with, married to, or working with a Nine, appreciate their peace-loving ways while offering them a safe place to freely express points of conflict.

Free to ask yourself:

These questions are drawn from themes covered over the past five days.

- Each of the Enneagram types has a vice associated with it – the 'passion' or lie of that type. We're all capable – and culpable – when it comes to all nine of these vices, but each type tends towards a particular sin more than any of the others. Ones are prone to anger, Twos to pride, Threes to deceit, Fours to envy, Fives to avarice (greed), Sixes to fear, Sevens to gluttony, Eights to lust, and Nines to sloth (laziness).

- Read 2 Corinthians 13:5. Test yourself! Where is the Holy Spirit convicting you, or kindly leading you to repentance?

FREE TO FEEL

Free to ask God:

JESUS,

Help me see and celebrate the strengths of my temperament. Help me see, too, where I've believed a lie, or chosen toxic patterns and habits of behavior to protect myself. Make me mindful of events from my childhood which I haven't seen or considered in the light of Your truth. Help me surrender those to You. Let's deal with them together, so I can be free. I give You my internal makeup – which You made up! As I become more like You, day by day, let my personality glorify You.

AMEN.

FREE TO FEEL

Crazy and lazy

Never stop praying.
1 Thessalonians 5:17, NLT

Walter Wink said, 'History belongs to the intercessors – those who believe and pray the future into being.' Prayer is a wondrous, mysterious, supernatural, obvious, accessible resource. How is it that a sovereign God – who already knows the end from the beginning and is actively, sovereignly, holding and handling every atom in the cosmos – would give us this tool so we can partner with Him in that process? I mean, we can scarcely be trusted to remember to stop for milk and loo paper on our way home from work. And yet, through prayer, God invites us – *freely!* – into His throne room where we find grace and mercy to help us in times of need (Hebrews 4:16). This same limitlessly rich, generous God, our Provider (see Genesis 22:14, Deuteronomy 2:7, 1 Samuel 2:8, 1 Chronicles 29:12, Matthew 6:26, Acts 14:17, Philippians 4:17 and dozens more!) – the One who owns the cattle on a thousand hills and all the gold embedded in rocks beneath those hills (Psalm 50:10) – He freely invites us into His storehouses. ·

Knowing all this, it's crazy how little we pray – and how *lazy* we are to pray. If we have this astonishing, free tool at our disposal with which to move the heart of God and change the course of the Kingdom and history on planet earth, why don't we use it more? Over the next few weeks, we'll press into the idea of being free to pray, anytime, anywhere. Let's ask God to uncover the things that hinder us from praying more.

Let's ask Him for renewed excitement to find Him in otherworldly, totally ordinary, conversation.

FREE TO ASK

Waking words

In the morning, LORD, You hear my voice; in the morning
I lay my requests before You and wait expectantly.
Psalm 5:3, NIV

Imagine for a moment all the Christians in the world, across every time zone, woke up in the morning and *did not check their phones.* What if – in those first groggy, what-day-is-it, just-hit-snooze, waking moments when we long for the duvet to swallow us for a few minutes more, or when we fumble on the bedside table to wake up our social media feeds before we're fully awake ourselves – what if, when the new day beckons, *we turned first to God?* Imagine the impact we'd have on the world if we all determined we'd win the day by beginning it, talking to God.

I don't get this right every day, but I've made it my habit, before throwing off the covers, to greet God with a few simple lines, the intention of which I trust Him to eloquently translate as: 'Lord, from breakfast to bedtime, position me for righteousness. Maximize my life today, for Your maximum glory, whatever shape that takes. Give me words of wisdom for every person I'll encounter.' I picture how the day will likely end, and work backwards from that, praying through my schedule or whatever big or ordinary things will probably happen. I borrow the words of an old hymn: 'Take my life and let it be ever only all for Thee.' No single day ever rolls out flawlessly. But I know my days derail a little less dramatically when I've prayed preemptively. We don't know what's at stake as we wake to the new mercies of each new day. Let's pray.

Straight answers

Trust in the Lord with all your heart and lean not
on your own understanding; in all your ways submit
to Him, and He will make your paths straight.
Proverbs 3:5-6, NIV

Life is a series of decisions. Some are small and relatively inconse-quential. (Peanut butter or jam on my toast? Or both?) Some are life changing. (Should I marry him or not?) Some alter eternity. (Is this the right time to tell my co-worker about Jesus?)

When it comes to making big decisions, Andy Stanley suggests four questions to prayerfully, helpfully, ask ourselves. And we may as well practice using these questions on small decisions too.

Surrender the decision completely to God, asking Him to lay His de-sires for you, on your heart. Then ask yourself, (1) Am I being honest with myself – *really*? (2) What's the story I want to tell? (3) Is there a tension that deserves my attention? (4) What would be most honoring to God? (And what would be most honoring to the people around me?)

Write down – no filters! – your hopes, fears, motives, or misgivings, as they relate to the decision you're making. Don't kid yourself. Don't *lie* to yourself. Be real. Then decide how you'd ideally love to relay the outcome of this decision, with a grandchild perched on your future knee. What kind of story would you be proud to tell? Pay attention to the gut tug of the Holy Spirit's conviction – or the excitement, expec-tancy, or anticipation of a God idea. Lastly, check that your decision is devoid of any sin and would not only glorify God, but be honoring (kind, considerate, loving, and gentle) towards others. Then go for it.

FREE TO ASK

Praying for a pony

This is the confidence we have in approaching God:
that if we ask anything according to His will, He hears us.
1 John 5:14, NIV

It feels scandalous to suggest it, but here it is: *you can ask God for anything.*

'Woah!' you say, shocked. 'Isn't that the prosperity gospel?' Nope. Perpetrators of the prosperity gospel spew the lie that you *deserve* anything that takes your fancy. Whatever you want, you can name it and claim it and God will deliver it, like some cosmic Santa Claus. And if He doesn't give you the car or the house or the healing or the promotion or the husband or the baby? It's your fault. Damningly and disappointingly, *you* just don't have enough faith.

All that is a gross distortion of the truth. Nevertheless, you *can* ask God for anything. He's your Father. He imagined you and created you. He sustains your life. He loves you eternally. The same way a child would ask her dad for a piggyback or a pony or an ice-cream on the beach or help tying her shoelaces, you can ask your Heavenly Father, with audacious confidence, for the biggest or smallest things that occur to you. Things you need. Things you want. With fearless trust in a loving Father, you can enter the storehouses of His resources and ask, trusting He knows far more than you do. He knows what you really need, and when. He knows what will distract you from His purposes for you. (He might say no to the pony. Or not!) Either way, you can celebrate that His given outcome will be the best one, at the best time, for you.

Up close and personal

This high priest of ours understands our weaknesses, for He faced
all of the same testings we do, yet He did not sin. So let us come
boldly to the throne of our gracious God. There we will receive
His mercy, and we will find grace to help us when we need it most.
Hebrews 4:15-16, NLT

You can ask God for anything, not just because He made everything, and owns everything, or because time and the universe rest in His power. You can ask God for anything because of His character. He's holy and powerful. He's also gracious, loving, and safe. You can ask without fear.

Rory Dyer says, 'God the Father has a long fuse, a short memory, a thick skin, and a big heart.' That means He's slow to anger. He doesn't get irritated with you for asking, the way we as parents (or is it just me?) get annoyed when our kids nag. He wipes out our sin and He decides to forget about it, as if it never happened. (*What sin?*) He places us in right standing with Himself. He isn't easily offended, the way we are. He's doesn't go and get His feelings hurt by anything we do or say. Mad at God? He's ok with that. If He is who He says He is, then He's way more than big enough to handle our temper tantrums and keep on loving us.

The writer of Hebrews says we can approach God *boldly* – confidently, shamelessly, intrepidly, courageously, unflinchingly. That means it's ok to draw near. Don't shout your requests from afar. Get into God's presence. Come up close and personal to the throne of grace.

FREE TO ASK

Free to ask yourself:

**These questions are drawn from themes
covered over the past five days.**

- Is prayer always your knee-jerk, first response to trouble of any kind? If not, why not?

- What kinds of situations prompt you to pray immediately? How might you turn that urgency and expectation to other areas of your life?

- Can you remember a time when God answered your prayer almost instantaneously? Which of your prayers did God take years to answer? For which prayers are you still waiting for answers or clarity?

- Psalm 118:5 says, 'Out of my distress I called on the LORD; the LORD answered me and set me free.' For the psalmist, praying resulted in freedom. Do you need to be set free from something? Is there something stopping you from calling on the Lord out of your distress?

Free to write it out:

Take a few minutes to write out the deepest desire of your heart, in prayer. If it's way too personal to record in this devotional, write it out on a separate piece of paper. Burn it or bury it afterwards if you must. But take time to be honest with yourself and your Savior, about what you truly long for. Trust Him.

_____

_____

_____

_____

_____

_____

_____

_____

_____

_____

FREE TO ASK

Everyone everywhere

I urge you, first of all, to pray for all people. Ask God to
help them; intercede on their behalf, and give thanks for them.
1 Timothy 2:1, NLT

Maybe for you, prayer is more shopping list than conversation. That's ok. As we've said, our Father has a long fuse, a short memory, a thick skin, and a big heart.

But rattling off your inventory of needs and wants is so vanilla. The kind of intimacy God's designed you to enjoy in His presence is every flavor and color conceivable. An idea would be to ask God, 'What do you want to do with me, and this day?' Spend some time waiting. Don't let the silence freak you out. Breathe deeply. See if a particular thought rises, clear and constant and colorful in your mind.

Perhaps, too, you might pray less for things that will satisfy you and pray more for others. Pray, 'God, bring to my mind the people You want me to pray for today.' As surely as I know I'm typing this sentence with my golden retriever snoozing at my feet, *I know God will answer you*. (In fact, email me at dalene.reyburn@gmail.com and tell me about it; I love hearing stories of answered prayer.)

Pray relationally. Pray for good ideas of how to love people well. Pray for insight into the temperaments of unpredictable friends, so you can be the peace and joy of Jesus to them. Ask Him if you can borrow His feelings for (difficult) people, so you can relax and engage with them warmly and kindly, as He would. That kind of other-centered prayer could revolutionize the days and decades of our lives.

From field to fork

The eyes of all look to You in hope; You give them
their food as they need it. When You open Your hand,
You satisfy the hunger and thirst of every living thing.
Psalm 145:15-16, NLT

When you sit down to eat dinner tonight, the food you'll find on your plate (or in your carton of takeout) started life a while ago. If you've planned a sandwich for lunch, the cheese or chicken started working towards the goal of getting between your bread a while back too. If you're vegan, the seeds that grew into whatever you're eating weren't planted yesterday. They've taken months to get to the point of harvest, then consumption. Fruit trees take years to start yielding.

Doubtless you'll get to nosh something today because God is your provider. He sees the end from the beginning way before we ever do, and in ways we never can. He works while you're sleeping, and when you're not even aware there's work to be done. He works in the dark beneath the soil growing roots that will nourish you with something you'll dice or chop and drop into a pan of olive oil weeks from now. This is the day the Lord has made (Psalm 118:24). He saw it before He'd even created the world. He knew the needs you'd have today, before even one of your days had dawned (Isaiah 65:24, Psalm 139:16) – and He promises to deliver.

Remembering this is the God you serve would probably change how you pray. Give thanks for His work in behind-the-scenes people, pastures, plants, and projects that freed you to enjoy the tastes and textures of whatever you're eating today.

FREE TO ASK

Beg, borrow, learn

Hear my prayer, O Lᴏʀᴅ; listen to my plea! Answer me because
You are faithful and righteous ... I lift my hands to You in prayer.
I thirst for You as parched land thirsts for rain ... Let me hear of Your
unfailing love each morning, for I am trusting You. Show me where to
walk, for I give myself to You ... Teach me to do Your will, for You are
my God. May Your gracious Spirit lead me forward on a firm footing.
Psalm 143:1, 6, 8, 10, NLT

FREE TO ASK

If you need a prayer coach, pick any one of the psalmists. When you
don't have words of your own because you're too overwhelmed to
think never mind pray, there's deep comfort in beseeching God with
the psalmist's borrowed words.

God's Word fights for us in prayer. It lends strength to our frail and fragile hearts, and focus to our scattered, frantic thoughts. In Psalm 143,
David is honest about his raw desperation and depression. He appeals
to God's character of love and righteousness. He flat-out begs God to
come through for him. And you can totally plagiarize his prayer.

It's ok to come to God in prayer with absolutely no answers of your
own. In fact, it's the very best posture of approach. 2 Chronicles 20:12
says, 'We do not know what to do, but our eyes are on You.' The answers will come, dear heart. All you need to do is come into God's
presence. Come honest. Come hurting. Come wordless and desperate.
Beg for mercy with words loaned from the Word. Lean into the freedom you have to learn from the prayer warriors of the past.

Needy

Most important of all, continue to show deep love for each other ...
1 Peter 4:8, NLT

FREE TO ASK

None of us wants to be a needy friend. We associate asking for help with weakness. We want to be known as self-sufficient and strong – not pathetic or overly sensitive. Except, God designed us to need each other. It's ok to ask for help. It's even ok to ask for a hug.

Shortly after moving countries, I was invited to a ladies' church meeting. I knew I'd be the youngest woman there by two decades. Usually, I would've politely declined. And yet! I was so excited to see friendly faces and find a safe space just to be. Mostly, I was craving a hug. I desperately hoped there would be someone at the coffee morning who wasn't too British to hug a foreign stranger on our first meeting. Driving to the church, I prayed out loud for a hug.

I arrived to warm greetings but there was definitely no hugging going on. We were in a global pandemic, after all. In Britain. But after the coffee and the Bible study, in the closing prayer, a woman said, 'Thank you God that at last, with lockdown restrictions lifting, we can hug again!' This was my cue. I told her I'd prayed for a hug. Would she oblige? She did, with enormous joy. And then another lady said that in fact *she* was the hug specialist. She hugged me too.

Perhaps it's time to get over ourselves and be brave enough to admit our neediness. God is kind and understanding, faithful to meet us in the smallest moments of our humanness. What do you need today?

Healer

> Are any of you sick? You should call for the elders of
> the church to come and pray over you, anointing you
> with oil in the name of the Lord. Such a prayer offered
> in faith will heal the sick, and the Lord will make you well.
> And if you have committed any sins, you will be forgiven.
> James 5:14-15, NLT

You and I are called to live by faith. When it comes to sickness, accidents, and other tragedies, it takes great faith to trust that God *can* and *does* heal. It takes great faith to trust that if or when He *doesn't* heal, every time, He's still infinitely kind, wise and powerful.

I think perhaps we don't pray for healing enough. Maybe because too many shady, pseudo-Christians have fake-healed too many times and any faith we had in God as our Healer has turned to cynicism. For years I didn't pray much for healing because I didn't *really* believe God was my Father. My wise, well-resourced, rich-in-love Father. These days? I know in the marrow of my bones that I can ask Him anything, any time. I can ask happily and brazenly, with unabashed audacity. Of course, my Father's *Yes* or *No* will always be in accordance with His love for me, and His best plans for me. But I'm His child, so I'm free to ask.

I've also realized we *should* pray for healing – enthusiastically and often! – because God heals (Exodus 15:26, Acts 10:38), and because He's never told us to stop praying for healing. Who needs your prayers for healing today?

Free to ask yourself:

**These questions are drawn from themes
covered over the past five days.**

- Who are you praying for this week?

- What's in your fridge right now? What has God provided for you today, from this good, green earth?

- If you're feeling vulnerable, low, or left out, what kind of help could you pray for today?

- Do you, or does someone you love, need healing? Read Isaiah 53. How do the sorrows and sufferings of Jesus – and His triumph over death – speak life into the situation?

Free to ask God:

HEAVENLY KING,

Help! I've got no answers. No clever ideas. I'm desperate and depressed, and I'm begging You for help. I can't see a way out, but You've promised not to 'abandon me to the realm of the dead' (Psalm 16:10). I'm choosing to believe Your Word that says, 'He lifted me out of the pit of despair, out of the mud and the mire. He set my feet on solid ground and steadied me as I walked along.' (Psalm 40:2) Remind me and refresh me with the truth that You will complete the good work You started in me (Philippians 1:6).

AMEN.

Maybe, maybe not

'If we are thrown into the blazing furnace, the God
whom we serve is able to save us. He will rescue us from
your power, Your Majesty. But even if He doesn't, we want to
make it clear to you, Your Majesty, that we will never serve
your gods or worship the gold statue you have set up.'
Daniel 3:17-18, NLT

When it comes to having faith for healing, we can take our cues from Shadrach, Meshach, and Abednego.

Years ago, my brother-in-law, a keen marathon runner, injured his back. No more races. Almost ten years after that, he read in his daily devotional: 'If you have pain in your life, you should pray.' So, he prayed. God healed him. And he's been running ever since. He's living by faith.

I get tension headaches and migraines. Sometimes they're debilitating. I can't speak or drive. I have half a personality for about three days. One night at our church a dynamic visiting preacher invited people to come forward for prayer. He laid hands on me. He prayed. I prayed. It was an incredible night. So many people were set free in amazing ways. I definitely wasn't healed.

But like my brother-in-law, I'm living by faith. My faith doesn't hinge on whether I'm healed so I'm ok to keep praying for healing. I was simply reminded that night of the splendid truth: 'Still, definitely no headaches in heaven! Maybe there'll be healing sometime in this life. Just not tonight.'

God is doing different things in my character, and in my brother-in-law's character, and in yours. He's got each of us on a different journey; and we can trust Him.

FREE TO ASK

Kingdom come

He will wipe every tear from their eyes, and there will be no more death or sorrow or crying or pain. All these things are gone forever.
Revelation 21:4, NLT

In our freedom to pray for healing, we keep our eyes on the Kingdom. Because, at some point, physical healing won't work for any of us, anymore. Like, Lazarus died. Jesus raised Him from the dead, to demonstrate His power and His love (John 11). Astonishing and miraculous! But Lazarus is no longer with us. He died again. He got to the end of his life (again) and that time, *for real*.

Our lives are pure grace, on borrowed time. Physical healing in any shape or form is just an extension. It's simply God's kindness, to give us a little less pain, or a little extra time with people we love, or more opportunities to be a Kingdom influence by living lives that offer hope to a desperate world. But because humans sinned and the planet broke, we all get to the point where healing doesn't happen, and we die. We get to the end of our stories.

Except, if we know Jesus, the end is just the beginning. No matter what has paralyzed us in this life, we'll run into the arms of the Father. There will be ultimate healing, and the most extravagant Kingdom dinner party imaginable. We'll be there, and Jesus will be there, and He'll look around the table and go, 'Look what I did with the sick and the selfish, the dying and the destitute. Look how beautiful they are. Look how I've healed them, and set them free.'

FREE TO ASK

Let's go

Yes, and the Lord will deliver me from every evil attack
and will bring me safely into His heavenly Kingdom.
All glory to God forever and ever! Amen.
2 Timothy 4:18, NLT

Eugene Peterson, who wrote *The Message* paraphrase of the Bible, died on 22 October 2018 at the age of 85. A week before his death he was admitted to a hospice facility. He'd contracted an infection which complicated his heart disease and dementia. In those last days he was constantly surrounded by family members, and the statement they released after his death said the following: 'During the previous days, it was apparent that [Eugene] was navigating the thin and sacred space between earth and heaven... We overheard him speaking to people we can only presume were welcoming him into paradise... Among his last words were, "Let's go," which suggest his anticipation and perhaps a glimpse of the beauty and eternal delight set before him... His countenance radiated that expectancy. And his joy: my, oh my; the man remained joyful right up to his blessed end, smiling frequently.'

The marvelous, mysterious truth is that God's Kingdom is *now*, and it's *not yet*. And healing gives us a glimpse of that. We're in a glorious dispensation of grace and Holy Spirit power – but the best is yet to be. When God heals physically, it's a tangible manifestation of how He heals spiritually – what He does on the insides of us – and it's an electrifying reminder of the eternal realities that await. I say, *bring it on*. Let's pray more that we'd all begin to pray more for healing – boldly believing in the power and goodness of God.

FREE TO ASK

Love

> But the Holy Spirit produces this kind of fruit in our lives: love, joy, peace, patience, kindness, goodness, faithfulness, gentleness, and self-control. There is no law against these things!
> Galatians 5:22-23, NLT

If there are no red-hot issues burning up your life and no glaring sins of which God is convicting you to repent and you're not quite sure what you should be praying about, *you could pray to bear more fruit.* After all, that's how we make God known. We're to bear more and more Kingdom fruit, so that, more and more, the world would feed off our lives and taste Jesus.

Love is the first descriptor on Paul's fruit-of-the-Spirit list. The Greek word translated 'love' is *agape,* and it means affection or benevolence. It's a pure, intentional, sacrificial love. It's ongoing and outgoing. It decides to put others' needs before its own. It's powerful, and it's in short supply all over the world. How incredible that as Jesus followers, we get to flood the global market. The Holy Spirit lives in us, growing love on our insides until it spills outside of us too. Perhaps you could pray today:

Loving Father, help me see others the way You see them. Please let me borrow Your feelings for them, so that I might love them better. Make me a good listener, and slow to speak. Let me only offer words that nourish the souls of those around me, not cutting anyone with unkindness and thoughtlessness. Help me always to go second, allowing others to go ahead of me through the doorways of life, that they might taste Your abundant love. Amen.

DAY 110

Joy

Always be full of joy in the Lord. I say it again – rejoice!
Philippians 4:4, NLT

Paul commands us to be full of joy – *always*. We know God's commands are enabling. He wouldn't tell us to rejoice always if it wasn't possible. Again, the Spirit who lives in us is the source of joy. He cultivates our characters, so our lives yield that fruit (Galatians 5:22-23).

Joy shouldn't be confused with ecstasy or fun or a sense of happy-go-lucky insouciance. Those are all real emotions, but joy is richer and truer than all those things, and independent of circumstances. It's the deep-seated, immovable peace, contentment and happy satisfaction of knowing, no matter what, *God.*

John Mark Comer reckons it's enough to ask God that we might be reasonably happy in this life, and exceedingly happy with Jesus in the next. That adds up to plenty of joy. It's unrealistic to expect unabating happiness for the full length of our lives in a broken world. *But the fruit of the Spirit is joy!* We are abidingly filled with the Spirit. If we know Jesus, the Holy Spirit is in us (Romans 8:9), so no matter what, joy is always a viable option.

Jesus, Creator of joy, You were surely the happiest person who ever lived, despite the abuse You took, and despite how You suffered and died. You promise us that Your joy is our strength (Nehemiah 8:10). Please give me some of that joy. Bring it alive in my heart in fresh, wondrous ways. Allow it to light me up from the inside – and radiate from me to bring bright sparks of levity to a dark world. Amen.

Free to ask yourself:

**These questions are drawn from themes
covered over the past five days.**

- Do you know of someone who prayed, and was healed? Has it ever happened to you?

- Is praying for healing something that comes naturally to you, whenever you or someone close to you is in pain? Why, or why not?

- Does the name or face of someone come to mind, when you ask God, 'Whom should I love today?'

- Read Psalm 16:11. When faced with people or places that threaten to steal your joy, how might you intentionally remain on the path of life, finding joy in the presence of God?

FREE TO ASK

Free to write it out:

**Take time to write out your thoughts on healing.
Are you frustrated, or full of faith? Do you long for healing
in your own life, or in the life of someone close to you?
Healing from depression, anxiety, cancer, Covid-19?**

Peace

> Now may the Lord of peace Himself give you His peace at
> all times and in every situation. The Lord be with you all.
> 2 Thessalonians 3:16, NLT

In the Bible, peace can be interpreted quite politically – in an almost military way. It can mean being *at peace* with God – in the sense that we are no longer His enemies. We're fighting on the same side as our King, in a war against evil. It also means to be *at peace* within ourselves and with the world around us: to be undisturbed and 'un-disturbing', to feel a sense of calm and serenity and tranquility. Peace is *not* a trance-like, Zen-like passivity (as in, 'Peace out, bro …'), but a deep, true, wide awake, fully alert assurance that all is as it should be in an eternal sense. It's the comfortable assurance that ultimately everything is going to be ok, and that we are in good hands.

You are free to pray for peace, and you are free to start today.

Holy Spirit, give me Your peace. My shoulders can't take it anymore! Please take my burdens, and drape over me instead Your blanket of peace. Give me wisdom to be a peacemaker and a peacekeeper, as far as it depends on me. When I walk into a room fraught with tension or tumult, use me to bring Your presence and Your peace. I don't want to ever be confused for being in the enemy's ranks. Ally me to Yourself forever – Jesus, Prince of Peace! I want to be at peace with You and in the palm of Your hand. Amen.

Patience

Always be humble and gentle. Be patient with each other,
making allowance for each other's faults because of your love.
Ephesians 4:2, NLT

If you've been tracking with me, you'll know we're learning to pray through Paul's revelation of the fruit of the Spirit in Galatians 5:22-23, and patience is next on the list. Christians can be oddly superstitious about praying for patience. You'll hear folks joking (but not joking), saying things like, 'Don't make the mistake of praying for patience! You'll end up having the most frustrating week! God will *test* your patience like never before!'

Yours is a good, kind Father. Sure, He wants to purify you from sin, so your life resembles that of Jesus. But don't be confused about His methods and motives: it's His *kindness* that leads you to repentance, not His spite. He's not out to trap you. He wants to see patience develop in your life as evidence of His Spirit in you. And you're free to ask for it.

God, You are perfectly patient, giving us time to seek You and find You. Help me move, like You do, at the gentle pace of love, so that my soul never needs to catch up with my body. Slow me down. Help me to be patient with myself, but mostly with others whose tempos and rhythms differ from mine, or whose idiosyncrasies get on my nerves. Remind me that I badly need others to be patient with me too. Sustain me in the moments of each day so I am patiently present in each of them, not lunging hurriedly ahead into a future that's still out of reach. Amen.

Kindness

Those who are kind benefit themselves,
but the cruel bring ruin on themselves.
Proverbs 11:17, NIV

As I write, the world is still largely in the death throes of a global pandemic. It's hardly an exaggeration to say that, here on the third rock from the sun, we've all been through a lot. And in times such as these, people don't need us to be right, or practical, or to give advice – though all those things have value and have their place. More than ever, and more than anything, people desperately need us to be kind. It's kindness that is remembered. It's kindness that changes lives, offering safe spaces and hope to people in distress.

What's more, the wondrous, supernatural thing about being kind is that it benefits *you*. That's seriously win-win. Why would any of us *not* want to change the world, and ourselves, for the better, through simple deeds of thoughtfulness and compassion?

Pray for kindness today.

Jesus, You are the kindest of all. Your kindness led You to the cross and leads us to repentance. Teach me to follow in Your soft footfalls. Teach me how to be kind. Help me show to others the same kindness I'd love them to show me. Give me gentle words of encouragement and compassion. Make me ready to offer them as I move through this day. Give me good ideas of practical things I can do for others – things that will pour kindness into their souls. And let me be totally ok – even excited – when most of my random, secret acts of kindness go unacknowledged, because it's not about me. Amen.

Goodness

> Therefore, whenever we have the opportunity, we should do good to everyone – especially to those in the family of faith.
> Galatians 6:10, NLT

The epic battle that rages across time and the universe, is between good and evil. It's between the benevolent, holy God we serve, and His enemy and ours. The fruit of goodness we bear in our lives as we're led and transformed by the Holy Spirit sets us apart remarkably as being on the winning side of this cosmic war – because we know that in the end, God wins.

We could and should also be wowing the world with the armaments of goodness we wield amongst our families, friendship circles, and church communities. When there's a family in need of meals because they're ill or cash-strapped or finding their new normal with a newborn? Their freezer should be overflowing with casseroles that shout *victory!* It's such a no-brainer – that we should be *asking God for more goodness*, because *goodness is such a good thing!*

Today, let's ask God to sharpen our weapons of goodness.

> *Heavenly Father, You are so good. I don't want to be a goody two-shoes. I want Your powerful, world-changing goodness to seep into me, and out of me, to change the world around me by bringing the salt and light of Your true love ways. Convict me, Holy Spirit, in instances when I am anything but good. Increase in me a desire to be truly good, as You are. Guide my thinking and decision-making, so that I'd be leaving a trail of goodness behind me, inspiring others to be good too. Amen.*

Faithfulness

Those who work their land will have abundant food,
but those who chase fantasies will have their fill of
poverty. A faithful person will be richly blessed ...
Proverbs 28:19-20, NIV

Faithfulness is a rare and elusive character commodity. Our culture has become increasingly faithless. Contracts are routinely broken with an air of clinical self-preservation, self-absorption, and pragmatism. Even covenants are broken, and the world calls it courage, self-actualization, and freedom. Loyalty is dismissed as quaint, and unnecessary. Yet our God is faithful, even when we are not (2 Timothy 2:13), and it's His faithfulness, worked out in and through our characters, that sets us apart as His children. Faithfulness makes us remarkable, lending integrity and others-centeredness to our roles as Christ's ambassadors. Faithfulness distinguishes us from the world.

On our own, we're bad at faithfulness. We're flakey and fickle and we opt for the easy way out whenever or wherever we can, forgoing the staying power that leaves spiritual and relational legacies. But the best news is that faithfulness is a gift grown in us by the indwelling Holy Spirit, and we are free to pray that He would increase the reality of faithfulness in our lives. Let's pray –

O God, strengthen our resolve and make us a faithful people! Help us to keep our marriage vows and our weekend commitments and our resolve to serve in community and bind us eternally to Yourself, despite our human failings and lack of stamina. Thank You for Your perfect, unswerving example of faithfulness, God. You are worthy of our faithful, unwavering worship. Amen.

Free to ask yourself:

**These questions are drawn from themes
covered over the past five days.**

- Are you at peace today? If not, what's robbing you of peace? Could you surrender it to God?

- Who rubs you up the wrong way? What would patience look like, in that relationship?

- Write down the names of some of the kindest people you know. How could you copy them?

- Prayerfully read Luke 16:10-12. What comes to mind? In which 'small things' of your life is God prompting you to muster up greater faithfulness – in preparation for bigger things He has in store for you?

FREE TO ASK

Free to ask God:

JESUS,

You are the Prince of Peace (Isaiah 9:6). You are patient with all people, not wanting any to die not knowing You (2 Peter 3:9). It's Your extraordinary kindness that leads us to repentance (Romans 2:4). You allow us to taste and see that You are good (Psalm 34:8). And You are faithful, even when we are not (2 Timothy 2:13). O God, would You grow this kind of fruit in me? I want to bring Your peace, patience, kindness, goodness, and faithfulness to the world.

AMEN.

FREE TO ASK

Gentleness

'Go out and stand before Me on the mountain,' the LORD told him. And as Elijah stood there, the LORD passed by, and a mighty windstorm hit the mountain. It was such a terrible blast that the rocks were torn loose, but the LORD was not in the wind. After the wind there was an earthquake, but the LORD was not in the earthquake. And after the earthquake there was a fire, but the LORD was not in the fire. And after the fire there was the sound of a gentle whisper.
1 Kings 19:11-12, NLT

If you think of those you most admire, they're probably gentle. Gentle doesn't mean weak and pathetic. Gentleness isn't a pushover. The God whom Elijah encountered – the God of the mountain and the mighty windstorm and the earthquake and the fire – ultimately revealed Himself as *gentle*. Gentleness is power under perfect, appropriate control. Like kindness, gentleness is a wise way of loaning someone your strength instead of reminding them of their weakness. It's curbing the clever, contrived retort you're perfectly capable of shooting back at someone to win an argument, choosing instead a soft response that isn't hurtful. Perhaps it's not responding at all, because shockingly, we don't always have to have the last word. Leave that to the still, small voice of God.

Friend, the world needs our gentleness. Let's pray:

Jesus, You could come at us guns blazing. We deserve it. Yet You speak tenderly and patiently, clearly but kindly, without a hint of frustration or condescension in Your tone. Gentle us, Lord Jesus, that we might be the whisper of Your grace to those caught in the storms of life. Amen.

FREE TO ASK

Self-control

> For the grace of God has been revealed, bringing salvation
> to all people. And we are instructed to turn from godless
> living and sinful pleasures. We should live in this evil world
> with wisdom, righteousness, and devotion to God ...
> Titus 2:11-12, NLT

In his letter to Titus, Paul describes the splendor and freedom of salvation – and how part of that is living a godly, self-controlled life. Conversely, advertisers beg us to abandon all self-control and indulge our every passion and whim. Spend. Eat. Put the vacation on another credit card. Do what you want, when you want, in the way you want, whenever you want, with whomever you want to do it. But if you've lived a bit, you'll know how all these things that promise us freedom end up enslaving us. The fruit of self-control frees us from the entanglements of sin and sets us up for a better, freer way of life.

In which of life's arenas do you struggle most to exercise self-control? Are you battling to reign in your time spent on social media? Do you find it difficult to control your words when you're triggered in tough conversations?

We're free to pray for self-control.

O God, I surrender all of myself – body and soul – to You. Transform me from the inside out. Change my thinking. Strengthen me to slow down and think when I want to rush ahead into pleasure, or unkind and unnecessary power over those in my path. Let others look at my life and see evidence of Your changing grace and influence as I embody Your wisdom and Your ways. Amen.

Thrive

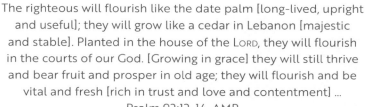

The righteous will flourish like the date palm [long-lived, upright
and useful]; they will grow like a cedar in Lebanon [majestic
and stable]. Planted in the house of the LORD, they will flourish
in the courts of our God. [Growing in grace] they will still thrive
and bear fruit and prosper in old age; they will flourish and be
vital and fresh [rich in trust and love and contentment] ...
Psalm 92:12-14, AMP

The word *flourish* describes how a living organism – like you – grows
or develops in a healthy or vigorous way in a particularly congenial
environment. For the next few weeks we'll delve into the idea of being free to flourish spiritually and in *every* way, so a good place to start
might be with the SEEDS acronym, which stands for Social, Exercise,
Education, Diet, and Sleep. How are your relationships? Are you making time to get some exercise? What are you learning? For the most
part, are you eating healthily? Are you getting enough sleep? Which of
these areas do you need to re-surrender to God?

Andy Crouch describes flourishing in terms of what Jesus came to bring:
abundant life, which is all about true authority (the capacity for meaningful action), and true vulnerability (exposure to meaningful risk). Put
another way, we are free to flourish because God has given us agency
and resources to do things that matter – things that will leave the world
better than we found it.

Doing those things will cost us courage. We risk egg-on-face, or worse.
But it'll be worth it, because we'll become channels of life that will
flood the dry furrows of a parched world.

FREE TO FLOURISH

First and ten

> But Daniel purposed in his heart that he would not defile
> himself with the portion of the king's delicacies, nor with
> the wine which he drank; therefore he requested of the
> chief of the eunuchs that he might not defile himself.
> Daniel 1:8, NLT

FREE TO FLOURISH

Daniel's courage and resolve were awe-inspiring. As he 'purposed in his heart', God caused him to flourish, even in the hostile milieu of a foreign culture.

We serve the same God Daniel did. We can also *purpose in our hearts*. Jeff Henderson has created a concept he calls 'First and Ten'. He reckons it's far more valuable and viable to commit to a new habit or goal for the first ten days of every month, than it is to make New Year's resolutions (which typically fizzle out by January 4th). The first ten days of each month add up to 120 days in a year. So, if you commit to a First and Ten habit, you'd likely be working at your goals for way longer than if you even made it to the *end* of January.

Whenever the next new month rolls around: what spiritual, intellectual, relational, financial or health goal could you set for yourself? Choose one simple thing – like drinking a glass of water before each meal, or reading a chapter, or stretching for five minutes. Commit to it for ten days. When ten days are over, you're welcome to stop – or not. Either way, you'll have purposed in your heart to increase your freedom to flourish.

Atomic flourishing

Joyful is the person who finds wisdom, the one who
gains understanding ... She offers you long life in her right hand,
and riches and honor in her left. She will guide you down
delightful paths; all her ways are satisfying. Wisdom is a tree of life
to those who embrace her; happy are those who hold her tightly.
Proverbs 3:13-18, NLT

In his book *Atomic Habits*, James Clear offers unique wisdom to guide us down what Solomon calls the 'delightful paths' of flourishing. An atomic habit is a goal or 'next step' so small it's almost impossible to fail to attain it. Like, putting your running shoes at the front door each night. It's super easy. Anyone can do that. And it's the thing that may galvanize you to *put them on* in the morning and go running.

It's the Holy Spirit in us who causes us to flourish. And by His presence and power in our lives we're enabled to institute these kinds of habits – with a view to greater flourishing. Maybe just before bed, you could write tomorrow's date in your journal, and place journal, pen, and Bible on your nightstand. It's a small, easy thing to do, which will set you up to head straight into a thoughtful time in God's Word in the morning.

Maybe you could fill a bottle of water each morning and place it next to the sink or the microwave – wherever you'll see it several times a day. It's easy to fill a bottle! And it'll remind and encourage you to drink what's in it before the day's end. You're free to form habits, which will set you up to freely flourish.

FREE TO FLOURISH

Free to ask yourself:

**These questions are drawn from themes
covered over the past five days.**

- Do you know someone who displays remarkable gentleness? How is their gentleness revealed through their words?

- Do you know someone with steely, steadfast self-control? How is their self-control revealed through their actions?

- If you were to make one decision, to do just one thing differently, for the first ten days of next month, what would it be?

- Is there an atomic habit God is prompting you to put in place? What's stopping you?

Free to write it out:

Read Psalm 1. Try paraphrasing this portion of Scripture, inserting your name, to describe what flourishing might look like in your life.

_____

_____

_____

_____

_____

_____

_____

_____

_____

_____

_____

FREE TO FLOURISH

Frenetic or fruitful?

'Thus, by their fruit you will recognize them.'
Matthew 7:20, NIV

A balanced diet is a brilliant idea. But I don't much like the idea of a balanced *life*. It sounds mediocre – like a good-enough spread of *bustlings* and *doings*, so I can say I filled my hours on earth by dishing up a bit of this and a bit of that. (Except, was I really satisfied, or effective?) Also, a balanced life can be the whip of unrealistic expectations. When I scoop flour onto my kitchen scale, I scrutinize the needle. Too much? Too little? Does the flour *measure up*? That question haunts women everywhere. Am I too much? Too little? *Balanced*?

For the most part, the cultural needle measuring a woman's worth has gone from zero (oppressed) to maxed out (empowered). And while that's right and marvelous, along with liberation we've believed the lie that we can do it all, be it all, have it all, *balance it all*, and win at life.

The truth is, while we *can* do anything, we can't do *everything*. And certainly not everything at once, with our sanity intact. Let's push aside the kitchen scale and reach for the fruit bowl, because God doesn't call us to be balanced. *He calls us to be fruitful.* I've never weighed my fruit bowl or eyed it analytically: 'Hmm. Too much? Too little? Does it measure up?' A bowl piled high with ripe pickings just makes me feel rich and grateful – not overwhelmed or unbalanced. If your life feels lopsided because you've been trying so hard to balance everything, I'm praying God would remind you today you're free to be fruitful, and flourish.

Big fruit first

For if a man cannot manage his own household,
how can he take care of God's church?
1 Timothy 3:5, NLT

The context of Paul's question to Timothy is the qualifications of elders in the church. He's talking about priorities, integrity, and life management. With this in mind, and following on from yesterday, it's important that we ask ourselves how fruitfulness might prevail against society's barrage of expectations to be balanced (and brilliant at it). Is it possible for us to steady the loads of marriage, motherhood, and marketplace – and still find time to meet with God, prioritizing obedience to Him in whatever life space we find ourselves?

Back to the fruit bowl we reached for yesterday: if you put the pineapples on top of the grapes in your fruit bowl, the grapes would get squashed. You'd put the big fruit in the bowl *first*, right? And perhaps to be fruitful we need to discern our priorities for the season we're in. What's the main thing? *What's the big fruit in your bowl?*

Balance of some sort – juggling the responsibilities of our various roles – will always be required of us. But it's really ok for a patch of land to lie fallow, for greater future fruit harvests. Like, there'll be seasons in which your kids may need you less, which will free you up to focus more on your career. There'll be seasons in which your husband will need you more, which may mean saying, 'Not now,' to ministry opportunities. Life is short, sure. But life is also long. There's enough time to do God's will. You're free to prioritize, and flourish.

FREE TO FLOURISH

Habits lead to harvest

Therefore be imitators of God, as beloved children.
Ephesians 5:1, ESV

Little children imitate the parents they adore. And imitation isn't a once-off thing. It's an over-and-over thing – it's *habitual*. Our kids won't learn to be generous because they once saw us tossing a few coins into the guitar case of a station busker. They'll learn to be generous – they'll *imitate* our generosity – when they see us giving freely of our time, money, words of encouragement or practical help, often and in every area of our lives.

So, for each of your current priorities, and as you seek to imitate God by habitually spending over-and-over time in His presence, perhaps your next step is to plant the seeds of habit. Because fruit grows from the inside out. There's no stick-on quick fix. The real thing takes patience, prayer, and over-and-over perseverance. And tiny, daily habits germinate and grow up to look like lives hung heavy with fruit.

Maybe you need to get into the habit of switching off your phone an hour or so before you go to sleep, so your husband knows he's more important to you than Pinterest. Or you may want to formulate the habit of winning the day by addressing your waking, pre-coffee thoughts to Jesus, relying on the Holy Spirit to make sense of your groggy, Lord-have-mercy mumblings. Turning the key in the ignition to drive your kids to school could be the habit trigger to pray with them. You might choose to habitually escape the office to meet a friend for a once-a-week lunchtime prayer walk.

Is there a harvest-producing, healthy habit God is nudging you to kickstart?

Behind your back

A good name is more desirable than great riches;
to be esteemed is better than silver or gold.
Proverbs 22:1, NIV

I use a daily phone reminder to activate a habit that I hope will lead to a more fruitful, less frenetic life. My phone beeps a calendar notification once a day that reads: *seven words*. I try to take a moment to reset and remind myself who I want to be for those around me. I've chosen seven words I hope my husband, my kids, and other people will use when they describe me behind my back. Newsflash: *they already use words to describe me*. So, I reckon I may as well decide what I'd love those words to be – and then live them.

For better or worse, people talk about you behind your back. They already use words to describe you too. What do you think those words are? What would you love them to be? You don't have to choose words or use a phone reminder. Perhaps you could weave another character-building habit into the rhythm of your life. But be intentional about habitually planting small seeds of character that will take root, and bear fruit, in every facet of your life.

Jesus didn't set us free so we could tick the boxes of a balanced life and wear our frenetic multitasking as a badge of honor. Jesus set us free, *for freedom* (Galatians 5:1). And the love-response of a life lived free, is fruit (Galatians 5:22-23). Let's encourage each other towards the simplicity of surrender to the God who grows our fruit, making us wise and effective, for our good and His glory.

FREE TO FLOURISH

Even so

'Even though the fig trees have no blossoms, and there are
no grapes on the vines; even though the olive crop fails,
and the fields lie empty and barren; even though the flocks
die in the fields, and the cattle barns are empty, yet I will
rejoice in the LORD! I will be joyful in the God of my salvation!'
Habakkuk 3:17-18, NLT

Relocating from South Africa to England was the hardest thing we've ever done, and probably the darkest season of our lives so far. I'm not being dramatic, just honest. We knew it would be tough on many levels. I probably made it tougher by putting tremendous pressure on myself to be able to say we were *settled*. I soon realized the truth that we're all adrift in a foreign land, until God calls us home, and while I couldn't necessarily say with certainty we were *settled*, I could *settle the day* (as we talked about earlier in this devotional) by asking myself if the day contained certain solid and lifegiving elements, even if just for a moment or in the smallest, simplest way.

I thought about what it would take for us, at the end of each day, to still be able to say, 'Yet I will rejoice in the Lord!' If we could find evidence of God's grace and goodness – and we could, each day – then, *even so*, it was a good day.

Try this at home. Think about the essential ingredients of a good, if ordinary, day. Then stand amazed at how God is setting you free to flourish even in trials and tough times.

FREE TO FLOURISH

Free to ask yourself:

**These questions are drawn from themes
covered over the past five days.**

- What are your 'big fruit', in this season? What might it look like to prioritize them, so your life becomes less frenetic and more fruitful?

- Is there another new, small habit you could implement, starting today, that will lead to a greater harvest of goodness in your life?

- Which adjectives would you love people to use when they describe you?

- Go back to Habakkuk 3 and read the whole chapter. How do the prophet's words inspire hope for renewed freedom and flourishing in your life?

Free to ask God:

Try these simple, one-liner habit-prayers for your 'big fruit' priority areas, and perhaps write out a few of your own:

GOD,

Keep my heart soft towards my husband.
Remind me to look my kids in the eye.
Make me a happy, uncomplicated friend.
In my career space, help me not to add to the noise but to do the things only I can do.
For every opportunity or invitation, help me say the best yes and the best no.
Help me not to worry about food or worship it. Choose my weight; choose my plate.
Help me find ways to be active every day, to look after this one body You've given me.
At home, help me to keep it tidy, but also to keep it real, making space for the raucous and the resting.
Give me wisdom to budget – and then to give, save, live, enjoy, repeat.

AMEN.

FREE TO FLOURISH

Supersize

Now all glory to God, who is able, through His mighty power at work within us, to accomplish infinitely more than we might ask or think.
Ephesians 3:20, NLT

A friend of mine took her two little boys clothes shopping at the end of one winter and any end-of-season kids' clothes she saw, she bought one size up, thinking to save the clothes for her boys for the next winter. Then she saw a shirt, on sale, for herself. 'This is beautiful,' she said, 'I think I'll get this.' And her six-year-old said, 'Mommy, you should buy two of those shirts. One for now, and one for next year's size.'

Most of us want to stay the size we are, or even *decrease* that size so next season we're wearing a size smaller. But just imagine we aimed to be wearing a *bigger* size, on the inside, a year from now. What if we trusted God for increased capacity – more heart-volume – greater Kingdom significance – a day, a week, a year from now? We all *want* to live significant lives, after all. No one ever says, 'You know, it's always been my dream to be really average. I just hope that I'll be able to look back on my life one day and say, I was absolutely mediocre!'

We're just small, ordinary people, yet we're called to make a big, extraordinary difference because we bear the image of an enormous, extraordinary, supersized God. We're called to be purveyors of hope. We're called to flourish. Let's go big, before we go home for eternity.

FREE TO FLOURISH

Milk and honey

'So I have come down to rescue them from the hand of
the Egyptians and to bring them up out of that land into a good
and spacious land, a land flowing with milk and honey – the home
of the Canaanites, Hittites, Amorites, Perizzites, Hivites and Jebusites.'
Exodus 3:8, NIV

God's incredible promise to His people in the book of Exodus speaks of rescue and redemption, hope and healing, expectation and abundant life. A friend of mine taught me to filter decisions and circumstances through five key words contained in this Promised Land Scripture: *good*, *spacious*, *flowing*, *milk* and *honey*.

So perhaps, for whatever you're currently facing, ask yourself whether this situation or course of action or invitation or opportunity is *good*? Does it lead you into a *spacious* place? Is the life of God in this place or prospect or circumstance *flowing* in you and through you – or has it pooled and stagnated? Is this prospective move or current event or decision sustainable – can it keep you going – like *milk*? And lastly, does it smack of the sweet, abundant life Jesus came to bring – like *honey*?

Of course, sometimes we find ourselves in arid, hostile circumstances. Life doesn't feel good and sweet and sustainable. Neither does it feel like anything's flowing, nor like we're in a spacious place. But the elements expressed in this verse remind us of the generosity of our loving Heavenly Father. They represent His best for us, in His desire that we flourish, and they show us how we might press into His presence and pray as we navigate decisions.

Perfect perimeters

'A person's days are determined; You have decreed the number
of his months and have set limits he cannot exceed.'
Job 14:5, NIV

We flourish when we're free from the fear that there's not enough time to get everything done. God bound your life in time and space. You can only be where you are right now, and you can only do what you can do with the twenty-four hours you get each day. Happily, those twenty-four hours are enough. There's time, today, to do God's will. Commit your schedule to Him, trusting He'll guide you to fill it wisely. And when things have gotten wildly out of control? Come humbly before your Father and pray that events might get scratched or postponed.

I do this all the time and God is so faithful in coming through for me with cancellations, even when it's my fault for over-committing. God knows my capacity, He wants me to be the best version of myself, and He's so kind. He's also teaching me to learn from my tendency to over-subscribe my time. We can't flourish when our toast is thinly buttered.

We also flourish when we're free from the fear that we don't have what it takes, and we'll never match up to whoever we're comparing ourselves. Swim in the lane God has cordoned off for you. Each unique human made in God's image has something unique to contribute to the Kingdom cause, within the timeframe perfectly chosen by God. When we play to our strengths – recognizing what we have to offer to the world, in the time we have, in the place we are – we flourish, and so do those around us.

FREE TO FLOURISH

Called

By His divine power, God has given us everything we
need for living a godly life. We have received all of this by
coming to know Him, the one who called us to Himself
by means of His marvelous glory and excellence.
2 Peter 1:3, NLT

Preachers and pastors tell us all the time there's a call of God on each of our lives. But what does that even mean and how do we go about answering that call – and *flourishing* in our calling?

There are three bits of good news, when it comes to knowing and embracing your calling. Firstly, Peter joyfully makes the truth clear, explaining that by God's empowering grace, we've got what it takes to fulfil His call on our lives. In Him, we have everything we need.

Secondly, we can demystify the complex concept of calling a little bit – because actually, it's not all that mystifying or complex. Jesus says, 'I won't lay anything heavy or ill-fitting on you. Keep company with me and you'll learn to live freely and lightly.' (Matthew 11:30) Thankfully, that doesn't sound mystifying or complex at all.

Thirdly, you needn't stress about your calling. Romans 14:17 says, 'For the Kingdom of God is not a matter of what we eat or drink, but of living a life of goodness and peace and joy in the Holy Spirit.' Your calling – your Kingdom life – should delight and excite you (and *not* stress you out). That doesn't mean there won't be resistance, sacrifice, pain, or doubt involved. Destiny will always be contested. But your calling is a right fit. It's becoming. You can give yourself permission to enjoy it, and flourish.

FREE TO FLOURISH

Flourishing under justice

'For the LORD your God is the God of gods and Lord of lords.
He is the great God, the mighty and awesome God,
who shows no partiality and cannot be bribed. He ensures
that orphans and widows receive justice. He shows love to the
foreigners living among you and gives them food and clothing.'
Deuteronomy 10:17-18, NLT

Perhaps you're fatherless. Perhaps you've been a victim of cruelty, neglect, sexual or emotional exploitation, or some other form of gender-based violence or mistreatment. Maybe you've lost your parents, your protector, your lover, or leader. And so, you're cynical and skeptical when it comes to being 'free to flourish'. How will it ever be possible for you to flourish, in this life, when you've been crushed, discarded, abandoned, or abused?

I can't begin to imagine your pain. I wouldn't dare give you trite clichés to cheer you up. I wouldn't tell you to build a bridge and get over it. But I want to remind you gently that God's Kingdom culture is one of kindness, equality, justice, protection, provision, and gender-based extravagance. He sings over you, lavishes you with His unthinkable love, and has already gone to the ends of the earth for you.

Paul tells us, 'Though [Jesus] was God, He did not think of equality with God as something to cling to. Instead, He gave up His divine privileges; He took the humble position of a slave and was born as a human being. When He appeared in human form, He humbled Himself in obedience to God and died a criminal's death on a cross.' (Philippians 2:6-8) He did all that for you, to set you free to flourish.

Free to ask yourself:

**These questions are drawn from themes
covered over the past five days.**

- Who towers above you, in spiritual size? Why do you look up to them? In which ways would you love to grow bigger on the inside?

- Which boxes does your life tick right now: is it good, spacious, flowing, sustainable and sweet? What needs to change?

- Do you believe there's enough time today to do God's will?

- Read Amos 5:24. Have you been wronged? Have you been handed justice – validation and vindication – for that wrong? If not, would you be willing to leave the case files with God, knowing He judges righteously, and knowing you *will* receive justice, in this life or the next?

Free to write it out:

When you hear the word 'calling', what's the first thing that comes to mind? Write out ideas of how you believe God is leading you, even if you think your ideas are farfetched or impossible.

_____

_____

_____

_____

_____

_____

_____

_____

_____

_____

_____

_____

FREE TO FLOURISH

Wake up to work

Even so, I have noticed one thing, at least, that is good.
It is good for people to eat, drink, and enjoy their work under
the sun during the short life God has given them, and to accept
their lot in life. And it is a good thing to receive wealth from
God and the good health to enjoy it. To enjoy your work
and accept your lot in life – this is indeed a gift from God.
Ecclesiastes 5:18-19, NLT

Flourishing in your day job is a beautiful freedom. Earlier in the year we explored the difference between *chofesh* (the freedom to do what you like) and *cherut* (the freedom to do what you should). On career flourishing and fulfilment, one commentator writes, 'What happens when men have "too much freedom"? The question is answered through the story of Noah, who, the rabbis say, invented the plow. For the first time, people did not have to work so hard to produce their food, and in their inability to use their new-found freedom productively, they became corrupt and depraved.

Many would say that we are again living in days such as those of Noah, filled with immorality and wickedness. It is perhaps no accident that many today are focused on the pursuit of *chofesh*, while the concept of *cherut* fades from view. As people of faith, may we become a beacon of real freedom, freely bound to God and His commandments, glorifying Him through our joyful, willing obedience.'

May you bravely step into the work God has prepared for you to do today. May you feel free and fully alive, working efficiently and effectively. May you flourish and be fulfilled.

Love your age

You saw me before I was born. Every day of my life was recorded in
Your book. Every moment was laid out before a single day had passed.
Psalm 139:16, NLT

We travel from birth to death along pre-determined timelines. The psalmist tells us the number of our days is already preset. And we don't know if we have a day left, or a decade, or much longer. (I've seen a birthday card that says, *Forget about the past, you can't change it. Forget about the future, you can't predict it. Forget about the present, I didn't get you one.*)

But seriously, to flourish freely, it's important to talk about age sometimes. Because, as time passes and our laughter lines deepen, the things we do and the way we live make the world different from how it was, and we want to make sure those changes aren't just trivial but build the Kingdom, glorify God, and alter eternity.

C.T. Studd said, 'Only one life, 'twil soon be past. Only what's done for Christ will last.' Though God is eternal (stretching backwards and forwards into eternity past and future) and though He's inside of time and outside of time at the same time, for perfect reasons we're bound by time and space. We live out our earthly existence in two-dimensional time, recognizing that we have a past, a present and a future.

However old you are, it's the very best age to be. You're exactly the age God planned you to be, today. What could you do today to make the world different – better – from how it was yesterday, for the glory of God and the good of those around you?

FREE TO FLOURISH

Preparing to prosper

Now Moses was very humble –
more humble than any other person on earth.
Numbers 12:3, NLT

If you've come this far on our freedom journey, I know you believe we're made for more than just trudging through the inexorable days of our lives until they're finished, and we die. And so, we want to learn to steward our time well: our past, our present, our future.

The timeline of Moses' life is fascinating in this respect. He's 120 years old when he dies. He spends forty years in Egypt, initially with his God-fearing parents, then as a son in the Egyptian palace. He witnesses one of his own people – a Hebrew – being beaten by an Egyptian taskmaster. He gets mad, kills the Egyptian, realizes that was dumb, and runs away.

He spends the next forty years working as a shepherd, for Jethro, in Midian. He marries Jethro's daughter, Zipporah, and they have two sons. For Moses, this is a season of waiting, and preparation. This is where God teaches him patience and trust. He's an ex-prince! And he finds himself looking after sheep – *for forty years*. But God doesn't waste the experience – He orchestrates it. He weeds things out of Moses' character, so much so that he's named Humblest Guy Ever. He teaches Moses to worship and equips him to wage war on the enemies of Israel. Finally, when Moses is eighty years old, God says, 'Ok, you're ready to look after some different sheep. Go back to Egypt and get them.'

Are you in a humbling season of waiting, and training? Take heart. God has not forgotten you. Your formation will result in your flourishing.

Flourishing for a future

Lord, through all the generations, You have been our home!
Before the mountains were born, before You gave birth to the
earth and the world, from beginning to end, You are God.
Psalm 90:1-2, NLT

Moses wrote Psalm 90. We looked at some of his story yesterday, and you know the rest. Moses: 'Let my people go!' Pharaoh: 'Forget it.' Plagues and chaos ensue until eventually Pharaoh's like, 'Sure! Go!' God splits the Red Sea, and the Israelites enter the wilderness where Moses leads them *for another forty years*.

Interestingly (and so different from the way we picture our lives panning out), Moses' biggest, most important, most difficult assignment from God comes right at the end of his life. Also, there isn't really a happy ending for Moses. He gets to his life's closing credits, and he doesn't even get to enter the Promised Land with the people. It's an incredible reminder to us that the tiny timelines of our lives are part of a sweeping saga, a much bigger story, and we are never the main character.

But this same Moses, who understood something about life's seasons and time passing, zooms out to give us big-picture perspective: 'From beginning to end, You are God.' Moses prays for God's favor to rest on His people. He asks God to establish the work of their hands because without God, their work amounts to nothing. Moses knows it's not about him – just like it's not about us.

Friend, as you take each next right step of obedience in your work in this world, you are flourishing for a future you may only witness from eternity. Keep going. It'll be worth it.

FREE TO FLOURISH

Made for more

Teach us to number our days, that we may gain a heart of wisdom.
Psalm 90:12, NIV

Psalm 90, written by Moses, who is described as the humblest man who ever lived, is too good not to dwell on for a few days. In the middle of this beautiful Scripture, he prays, 'Teach us to realize the brevity of life, so that we may grow in wisdom.' (Psalm 90:12, NLT) This is such a significant prayer to pray because we're made for more than getting stuck in our pasts. It's for freedom that Christ has set us free. The old has gone, and we're new creations. We're made for more than losing ourselves in relentless discontent with our present circumstances, unable to lift our heads.

We're made for more than being crippled by fear of the future or rendered useless today because we're idolizing something we hope will happen tomorrow. This is serious stuff. Hence, a grammar joke to lighten us up: *The past, the present and the future walked into a bar. It was tense.*

Jokes aside, we do need to realize the brevity of life, and get wise. Because every day we carry the tension of a past, a present and a future, and we need wisdom to carry that tension well. Over the next few days, we'll explore what it looks like to be grateful for the past, content in the present, and ready for the future – which will position you to step into your calling. Pray that God would bring things to mind – people, places or situations linked to your past, present or future – that are best surrendered to His transforming grace.

Free to ask yourself:

**These questions are drawn from themes
covered over the past five days.**

- Are you flourishing in your work right now? If not, does something need to change internally or externally?

- Are you embarrassed about, or uncomfortable with, your age? Why? What might change if you surrendered those issues or insecurities to God?

- Are you content to flourish in your work today, for the benefit of others in a future you may not live to see?

- Read all of Psalm 90. What strikes you? How do Moses' words encourage you or inspire you to fulfil your potential?

Free to ask God:

MIGHTY GOD,

You didn't miss a moment of my past. You're with me now in my present. You're already in my future. In parts of my story there's pain and regret. In parts of my story there's joy and excitement. Give me grace and wisdom and strength and resolve to surrender every part of my story – past, present, and future – to You. Please work it all out for my good and Your glory.

AMEN.

FREE TO FLOURISH

Neither here nor there

For You, a thousand years are as
a passing day, as brief as a few night hours.
Psalm 90:4, NLT

Once, after a magical white Christmas in Canada with friends, we flew back to South Africa on December 31st. We only landed back home on January 2nd, because of time zones and a layover in London. Waiting at Toronto's Pearson International Airport on New Year's Eve, we knew it was already January 1st back home in South Africa. We boarded the plane at 10pm Eastern Time. Dinner was served – quietly and politely – 'Chicken or beef?' – just after midnight. The captain didn't suggest we leap from our seats to chest bump the people across the aisle. No one sang Auld Lang Syne. Because we weren't in Eastern Time anymore. We were that much closer to Greenwich – where midnight had (also) already ticked by hours before. We were in a time warp. We missed the midnight countdown because we were straddling a neither-here-nor-there space flanked by time zones, continents, and in this case, actual calendar years.

Somewhere over the Atlantic, I was acutely aware that our earth-lives are always, in a sense, lived in an in-between space. God *calls* us to live in two places at once – the chaos of life, and the quiet of His presence. There's constantly a tenuous tie between temporal and eternal. We don't ever know, really, where we are on the timeline of fragile existence.

Maybe life has you dizzy and disorientated. If you're not quite sure where you are, where you're going, or why: rest assured that God does. Your times are in His hands (Psalm 31:15).

Grateful

One of them, when he saw that he was healed,
came back to Jesus, shouting, 'Praise God!'
Luke 17:15, NLT

This guy was one of ten men healed. The other nine forgot their manners. Jesus challenged their entitlement, saying, 'Didn't I heal ten men? Where are the other nine?' (Luke 17:17)

Gratitude for what God's done for us in the past unlocks our freedom to flourish. And looking back, you have at least one thing to be grateful for: at the cross, Jesus did enough good to last you a lifetime. He did enough to last you all eternity. What Jesus already did for you, in the past, can't be undone, by any person or circumstance. *It is finished.* And incredibly, for most of us, the blessings didn't stop at the cross. As we look back over the numbered days we've already lived, we have tons of other past experiences for which to be grateful, *as well.* We can settle the past in a place of peace by voicing our thanks to God.

And if your past has been unspeakably traumatic, perhaps the challenge is to wrestle with God in prayer until you can accept the truth that even the trauma, God will somehow cause for your good. Give thanks that by God's grace, you can put the past where it belongs, which is, behind you. Thank God that despite what's happened in your past, He's never relaxed His grace-grip on your life. Thanksgiving may feel impossibly difficult, but it may be the step of scary faith in the direction of trusting that God can give you gladness in proportion to your former misery (Psalm 90:15), turning regret into redemption.

Neither victim nor hero

I will give thanks to the LORD because of His righteousness;
I will sing the praises of the name of the LORD Most High.
Psalm 7:17, NIV

Andy Crouch suggests the stories we tell about anything that's happened to us – five minutes ago or five years ago – mostly fall into two categories: hero stories and victim stories. This is so convicting as I listen to the narrative I spin of my own life. We tend to tell our stories leaning towards either arrogance or self-pity. Or we tell stories that are a combination of both: stories where we're the victim who overcomes and ends up the hero.

Our victim stories are designed to shift blame, or to get people to feel sorry for us, or to give airtime to our venting and ranting and complaining and fault-finding. Our hero stories are woven to draw attention to ourselves (subtly or not so subtly). We find ways to refer to ourselves in conversation. We namedrop and mention our achievements and make ourselves out to be generally awe-inspiring humans. And our combination stories start off with us being in some way hard done by ('I was unfairly passed over for promotion!'), and end with us being lauded victorious through our own marvelousness ('I was head-hunted by the opposition organization and given a job two rungs up the corporate ladder from my boss! Ha!').

To flourish? Let's choose to recount our pasts with more than just self-pity or arrogance. As we number our days by telling the stories of our lives, let's tell stories of rescue and redemption. Stories that promote God and others. Stories that showcase our joy, humility, and selflessness. Grateful stories.

Content to be ready

I remain confident of this: I will see the
goodness of the LORD on the land of the living.
Psalm 27:13, NIV

Despite how much good God has already done for you in the past, He will doubtless continue to do plenty of good things through you, in you, for you, in the present. It's in His flawless, holy, loving character. He can do no other. Maybe this morning you caught the aroma of someone else's coffee on your way to work, or your teenager acknowledged you in the school carpark. That's the goodness of the Lord in the land of the living! If we take an honest look around the world, it's unfair how much we have. We dare not be discontent.

Contentment means that today, while you have life and strength, you're clinging to your sense of wonder. You're willing to get your hands dirty for Kingdom causes bigger than you. And because you've no idea how much time you've got left, you're living at peace – content – with others, as far as it depends on you.

Living like this – grateful for the past and content in the present – positions us to be ready for the future, because we're *satisfied*. Anything else God adds to our lives – like knowing the next step for your family, career, relationship, studies, or start-up venture – is a total bonus. We don't necessarily need to know the next step. We just need to be ready to take it. Jesus is a good Shepherd. He leads us into pastures and promised lands. You can trust Him to lead you on, in good time.

You've got something

Then the LORD said to him, 'What is that
in your hand?' 'A staff,' he replied.
Exodus 4:2, NIV

If we learn to live fully and fearlessly where God has us, we'll be ready to live fully and fearlessly wherever He leads us in the future. When God tells Moses to go back to Egypt to fetch the Israelites, Moses is insecure. He doesn't feel like he has anything to offer in terms of the future of his nation. God asks him, 'What's in your hand?' Of course, it's his shepherd's staff, and God uses the staff to perform the signs and wonders that convince Pharaoh to let His people leave Egypt.

Maybe you're thinking, 'I'm definitely not ready for the future!' Could you glance down at your hands, and make ready to offer whatever you see there to God, for His future use? God hasn't left you emptyhanded. You've got something. If you've lost what you once had in your hands, resist yearning for the good old days, the way the Israelites hankered after the food they ate in Egypt. Choose to be grateful that God has seen fit to weave you into the ongoing story of His Kingdom. Choose to be content in the present. And get ready for whatever the future will look like. Who knows what God will do with your one short life?

In the meantime, you can grow in wisdom and insight by numbering your days, cramming each one full of life. By God's sustaining and empowering grace, you've got what it takes – and you're readier than you think – to be free to flourish.

Free to ask yourself:

**These questions are drawn from themes
covered over the past five days.**

- Are you stuck somewhere in your past? Is God highlighting something about your past journey that's holding you back? What might be the first step towards gratefully coming to terms with what has been?

- Are you stuck in a rut of discontent, in the present, because you've somehow lost sight of the goodness of the Lord, today, in the land of the living?

- Are you hung up on what *may* be – awfulizing and catastrophizing the future? Could you trust all that to God, and just ready yourself to obey?

- Read Ecclesiastes 3:1-8. How has this Scripture played out in your own life?

Free to write it out:

Jesus was also once bound by time and space. His life on earth was a collection of yesterdays and todays and tomorrows, like ours. And yet even constrained to a timeline, He was the epitome of abundant life, and it was abundant life that He came to bring. He's the same God who numbers your days, and gives you a heart of wisdom, and He didn't just make you, He made you for more. Journal your response to this truth.

_____

_____

_____

_____

_____

_____

_____

_____

FREE TO FOLLOW

Right road, or regret?

Show me the right path, O Lord; point out the road for me to follow.
Psalm 25:4, NLT

Our faith in God comfortably contains the beautiful paradox that we are simultaneously free to choose, and wholly carried by the sovereign providence of God. It's an easy yoke. We have nothing to fear because He holds us and unfolds for us His perfect plans. And we can walk freely, celebrating the truth that He gives us wisdom, common sense, leanings, desires, and opportunities, and we are free to walk in them. We are free to navigate decisions, massive and miniscule. We are free to move and adventure, following in the footsteps of our Shepherd as we hear His voice.

In being free to follow, a powerful question we can learn to ask ourselves is, 'What will I regret doing, or not doing, ten years from now?' It makes for compelling and clarifying self-interrogation. It demands a courageous response, and one we can't help but to follow through on, because none of us wants to live with regret. As you ask yourself this question, pray for wisdom, discernment, and insight into your motives. For example, Ephesians 4:32 instructs us to be kind, tenderhearted and forgiving. So, if you're *not* in that emotional space, it's likely your decisions won't be in line with God's best for you.

Assess your relationships and reactions. Do you wish people well? Are you holding a grudge? It's hard to hear from God above the noise of our own bitterness. Pray for the Holy Spirit to bring to mind perspectives and principles you may have lost sight of. And thank Him for the freedom to follow Him.

Kingdom mobility

'For from His fullness we have all received, grace upon grace.'
John 1:16, ESV

Our mobility in God's Kingdom looks different from mobility in the world. The world's metrics for success are immediate and tangible and displayable. The Kingdom's metrics for success are eternal and supernatural and often unseen. Yet we can be sure it's God's nature to move us from 'glory to glory' (2 Corinthians 3:18) as we receive 'grace upon grace.' Our life in the Kingdom never involves a step down in terms of character or purpose or effectiveness. Our Kingdom movements are never lateral, A-to-B moves. They're always a step up as we move towards greater and greater likeness to Jesus.

When you're following Jesus – undertaking to live and love as He did and navigating your life in ways that glorify Him – you may sometimes think that what felt like your bravest move was actually your biggest mistake. It's helpful then to remember that Jesus is a *good* Shepherd. He's not spiteful or capricious or irresponsible with your life. He won't ever trick you or ambush you. His leadings are always for your good and His glory.

That's not to say when we follow Him life is always a picnic. For our growth and for the furthering of His Kingdom, God will, at times, lead us through difficult, challenging landscapes. Hold steady. Don't give up. The Shepherd never leaves the sheep in danger or without resources. Call out to Him constantly – 'God, left or right?' – so you don't wander off too far to hear His voice, calling you.

Roots determine routes

Let your roots grow down into Him, and let your lives be
built on Him. Then your faith will grow strong in the truth
you were taught, and you will overflow with thankfulness.
Colossians 2:7, NLT

Your life will go somewhere. There's a personal route for you to take, in your friendships, careers, studies, finances, marriage, singleness, parenting, or travels. We reinforce this idea by saying Christian-sounding things like, 'We're on a journey with God.' Or, 'I really believe this is the road God has for you…' But if you're anything like me, you may not always know what those things mean.

If you're reading this, you probably believe God has a purpose for your life – a road for you to walk. Or maybe you don't believe that at all. Maybe you don't even believe in God but someone gave you this book and you've opened to this page out of guilt, obligation, or mild curiosity. (I'm so glad you did.) Even so, you possibly – probably – deep down hope there *is* a God who has a purpose for your life, because otherwise, what's the point? Either we're alone in the universe, which is terrifying, or God is with us and there's hope.

So, assuming God is real and has a discoverable plan for you, it's vital to recognize that our *roots* determine our *routes*. God's Word tells us who He is, and who we are in relation to Him, which grounds us the way roots do. And then it tells us the routes we're to take into all the world, to make Him known. Start with the roots. Stick at it. The routes will become clear.

Deep roots, straight routes

This is what the LORD says: 'Cursed are those who put their trust in mere humans, who rely on human strength and turn their hearts away from the LORD. They are like stunted shrubs in the desert, with no hope for the future. They will live in the barren wilderness, in an uninhabited salty land. But blessed are those who trust in the LORD and have made the LORD their hope and confidence. They are like trees planted along a riverbank, with roots that reach deep into the water. Such trees are not bothered by the heat or worried by long months of drought. Their leaves stay green, and they never stop producing fruit.'
Jeremiah 17:5-8, NLT

This chapter of Jeremiah starts with God talking about how His people's sin is etched on their hearts with an iron chisel. His plan was for their hearts to be engraved with His Word, but instead they've scratched into their hard hearts a record of their wrongdoings.

We're all going somewhere and doing something, in this life. We're carving out routes, and filling up our time, somehow. We'll get from January to December, many times over no doubt, before our time on earth is up. But if we're not properly rooted, we'll probably waste a lot of time, and get ourselves into the mess of sin Jeremiah was warning God's people to avoid.

The Hebrew word translated 'confidence' in verse 7 means *refuge*, *security*, or *assurance*. Imagine how it might deepen your roots and straighten your routes if you were able to say, 'I have a refuge. I'm secure and assured because I've made the Lord my hope and confidence.'

Wow

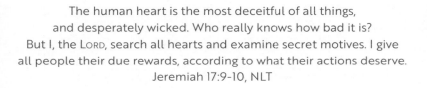

The human heart is the most deceitful of all things,
and desperately wicked. Who really knows how bad it is?
But I, the Lord, search all hearts and examine secret motives. I give
all people their due rewards, according to what their actions deserve.
Jeremiah 17:9-10, NLT

The gospel according to Pixar and Disney is, 'Follow your heart!' Make like Elsa. Let it go. You do you. I love all those movies, but the gospel according to Jesus is, 'Please don't follow your heart! It's the most deceitful of all things, and desperately wicked. It'll take you down the wrong route. It'll take you down, period. Follow *Me*. I'll *change* your heart.'

In our quest for changed hearts, deep roots, and straight routes (and considering the dead trees and the green trees we read about yesterday), we're going to reflect on mental pictures of four different trees. We'll call the first one the *wow* tree. (The other three are called *oh dear*, *oops* and *shh*. Read on!)

Imagine a magnificent tree on the banks of a tranquil river. That's who we're called to be. Trusting, hopeful, confident trees planted along a riverbank, with deep-reaching roots. Trees with perpetually green leaves, always producing fruit. In Matthew Henry's commentary on Jeremiah 17 he wrote, 'Those who make God their hope, have enough in Him to make up the want of all creature-comforts.' That's *wow*.

May you lead a *wow* life. May you be rooted on the water's edge. May you sprout green leaves and plentiful fruit. Even in the disaster of floods or droughts, may you be fully alive as you follow, not your own heart, but the One who made it.

Free to ask yourself:

**These questions are drawn from themes
covered over the past five days.**

- Are you faced with a big decision? What will you regret do-ing, or not doing, ten years from now?

- For a moment, forget upward mobility as the world defines it. How has God moved you from glory to glory, heaping grace upon grace upon you, over the past five or ten years?

- Has following your heart ever ended badly for you? How might the situation have turned out differently if, instead, you'd followed Jesus?

- Read Psalm 25. Then think about how the psalmist's roots determine his routes.

FREE TO FOLLOW

Free to ask God:

HEAVENLY FATHER,

I come into Your presence which is everywhere and here and now. I can't escape it. I'm in good hands. You know the end from the beginning, so I can rest in the messy middle. You're the God who sees every soul obliterated by the cancel culture. You see the knife slipped between the ribs, even by those near and dear. Thank You that my calling is irrevocable, and that it's in a laying down of self – a death to self – that there's a resurrection of purpose. Remind me that good leaders are just good yielders to the leading of the Good Shepherd.

AMEN.

Oh dear

...He lives rootless and aimless in a land where nothing grows.
Jeremiah 17:6, MSG

I'm sure you'd love to be a *wow* tree. Me too. But maybe you're thinking, 'Get real. That's a load of happily-ever-after Disney right there. It's an impossible fairy tale, not real life.' Maybe your life looks more like an *oh dear* tree. If others looked at the tree of your life? They'd feel sorry for it because it's just so ... *oh dear*.

Jeremiah's a straight talker. He says, '*Oh dear* indeed. Except, the tree kind of did this to itself.' An honest conversation with an *oh dear* tree might go like this: 'Oh dear, tree. Sorry you're so dead. What happened?' 'Well, I put my trust in mere humans. I relied on human strength and turned my heart away from the Lord. So, I'm like a stunted shrub in the desert, with no hope for the future, and I live in the barren wilderness.'

Sometimes our own sin puts us in the wilderness. Sometimes someone else's sin puts us there. Sometimes because sin broke the world, life just isn't ideal. Maybe your marriage is more of a stunted shrub in the desert than a willow on the bank. Maybe your finances have dried up completely and you're desperate. Maybe you've got thousands of Facebook friends but scrolling through your feed feels like traipsing through a lonely wasteland. Maybe you're not sure how you're going to get your kids to trudge through another year in the deserts of anxiety, dyslexia, or digital addiction. Maybe you're bone weary of being single.

Read on. There's hope. God is the great gardener who can transplant you to the riverbank.

FREE TO FOLLOW

Oops

But Jesus said, 'Someone deliberately touched Me,
for I felt healing power go out from Me.'
Luke 8:46, NLT

It's possible you're less of (yesterday's) *oh dear* tree, and more of an *oops* tree. An *oops* tree might be beautiful, ubiquitous, and fast growing. But its roots are shallow. As soon as there's a storm, it falls over. *Oops.*

Shallow-rooted people tend to put their hope and confidence, not just in human strength, but in human activities. Luke tells the story of a woman who's been menstruating constantly for twelve years. She's tried everything. Jesus is in town, and she thinks, 'What if there's a chance this guy can help me?' A social outcast, she risks the hustle, jostle, and shame of the crowd. She comes up behind Jesus, touches the fringe of His robe, and the bleeding stops. Jesus asks, 'Who touched Me?' (Luke 8:45) In this up-close-and-personal mass of humanity, He knows one person deliberately touched Him. Everyone else was just part of the vibe.

Perhaps there's an insidious danger of us convincing ourselves we're hanging out with Jesus when really, we're just part of the church vibe. Our hope and confidence are more in the *things* of God, than in God Himself. We sign up for serving teams. We follow Christian influencers on Instagram. We live a churchy life. We press up against Jesus and hang out with all His other friends in the crowd, but we don't deliberately reach out to just Him. So, our roots are shallow. Life happens, and we fall over. *Oops.*

If you find your roots torn loose by the storms of life, reach out to Jesus and read on. There's hope.

Shh ...

'My servant grew up in the LORD's presence like a tender
green shoot, like a root in dry ground. There was nothing beautiful
or majestic about His appearance, nothing to attract us to Him.'
Isaiah 53:2, NLT

The famous Tree of Ténéré in the Sahara Desert was around 300 years old in 1973 when a drunken truck driver veered into it, killing it. For centuries, it was the most isolated tree in the world, even marked on maps. It was a beacon of shade and hope, used by travelers to get their bearings. It also posed questions. How had it survived? How was it continuing to survive in the blistering Saharan sands? In 1938, some guys dug a well shaft near the tree. Thirty-six meters down they hit the answer: groundwater and the tree's taproot.

Taproots are strong and grow vertically towards the water table, which is hidden. They grow deep, quietly and in secret. *Shh.* Trees with a taproot dare not be underestimated: they grow deeper below the ground, often, than they grow tall above ground. The Tree of Ténéré wasn't a big tree. Nothing to look at, really. Kind of like Jesus. And yet Jesus was unshakeable, and His name would be the hope of all the world (Matthew 12:21).

Friend, the *shh* tree is the *wow* tree. The *shh* tree doesn't fear heat or drought. Its leaves stay green because it tenaciously digs deep, to the source of life. *Wow.* This was the life of Jesus, and the life He calls us to. He never promised there wouldn't be heat and drought. He promised to be the ever-present river of life running over our roots.

Mimic the Master

'But when you pray, go away by yourself, shut the door
behind you, and pray to your Father in private.
Then your Father, who sees everything, will reward you.'
Matthew 6:6, NLT

In this past week's readings, we've established that Christianity is not the gospel according to Pixar or Disney. It's not a fairy tale. There's one very real Person – Jesus – who walked the earth like we do. He wasn't an *oh dear* tree or an *oops* tree. He was the *wow, shh* tree. His leaves stayed green. He never stopped producing fruit. He invites us to follow Him, and if we explore how He lived we start understanding what it means to trust in the Lord and make Him our hope and confidence.

Jesus knew His Father's Word. In the face of doubts, distractions, accusations, He quoted Scripture. He was *rooted* in Scripture. He frequently – often – regularly – drew away alone to pray, and He intentionally taught others to do the same. He was mobbed by crowds, and He stopped for the one. He had strong, close friendships, and He engaged with strangers and pariahs. He's our perfect example of how to do healthy community, and He was passionate about making His followers understand that we won't do community well if we don't do solitude well.

He had deep roots because He would consistently, deliberately, alone and in secret, seek first His Father. And because of that, He knew the *route* He had to take. He took His message on the road, set His face like flint, and went on a preaching tour that ended in Jerusalem – and death on the tree that set us free to follow Him.

Netflix theology

Be still before the LORD and wait patiently for Him.
Psalm 37:7, NIV

If you're still tracking with these readings, I believe you want to dig deep wells into God's living water, to be refreshing to others. Me too. I dream of putting down strong roots so my branches will spread far and wide, giving shade to weary wanderers.

Except, I'm ridiculously impatient. I want instant results. In the olden days, we had to wait a whole week before we could watch the next episode of a series. A *week*. Now it takes all our self-control to quickly hit that back arrow before the next episode starts in 5-4-3-2 – and then – how did that happen? – we're on Season 5.

We tend to apply Netflix theology to God. We want instant gratification. We say, 'Excuse me, God, I had a quiet time today. I clicked on three different reading plans in YouVersion. Do you even love me? Because this situation not been resolved! I would really like to watch this next episode of my life play out in 5-4-3-2...' We're loathe to form the habit of regular time in prayer and God's Word, because we don't see a difference quickly enough. We don't necessarily *feel* a difference. But like anything worthwhile in life (like staying healthy or out of debt): a lifetime of small decisions add up to enough. Same-same spiritually. Nothing beats consistency. Small investments of time, over time – the astonishing, cumulative power of patience and daily obedience – will change our lives, and enough changed lives build up to the critical mass that changes community, and changed communities, change the world.

Free to ask yourself:

These questions are drawn from themes covered over the past five days.

- If someone were to ask you today, 'How are your roots?', what would your one-word answer be?

- Have you passed through a season of life during which it became evident that your roots were too shallow?

- How would you explain to someone that our roots determine our routes? What practical advice would you give them?

- Does your secret obedience to God feel overrated? Does it feel like you're sweeping parts of a floor no one will ever even walk on? How does Luke 8:17 encourage you?

Free to write it out:

**Take time today to send down deep roots.
Pour out your frustrations if it feels to you as if
God has been slow to respond to your desperation.
Write down any thoughts that come to mind as you
consider ways to grow strong roots and lay straight routes.**

The ultimate tree

> But Christ has rescued us from the curse pronounced
> by the law. When He was hung on the cross, He took upon
> Himself the curse for our wrongdoing. For it is written in
> the Scriptures, 'Cursed is everyone who is hung on a tree.'
> Galatians 3:13, NLT

Between now and heaven, there'll be tough times. We live in a fallen world where crazy, terrible things happen. Whether it's heat at work or relational or financial drought, sin entered the world bent on turning us into stunted shrubs in the desert with no hope for the future. The world's a mess. Fascinatingly, it was a tree that got us into this mess, and it's a tree that gets us out.

Back in Eden, God puts Adam in charge of all the trees. He tells Adam and Eve, 'Help yourself to the fruit of any of these trees. Just not the tree of the knowledge of good and evil.' (Genesis 2:16-17) But Adam and Eve get sidetracked by the enemy. They decide not to make God their hope and confidence. The rest is literally history.

Fast forward some millennia. God makes another tree grow, giving it a ring for its birthday every year. He knows it'll be chopped down and hacked into a cross. It's carried up a hill and planted back into the ground – dead. And God hangs from it. He grafts His ordinary, killable body onto that dead tree so we can be grafted into the living tree of His Kingdom.

Because of that historical fact, we have a future hope despite deserts and droughts. We've been made alive – our roots resting in His rushing streams running deep.

Quiet time

Come close to God, and God will come close to you.
James 4:8, NLT

I've never loved the term 'quiet time'. It's a churchy word that, depending on your temperament, could put real condemnation on you. (Cue the reproachful question: 'Have you had your quiet time today?' If your answer is no, you heap burning coals on your own head. If it's yes, you give yourself a self-righteous gold star on heaven's big behavior chart.)

Perhaps we could reframe the concept. Because really, it's simply this: every day the King invites you to meet with Him. He'll be waiting. Will you show up? Even just for five minutes? Imagine your president, prime minster or monarch phoned you and invited you for lunch, saying, 'I've made a reservation at the city's top restaurant. I would love to just hang out with you, random citizen.' You'd cancel whatever plans you had, and you'd be there, wouldn't you? With a long list of questions, and maybe even one or two suggestions.

Every day, the King of kings says, 'I'm available 24/7. I'd love you to practice prioritizing time with Me, because although I'm beyond figuring out and will blow your mind, as much as your brain can handle, I'll allow you to get to know Me personally. I'll never waste your time. I'll let you feast on wisdom that changes everything. And you're welcome to put in requests.'

If you've fallen out of the habit of spending time with God, it may feel awkward to start again. Just start. Say something to God. Read something of what He's written. He'll guide you.

Free to follow ... and suffer?

I am glad when I suffer for you in my body, for I am participating
in the sufferings of Christ that continue for His body, the church.
Colossians 1:24, NLT

Paul isn't saying there was anything lacking in the afflictions of Christ. There's nothing deficient in the completed work of the cross. You don't need to go down to your local hardware store, buy a packet of 9-inch nails and drive them into your own hands to punish yourself for your sin. Jesus already did all that suffering on our behalf.

Paul's just explaining that there's an ongoing, gospel-spreading work happening through the church, the body of Christ. When Jesus was here on earth, He didn't make all the disciples that were ever going to be made. That work is still lacking. He left us to do that. And some-times that work involves suffering. The suffering doesn't add to the atonement. It's a biproduct of getting the word out there. Growing the church and making disciples can be grueling work and it does involve sacrifice.

What Paul is *not* saying is that he can't wait to be shipwrecked for a *third* time, because he can't get enough of suffering. He's not a mas-ochist. He's just ok to suffer. It's as if he's saying, 'More than anything, I want to see people set free. This anguish and distress? It's so worth it. Because Jesus is creating a new, multi-ethnic family made up of Jews and Gentiles and everyone in between and it's going to be glorious.' For whatever you face, God is with you. His free grace is freely available and sufficient (2 Corinthians 12:9).

Bring it on

*'I have told you all this so that you may have peace in Me.
Here on earth you will have many trials and sorrows.
But take heart, because I have overcome the world.'*
John 16:33, NLT

We shouldn't be surprised by hardships we encounter for following Jesus. Life is already hard in a fallen world. But when we enlist in Team Jesus? We're adding extra hardships. (You're welcome!) In all seriousness, though, I'd rather you know upfront that, in surrendering your life to Jesus, you're signing up for some hostility and opposition: the world, the flesh, the devil.

The world's systems will come against us because the truth about sin and repentance is extremely irritating and offensive to pretty much every world culture. Our own flesh will come against us because we'll want to be 'free' to do and be certain things. It'll feel like God is a buzz-kill holding out on us, when really He's calling us to something better and freer because He knows the thing promising us freedom will end up ensnaring us. The devil will come against us because he's not fond of life, light, love, growth, and freedom.

But if you've been following Jesus for longer than five minutes, I know you wouldn't trade it for anything. Me neither. Because being in Christ, in the midst of chaos, means that no matter what, it is well with your soul. Jesus *does* make life better. It's always going to be better to be free than to be trapped. One day in His courts will always be better than a thousand elsewhere (Psalm 84:10). Bring it on.

FREE TO FOLLOW

Master of mystery

God has given me the responsibility of serving His church
by proclaiming His entire message to you. This message was
kept secret for centuries and generations past, but now it has
been revealed to God's people ... And this is the secret: Christ
lives in you. This gives you assurance of sharing His glory.
Colossians 1:25-27, NLT

Humans love mystery and intrigue. It's why Agatha Christie's books have sold over two billion copies, an amount surpassed only by the Bible and Shakespeare's works. Scandalously, it's why we're drawn to gossip, why we get our knickers in a knot over conspiracy theories, and why we rubberneck when we drive past road accidents. Innocently, it's why even as grownups we love Easter egg hunting and wondering what's in our Christmas stockings and we're thrilled by stories of surprise marriage proposals.

Here Paul refers to the gospel as a mystery: a secret God had been keeping for centuries and was now revealing. The Greeks and Romans of Paul's day also really loved a mystery. Gnosticism was showing signs of life. Mystical pagan practices were rife. And Paul is saying, 'You want mystery? I'll give you mystery. You don't need to join an enigmatic cult. I'll tell you about the greatest plot twist in all human history. I'll tell you *who dunnit*: Jesus Christ. And this mystery isn't a secret teaching known only to an exclusive few and unknown to the masses. This mystery, now revealed, is for everyone.' Paul knew mystery was a buzzword in this culture. He capitalizes on that to recapture the attention of God's people. Let his words recapture your attention too, as you freely follow the mystery revealed: Jesus.

Free to ask yourself:

These questions are drawn from themes covered over the past five days.

- How would you explain to someone who has recently become a Christian what it means to 'spend time with God'?

- Have you ever suffered for being a Christian?

- On your journey of following Jesus, what comes against you most often: the world, the flesh, or the devil? What is your combat strategy?

- Read Colossians 1:9-14. For whom can you pray this, today?

Free to ask God:

JESUS,

You suffered unimaginably, for me. Grow in me a spine of steel, willing to stand straight and strong for You and Your Kingdom. Show me where I'm weak or un-willing to nail my colors to the mast, for Your glory. Give me courage and resolve and a stalwart faith that happily engages with the rejection the world is sure to throw my way. And keep my heart soft towards those who don't know You yet.

AMEN.

Aha!

> Now all glory to God, who is able to make you strong, just as
> my Good News says. This message about Jesus Christ has revealed
> His plan for you Gentiles, a plan kept secret from the beginning of time.
> Romans 16:25, NLT

FREE TO FOLLOW

Before Jesus came to earth, no one knew exactly how God planned to fulfil the many predictions of the Messiah. The Old Testament, from Genesis to Malachi, is full of gospel shadows, symbols, pictures, and prophecies of Jesus. It's all about the Father rescuing His creation by sending His Son. We know, from Abraham, that we're saved by grace through faith. We know the Messiah would be born of a virgin in Bethlehem, that He would be Emmanuel, God with us, that He'd have His hands and feet pierced, and He'd die an excruciating death. The Old Testament tells us the Messiah would rise on the third day and be seated at the Father's right hand.

But no one knew exactly how and when all that would play out. It was only when Jesus actually came, and died, and rose again that the Tetris blocks of those prophecies fell into place and the universe went, 'Aha! It was Him!' Even during His life, Jesus kept the gospel a secret. He spoke in parables, leaving some dots unconnected in the minds of His audience. He healed people and said, 'Don't tell anyone.' Even demons were shushed. He was waiting for the moment of His death and resurrection when truth exploded and the masterful plan, hidden for ages, was put on glorious display. Praise God you're reading this on the other side of Christ's big reveal, free to follow Him!

Defeating evil

God has now revealed to us His mysterious will
regarding Christ – which is to fulfill His own good plan.
Ephesians 1:9, NLT

Maybe you're still wondering *why* God kept the gospel a secret, for so long. Why was the gospel this mystery that was hidden – and then revealed? We'll look at three reasons over the next three days, the first of which is that God was defeating evil. He was at war with the enemy. And in war, you don't tell the enemy your plans.

Churchill didn't phone Hitler in 1944 and say, 'Hey, Adolf? *Wie gehts?* So, we're planning to send some boats across the Channel on 6 June. Yip ... Why, thank you! We also thought it was a neat idea. So perhaps you want to check if your guys are free to fight us on the beaches?' Quite the opposite.

In 1 Corinthians 2:7-8 Paul writes, '... the wisdom we speak of is the mystery of God – His plan that was previously hidden, even though He made it for our ultimate glory before the world began. But the rulers of this world have not understood it; if they had, they would not have crucified our glorious Lord.' So, God was hiding His plans from the enemy – keeping them secret. In that cataclysmic moment – Christ on the cross – God the Father wrecked like a ninja. Satan thought he'd won. 'Ha ha! They're killing God,' he might've thought. He didn't know the death of Jesus signified his greatest defeat and our greatest redemption, victory, and freedom. Praise God for His magnificent mystery now revealed.

FREE TO FOLLOW

All glory

It is the glory of God to conceal a matter ...
Proverbs 25:2, NIV

We read yesterday how God kept the details of His salvation plan secret as a strategy of war against our enemy, the devil. The second reason He kept Operation Planet Earth on the down low is that it gave Him glory to do so.

In Ephesians 1, Paul talks about the gospel as 'God's mysterious plan regarding Christ,' and then tells us in Ephesians 2 that we're saved by grace through faith – the gospel – so that *no one can boast*. Our salvation was *all* God's idea. We can take exactly zero credit for being clever and helping Him out in any way at all. If God had left it up to humans to invent a plan for salvation, we would've come up with religion. That's what humans do. Left to our own black-and-white devices, we would've said, 'Ok people, here's how it's going to work. Do all these good things. Don't do all these bad things. And you better just hope the good things outweigh the bad things!'

God's full-color version sounded like this: 'I'm going to send My Son to be born as a tiny baby person. He'll grow up to lead a perfect life, die a sacrificial death, be raised to life on the third day, and offer salvation freely to anyone who believes in Him.' Only a God far beyond the capacity of our brains could have come up with that, and only God gets the glory because from start to finish of that plan He was in control. He. Does. Everything. All glory and gratitude to God for stooping to save us.

Divine clickbait

This God, whom you worship without knowing, is the one
I'm telling you about. He is the God who made the world
and everything in it. Since He is Lord of heaven and earth,
He doesn't live in man-made temples, and human hands can't
serve His needs – for He has no needs. He Himself gives life
and breath to everything, and He satisfies every need.
Acts 17:23-25, NLT

There's a third reason God in all His brilliance kept the gospel a mystery until it was fulfilled in Christ. He knows there's nothing like a good secret to get our attention. Think of Jesus saying to folks, 'Don't tell anyone I healed you.' What do they immediately do? 'You won't believe it! This guy just healed me! It's amazing!' That's humans for you. We're so predictable.

In Acts 17, Paul is in Athens. He notices among all the altars to many pagan gods one that has the inscription, 'To an Unknown God.' These people didn't have it all figured out. They were searching. They knew there had to be something – *Someone* – more. And God uses this, like divine clickbait. Paul goes on to say, 'His purpose was for the nations to seek after God and perhaps feel their way toward Him and find Him – though He is not far from any one of us. For in Him we live and move and exist.' (Acts 17:27-28)

God is sovereignly working to woo us all the time. When He whispers, may you long to know His secrets, and so lean in closer and closer to hear Him.

Big juice

> To them God has chosen to make known among the Gentiles the
> glorious riches of this mystery, which is Christ in you, the hope of glory.
> Colossians 1:27, NIV

The result of God's gospel revelation to humanity is found in Paul's words to the Colossians: *Christ in you, the hope of glory.* To which we say, 'What does that even mean? Also, it's so simplistic.' Exactly. The gospel is incomprehensible, and absolutely that simple.

I've heard the story of a two-year-old girl seeing the ocean for the first time. When she and her family arrived at their seaside holiday destination, they immediately headed for the beach. They crested an enormous dune and before them lay the vastness of the ocean from horizon to horizon. The little girl just gasped and said, 'Big juice!' She didn't have the vocabulary to say, 'I've never seen so much liquid! It's endless! It's so blue and so beautiful.' She just reached for the words she knew.

We don't have the vocabulary or mental space to understand how Jesus existed before anything else and holds *all creation* together (Colossians 1:17). Every molecule in the universe is held together by Jesus, in Jesus, for Jesus. And yet the Spirit of this same Jesus is *in us*. You're in Christ. And Christ is in you. Paul also tells us all the treasures of wisdom and knowledge lie hidden in Jesus (Colossians 2:3). He possesses all the truth there is. And Paul says He's *in us*. He's also everywhere else, and we are in Him – because in Him we live and move and exist (Acts 17:28). It's a mystery, and that's ok. *Big juice.*

Free to ask yourself:

These questions are drawn from themes covered over the past five days.

- How have the mysteries of God drawn you closer to Him?

- What thoughts, questions or experiences are inside your mental box labeled *Things I Will Never Understand*? Do you think it might be worth writing those things out, and putting them inside an actual box, so you no longer need to carry them with you?

- How have you seen the enemy defeated as you've brought the gospel to bear on a particular area of your life?

- Read Deuteronomy 29:29. What is God calling you to do today, despite what He hasn't yet revealed to you?

Free to write it out:

Take a few minutes to be completely, unreservedly honest with God. Bring before Him your unedited questions, fears, doubts, and anxieties. If you're frustrated because God hasn't revealed something to you, write it down. He can handle it.

Free to forgive

Be kind and compassionate to one another,
forgiving each other, just as in Christ God forgave you.
Ephesians 4:32, NIV

Because we're humans, living alongside other humans, we've all had to forgive someone. Maybe you were cut off in the traffic. Maybe you've experienced crushing betrayal by the person you thought loved you best. Forgiveness can feel impossible – like you're *rewarding* your enemy – particularly if you're pretty sure the wrong you've suffered won't ever be validated, and you may never be vindicated. Jesus gets it. No one in history has endured greater injustice. And yet Jesus didn't retaliate or threaten revenge. He left His case in the hands of God, who always judges fairly, and we can do the same (1 Peter 2:23).

Jesus died to free us from sin's grip. He's already done the hard work of forgiveness, for us. Ask Him to do it again – to do in you that which you can't do yourself. Let His grace flow through you towards your offender. As you cancel their debt and release them into the hands of the living God, you'll find that *you're* the one set free. There's never going to be a better time to forgive, than right now.

Another idea is to *pre*-forgive people – even before your day starts. Other people don't own your joy. Make sure they don't steal it, by deciding *before* they've had a chance to hurt or offend you, that you're releasing them into the hands of the God who judges fairly, and always has your back. Freely we've been given (Matthew 10:8). Let's freely give forgiveness to those who owe us, as much as we'd love them to forgive us.

Free to belong

*... so it is with Christ's body. We are many parts
of one body, and we all belong to each other.*
Romans 12:5, NLT

You might not feel particularly connected to the people in your church or community group. You might not feel connected to Christians in Thailand or Argentina or India or Scotland. But the truth is, you are. If you love Jesus, then the same Holy Spirit who lives in you – guiding you and comforting you – lives in all those believers all over the world, and in the ones who sit behind you in church.

Jesus is building His church through us all. Whether or not it looks or feels that way, we're all tugging in the same direction: the direction of His Kingdom on earth as it is in heaven, for His glory and the fame of His name. Just knowing that frees us from the tendency to put up barriers, or to get hung up on our differences.

It's also a humbling reminder that we're no better than anyone else God has saved by His grace and added to His body. The ground at the foot of the cross is flat. Considering that, it's ludicrous to withhold any good – like the gift of forgiveness, which has been freely poured out on us – from anyone in His church body, local or global. Forgiveness is a gift we can freely, lavishly bestow on others. And again, we'll be the ones set free. Bitterness and grudges eat away at us like rodent tumors, making us sick and ugly on the inside – and eventually on the outside too. Do yourself a favor. Accept. Forgive. And set yourself free to belong.

Pray don't patronize

'Be merciful, just as your Father is merciful.'
Luke 6:36, NIV

Haters will hate. And when you're maligned or misunderstood or judged or criticized, it's unthinkably hard not to lash out in retaliation. There's a time to defend yourself, sure. There's a time to bring truth to light, and we can trust God for the discernment to know if or when we should stand up for ourselves, against others. We can also trust His promptings to leave our case in His hands, because He's the righteous judge who is perfectly powerful and perfectly fair (1 Peter 2:23).

But whether you're compelled to act or content to let a situation unfold under God's judgment and justice, it helps to remember that prejudice is almost always the result of ignorance or insecurity. Either the people being racist or sexist or ageist or just plain mean are *ignorant* of the truth that you're a beautiful human, loved by the King and made in His image, or they're *insecure* within themselves, driven to demote or demoralize you – hurt you or disregard you – so as to elevate themselves.

When you recognize injustice leveled against you as coming from either ignorance or insecurity, it's easier to make the leap to mercy, and prayer. You can pray for the perpetrators to come to greater knowledge and a deeper understanding of the truth. Or you can pray they'd find their security and identity in Jesus, which would go a long way towards alleviating them of the need to feel better about themselves by making you feel worse. When you find yourself subjected to prejudice, may you resist stooping to patronize, and rather, rise up in prayer.

Two ears, one mouth

Understand this, my dear brothers and sisters: You must
all be quick to listen, slow to speak, and slow to get angry.
James 1:19, NLT

God has set us free to communicate with Him and with others. He created communication. We're made in His image. And when our lives come under His Lordship, our communication capacity and strategy and effectiveness are all redeemed and increasingly sanctified. Miraculously He transforms us by the power of the Spirit so our communication can begin to reflect the mind and manner of Jesus.

Perhaps a place to start is to remember that the purpose of communication is to *connect* with others (as in, talk *to* people, not *at* them, and listen). It's a two-way street. There's a time for yelling out fast commands without waiting for a response. But the context of most of our communication is not a battlefield, or a fire drill, or preventing a toddler from running into the road. Most of our communication is with friends or family we love and live with, people we work alongside, or fellow world-sojourning strangers who cross our paths on any given day in any given situation. And we're to lovingly send and receive messages to establish and strengthen ties of love and respect.

Communication is not about us. It's about others, and it's about glorifying God. Let's use our freedom to learn to listen. Let's hold space for people's stories and opinions. Let's even get comfortable with silence – allowing someone's spoken words to rest in a room for a bit before we leap in with solutions or suggestions. Two ears. One mouth.

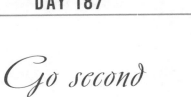

Go second

Don't be selfish; don't try to impress others. Be humble,
thinking of others as better than yourselves. Don't look out
only for your own interests, but take an interest in others, too.
Philippians 2:3-4, NLT

One of the pervasive lies of our culture is that we should first and foremost Look Out for Number One. We're an insular, individualistic, selfish bunch, bent on self-preservation at the expense of others and with little regard for the welfare of the world. Stepping back and allowing someone to get ahead of us goes against our most primal instincts.

It doesn't have to be that way. I mean, sure, *someone* has to be the first in line at a buffet. But I try to remind myself *it doesn't always have to be me*. Take a moment to think about what might happen in your city or community if, for the next month, all God's people stepped aside for the person in the grocery store behind them, letting them go ahead in the queue. Think about the societal shift that might ensue if we challenged each other to a different kind of competition, saying, 'The first one to go second – *that* person's the winner!' That kind of beautiful revolution really is possible if we stop saying 'One day ...' and say instead, 'Day one.' Just start.

You may be skeptical about whether going second can have wondrous effects. That's ok. Understanding can wait. Obedience cannot. And God's command is clear: think of others as better than yourself. Relief floods in, along with freedom from hustle and self-importance, when we stop putting ourselves forward and instead do all we can to elevate others.

FREE TO LOVE

Free to ask yourself:

These questions are drawn from themes covered over the past five days.

- Who do you need to forgive? What's your next step, to get there?

- Have you ever judged someone unfairly, or been less than kind, because you were ignorant about that person's situation or because you were battling your own insecurities?

- What might going second look like for you, today?

- Read Proverbs 18:2, 13. What provokes us to interrupt others, or to give our loud opinions even when they're not requested?

Free to ask God:

FREE TO LOVE

JESUS,

You put Yourself last to put us first. Teach me Your selfless ways! Help me communicate and connect with the people You have written into my story. Show me how to show others that they belong. Help me to listen, love, and let go of offences. Convict me, where my own ignorance or insecurity causes me to dismiss someone.

AMEN.

Ninety-nine for one

'If a man has a hundred sheep and one of them gets lost,
what will he do? Won't he leave the ninety-nine others in the
wilderness and go to search for the one that is lost until he finds it?'
Luke 15:4, NLT

At the risk of stirring up negative emotions: think of that person in your family or circle of friends or acquaintances who has hurt you or angered you or heinously wronged you in some way. Or think about the unlovely person whose life has rubbed up a little too closely to yours – the dirty and destitute, the embarrassing or the awkward. It's possible you feel something quite close to hatred for that person.

Now, try to envision Jesus leaving the ninety-nine – leaving *you* and all His other beloved, loyal, and lovely sheep – to go after that one person. Because that's exactly what He would do. And He would do that with the express intent of lovingly redeeming and restoring that person, for His pleasure and purposes.

Think about how it might change your relationship with people, or your responses to politicians, or bad-mannered children, or the family member who gets under your skin and seems to know just how to rob you of joy, if you saw them the way Jesus does: a beloved lamb, lost and loved and earnestly looked for. Jesus' great love for the person you *struggle* to love doesn't nullify the hurt they've caused you. It doesn't excuse their sin. But as much as you've been reclaimed by the Shepherd, so have they. May that perspective keep you soft-hearted and steady in all your doings and dealings today.

FREE TO LOVE

Graves to gardens

'I am my lover's, and he claims me as his own.'
Song of Solomon 7:10, NLT

Song of Solomon is a multi-layered story about the love affair between a husband and wife, God and the church, and Jesus and the individual believer. It's filled with garden language: color, fragrance, and fruit. The young woman's lover casts shade over her, protecting her from the harsh elements. Her identity is transformed as she accepts that she is deeply, truly loved. Then he calls her out to adventure with him, to abide in him, to stay tender and flexible to his leading. Her past no longer defines her, and her grave language changes to garden language.

That's my story, and yours. Jesus has covered our shame, redefined us, and called us to Kingdom adventures. And as we walk through our days abiding in Him, staying tender and flexible, we get to change grave atmospheres into garden atmospheres. We begin to see how we're not in the world to adapt, but to influence.

And so, in our marriages, friendships and connections with family and co-workers, we're to be known for what we're *for*, more than what we're *against*. We're to ask ourselves, 'Am I just finding fault, or am I seeing a future?' Or, where our kids are concerned, 'Does my child need love or a lecture?' Lectures are great, sometimes. Mostly, I need to bend flexibly around my kids and lean in with tender loving garden language. And beyond our own garden walls, we're called to courageously declare to everyone everywhere, 'His banner over you is love!' (Song of Solomon 2:4)

Finding feet

Don't just pretend to love others. Really love them. Hate what
is wrong. Hold tightly to what is good. Love each other with
genuine affection, and take delight in honoring each other.
Romans 12:9-10, NLT

Years ago, I saw a film about a married couple who very nearly got
divorced. Most days the only common ground they could find
was at the end of their bed, where they would find each other's feet
under the duvet. By maximizing that small point of connection, they
managed to rescue their marriage from the brink. That concept – of
keeping on *keeping on* finding one another – is a key ingredient in the
secret sauce of a strong marriage. And beyond marriage, *finding each
other* as friends, or siblings, or fellow volunteers is incredibly powerful
and valuable too.

What might it look like for you to keep on *finding* someone with whom
you're in relationship? What would it take for you to speak their love
language? How could you show an interest in someone's life in such a
way that that person feels loved, seen, *found*, wherever they find their
feet? It may look like keeping your own feet still for a bit. Pausing in
someone's company. Not rushing off but standing still long enough to
really listen. Lingering in someone's presence so they know they are a
legitimate priority to you.

Jesus has set us free to build genuine connections with the people
to whom He has linked our lives. In barely noticeable, mundane moments, and under the bright lights of magnificent moments, let's *find*
people's feet wherever they are stood, and love them well.

Beautiful difference

After this I saw a vast crowd, too great to count,
from every nation and tribe and people and language,
standing in front of the throne and before the Lamb.
Revelation 7:9, NLT

We all click or clash with people of varying temperaments or personality profiles. Sometimes opposites attract. Sometimes opposites drive us crazy. And to be free to love people well, it's crucial for us to take note of our reactions to how others make decisions or process situations.

If you're an adventurous risk-taker (sometimes too impulsive, which is *not* a good thing, and sometimes inspiring others to take bold action, which *is* a good thing), you may be irritated or frustrated by someone who is risk averse and more analytical (sometimes shrinking back from decisive action, which is *not* a good thing, and sometimes clarifying the realistic options or outcomes of a situation, which *is* a good thing). If you're Person A in the above example, try not to devalue the low-risk person in any given process. Don't negate their contribution by calling it fear. You may well need their worst-case-scenario planning. If you're Person B in the above example, try not to write off the optimists and enthusiasts. Don't negate their contribution by calling it delusional or dangerous. You may well benefit from their blue-sky thinking and optimism bias.

Loose lips sink ships. Let's speak well of others, no matter how different from us they are. Each human with whom you live, work, worship or socialize is an image-bearer of our great God whose genius is on display in the diversity of all He has made.

Foxtrot in the flowerbeds

A person's wisdom yields patience;
it is to one's glory to overlook an offense.
Proverbs 19:11, NIV

Marriage is a foxtrot. One of you is the *slow ... slow ...* and one of you is the *quick-quick*. That's how it should be. That's what makes it a dance. That's what lends rhythm to your days and your decisions. Celebrate your differing temperaments and traits by leaving them all on the dancefloor because opposites make magic. When you step on each other's toes, laugh (*with*, not *at*). Take a beat to find the beat. Find each other. The dance only works if you keep holding on. Maybe, dance barefoot. Humility ushers in the extraordinary presence, power, and purposes of God.

Also, you might try dancing in the garden, where marriage began. Marriage was invented by God and the very first marriage ceremony took place in the very first garden, *before* the Fall. Sin hadn't yet entered the world, and the only thing that was 'not good' in this perfect world, was for man to be alone. And so, marriage. As the designer of marriage, God has all the information on it and all the best ideas.

Sadly, back in that Genesis garden, things went horribly wrong. Eve was gullible, bossy, and manipulative. Adam was spineless. And the rest is history. But the moment Adam and Eve fell into sin, God stepped in with a promise of redemption (Genesis 3). That promise was a person. Jesus came to redeem all things, including our marriages. Praise God that He has freed us to re-inhabit the garden: to enjoy marriage as the intimate dance He intended it to be.

FREE TO LOVE

Free to ask yourself:

**These questions are drawn from themes
covered over the past five days.**

- Who drives you insane? Who has hurt you, or angered you, or mistreated you in some way? How does it change your posture toward that person when you remember that Jesus would leave the ninety-nine and go on a search-and-rescue mission for that one person you're laboring to love?

- Is there someone in your family, circle of friends, or office space whose temperament is diametrically opposed to yours? If so, how can you celebrate the strengths they bring to the table, and so diffuse any conflict or tension that may have built up?

- How is God prompting you to pray for your marriage, or for the marriage of people close to you?

- Read 2 Corinthians 2:15. In which area of your life do you have an opportunity to change grave language into garden language, and so be the sweet perfume of Christ?

Free to write it out:

Ask God to bring to mind the people in your life He wants you to pray for. Then start writing. Just write down whichever names surface, even if you have no idea why those people may need prayer, and even if you haven't seen or spoken to them in years. Write out your prayers for these people, or just ask the Holy Spirit to intercede on your behalf.

Good grapes

Since God chose you to be the holy people He loves, you must clothe yourselves with tenderhearted mercy, kindness, humility, gentleness, and patience. Make allowance for each other's faults, and forgive anyone who offends you. Remember, the Lord forgave you, so you must forgive others. Above all, clothe yourselves with love, which binds us all together in perfect harmony.
Colossians 3:12-14, NLT

Conflict with other people often makes us see them as *wholly* bad – like rotten apples. We mentally or emotionally throw them away. They're inedible. Unpalatable. Unlovable. Any sweet times we enjoyed with them are soured. Bright memories turn dark. The relational trauma leaves us re-processing whole seasons of life we shared with our offenders.

There's a beautiful social reframing tool we're free to use. Instead of seeing the affronting person as an apple, see them as a bunch of grapes. Sure, some of the grapes are rotten or moldy or squished. No one would expect you to eat them and you'd certainly be smart to throw those onto the compost heap, where God will use them to grow something beautiful because He does cause *all* things to work together for the good of those who love Him (Romans 8:28). But you would probably be able to find plenty – or at least a few? – sweet, firm, ripe grapes on that same bunch, to enjoy.

It may feel tough to compartmentalize your experience in this way, but it's a helpful picture of boundaries, which I've heard described as 'the distance at which I can love you and me simultaneously.' May you grow in kindness, discernment, and rational wisdom, and may God shield you on every side from hurt and harm.

FREE TO LOVE

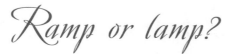

Ramp or lamp?

Don't be concerned about the outward beauty of fancy hairstyles, expensive jewelry, or beautiful clothes. You should clothe yourselves instead with the beauty that comes from within, the unfading beauty of a gentle and quiet spirit, which is so precious to God. This is how the holy women of old made themselves beautiful.
1 Peter 3:3-5, NLT

Peter suggests two possibilities as we exercise our freedom to love those God has placed in our homes: *Ramp or Lamp?* Are you living like a ramp model? Or are you lighting the lamp of your inner beauty? Peter's writing to encourage suffering Christians. And what he's getting at is that external beauty makes an impression; internal beauty makes a difference. And in demanding times we need difference makers. He's *not* saying you can't be an extrovert or wear makeup and jewelry. There are accounts all over Scripture of beautifully adorned women, leading confidently. He's saying, don't obsess over or worship your outward beauty. There's so much more to you than that.

So, look after your body. It's a temple of the Holy Spirit. Be a good steward of your outer beauty within the realms of reality and your budget, because we've each only been given so much to work with. Just don't make it an idol. It *will* let you down. In the end, gravity wins. Inner beauty, Peter says, is *unfading*. In fact, Paul tells us that though our outer bodies are getting older and older, our spirits are being renewed every day (2 Corinthians 4:16). We're growing *younger* on the inside. Psalm 34:5 says, 'Those who look to Him for help will be radiant with joy ...' Keep lighting your lamp.

FREE TO LOVE

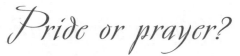

Pride or prayer?

In the same way, you husbands must give honor to your wives.
Treat your wife with understanding as you live together. She may
be weaker than you are, but she is your equal partner in God's gift of
new life. Treat her as you should so your prayers will not be hindered.
1 Peter 3:7, NLT

If *ramp or lamp* are two words for women (see yesterday's reading if you missed it), then *pride or prayer* are two words for men. Within the context of marriage, Peter shows us what it looks like for men to stand firm in a shaky world, and it comes down to asking, 'Will I live a life of pride or a life of prayer?'

The word *honor* as it's used in 1 Peter 3:7 is the same *honor* found in 1 Peter 2:7. It's the *honor* God the Father bestowed on Jesus. It's the Greek word *timé*, spelt T-I-M-E. If a man has no idea where to start honoring his wife, maybe this is a clue. Spend some *time* in prayer. Spend some *time* on her.

The last part of 1 Peter 3:7, in *The Message* translation, reads: 'Treat your wives, then, as equals so your prayers don't run aground.' We live in tumultuous times. Peter's saying, 'There's already enough of a storm raging *around* your boat. Make sure the storm isn't also raging *inside* your boat, because that's going to make it tricky to stay afloat.' Let's pray the men in our communities wouldn't dominate, condescend, and control, shipwrecking their prayers and partnerships, but rather serve, honor, and partner with their wives.

FREE TO LOVE

Love like a superhero

'And I will give you a new heart, and I will put
a new spirit in you. I will take out your stony,
stubborn heart and give you a tender, responsive heart.'
Ezekiel 36:26, NLT

I once took a tour of an insurance company. It had been rated one of the top organizations in the country in terms of employee buy-in and satisfaction. In the staff rec room, which included pinball and popcorn machines, couches, books, and loads of other fun stuff to enthuse and reward the staff, there was a closet hung with super-hero costumes. Batman, Wonder Woman, Spiderman, Superman – the whole shebang. If an employee messed up, or was negligent, or displayed an inappropriate attitude, or abused company policy in some way, he or she would be invited to wear a superhero costume for a day. This wasn't to shame the person. It was to remind them of *who they really are*. Because Superman would never take the office stapler home with him. He would surely whoosh between the desks of his department, helping his co-workers with their stapling to save them time and improve organizational efficiency.

It's a brilliant parenting technique: a way to remind our tiny super-heroes who they really are as God's image-bearers. It's a brilliant *adulting* technique. Because if I walked through my days acutely aware of the truth that I'm a King's daughter dressed in the holy robes of righteousness which He paid an inordinate price to purchase on my behalf, I think I'd behave better and live well. It would free me to love others with the grace, dignity, selflessness, and humility of a super-naturally powered, soft-hearted superhero.

Beyond your garden walls

Live wisely among those who are not believers, and make the
most of every opportunity. Let your conversation be gracious and
attractive so that you will have the right response for everyone.
Colossians 4:5-6, NLT

We got a lot of pedestrian traffic past the house we lived in, in South Africa. People who worked in our suburb caught buses from the next street. So, we planted a bed of spinach outside our front gate, close to the street, so our neighbors and anyone walking past could pick some and take it home for supper.

The cynics said, 'Isn't that asking for theft and trespassing?' Nope. We were *inviting* people to help themselves. Some asked, 'Won't people take advantage of you? Won't they take more than they need? Won't people steal all the plants?' One or two were stolen. The rest kept growing and people kept picking. We planted the spinach, knowing it was a risk and it might not work. We did it anyway. Things *inside* our garden walls were safe and stable enough that we had surplus energy and cheerfulness to risk loving people *outside* our garden walls. Sure, folks might take advantage of our love. We felt ok to love them anyway.

When we think of our friendships, marriages, family relationships, and work or sporting connections, let's look to Jesus for foundation, and direction. Let's pray that from the safe spaces of our solid relationships – from our havens of mutual love and respect – we'd see opportunities to make a difference in the big-out-there. Let's pray for courage to risk and capacity to reach into the lives of those around us to build and bless our communities.

Free to ask yourself:

**These questions are drawn from themes
covered over the past five days.**

- Have you written someone off? Is there a way you could be wise and protect your heart, but also love them or engage with even just a small part of their life? Could you find one good grape on their bunch, and enjoy the sweetness of just that?

- If you're honest, do you spend more effort making yourself ready for the ramp (concerning yourself with the opinions of others as you strut your stuff on the catwalk of life), or lighting your lamp (glowing with the inner beauty that comes from seeking first His Kingdom)?

- When last did you have a superhero day? What would it look like for you to, metaphorically, wear a cape today?

- Read Proverbs 27:23. Do you know 'the state of your flocks', or what's growing in your garden? What could you do this week to share with others from the overflow of your home?

Free to ask God:

GOD,

I want to love others freely, the way You do. You've given Your love so freely to me, and I want to pass it on to others. Help me overlook offences as often as possible and see the loveliness in the people You've placed in my life. Help me remember who I really am, in You, and let the truth of my identity make me bold and free to live and love graciously and generously.

AMEN.

FREE TO LOVE

Boundaries for freedom

Direct your children onto the right path,
and when they are older, they will not leave it.
Proverbs 22:6, NLT

Counterintuitively, boundaries are essential to freedom. God's design for the family is for peace and freedom to reign (Psalm 127 and 128), so it figures that home boundaries are crucial. Hence, it's really ok to say 'Wait' to our kids, when my husband and I are catching up on the day. Marriage should be honored by all (Hebrews 13:4), *including our kids*. They aren't the center of our marriage. They don't complete it. I'd love our kids to understand that our marriage was whole before they came along, and it will be whole long after they leave. I'd love for the truth of that to set them up for their own lifetime-lasting, happy, whole marriages.

Boundaries and priorities also free us from the pressure of our culture, which begs us to make idols of our kids, living our dreams through them and racing against other parents in the quest to give our kids everything that opens and shuts (which doesn't feel like freedom at all). Family freedom looks like us being wise and honest about the gifting on each of our children. It's tempting, but we don't need to sign up our darlings for every activity on offer. It will hurt them, and us, and our budget. Rather ask: What will be *good* for this child? What extra pressure can our family withstand, without throwing out the rhythm or robbing our marriage and family of rest, creativity, and time to talk about the highs and lows or each day? Let's be boundary-wise, and free to love our families well.

FREE TO LOVE

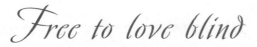

Free to love blind

> But Ruth replied, 'Don't ask me to leave you and turn back.
> Wherever you go, I will go; wherever you live, I will live.
> Your people will be my people, and your God will be my God.'
> Ruth 1:16, NLT

Ruth's courage to surrender to the God of the family she's married into is remarkable. She doesn't know how the story will end. Her life's been hard. From where she's standing, it might even get harder. It's not as if God had said to her, 'I know things have been super tough for you. But I just want you to know you're going to be named in the lineage of the Messiah! You're welcome.' She died, not knowing that. And yet she chooses to love her new family, anyway. She's not passive. She's operating in extraordinary, countercultural strength by showing kindness, generosity, and self-sacrifice.

Ruth could have chosen the opposite of love. She could have been harsh, stubborn, selfish, and arrogant. When her husband died and her mom-in-law moved on, she could have said, 'Sucks to be you, Naomi! I'm staying here because it's hard being a foreigner. I'm going to stay where I am because I'm comfortable, and I'm scared.' Instead, she accepted the Vinedresser's pruning of her life (John 15).

You know as well as I do that pruning is painful. We know it's for greater growth, but when we're in the pruning process, the growing can look like shrinking. And yet, love never fails (1 Corinthians 13:8). Ruth's love *works*, and *works out* – in her life, and to thousands of generations after her. Let's step bravely when love requires us to step blindly.

FREE TO LOVE

Like-minded love

> Therefore if you have any encouragement from being
> united with Christ, if any comfort from His love, if any common
> sharing in the Spirit, if any tenderness and compassion,
> then make my joy complete by being like-minded,
> having the same love, being one in spirit and of one mind.
> Philippians 2:1-2, NIV

John Mark Comer gives this beautiful definition of *agape* love (the godly love we're called to show others): 'A compassionate commitment to delight in the soul of another and to will that person's good ahead of your own, no matter the cost to yourself.'

Philippians 2 is all about showing this kind of love to the people with whom we share a community – or a home, office space, school, or church. We're to adopt the attitude of Jesus, who understood that to be seen is fantastic; to be overlooked is even better. This kind of love fights to create a culture of encouragement, tenderness, and compassion, building the fort of com*fort* and protection around team members and loved ones.

And of course, being like-minded isn't the same as group think – that dangerous space of following the crowd at all costs and creating echo chambers that validate our views. The vortex of confirmation bias is a dangerous thing. When we lean into group think, we lose God, and we lose out on opportunities to love the world He's placed us in. But to carry in our hearts the same love Jesus showed us – this love that delights in the soul of another and wants to see others go further – will put supernatural force behind our teams, families, and communities that will propel them into the unstoppable purposes of God.

FREE TO LOVE

Friends before function before fight before field

Meanwhile, I thought I should send Epaphroditus back
to you. He is a true brother, co-worker, and fellow soldier.
And he was your messenger to help me in my need.
Philippians 2:25, NLT

I tend to overlook Bible verses like this. Sure, Epaphroditus was a cool guy. But is anything about him relevant to us? Truth is, we can build a theology of how to do church – and love people well in the process – from Paul's recommendation of Epaphroditus.

Epaphroditus was first Paul's brother in the Lord. They were *friends*. They had a relationship based on common faith and Christ-like compassion. They worked together, mutually focused on their *function* of spreading the gospel and building the first-century church. They were willing to go to war with and for one another and they understood that their Kingdom *fight* wasn't 'against flesh-and-blood enemies, but against evil rulers and authorities of the unseen world, against mighty powers in this dark world, and against evil spirits in the heavenly places.' (Ephesians 6:12) And Epaphroditus was a messenger on the Mediterranean mission *field*, part of the apostolic team that laid the foundations of the global church.

The order of all this is important. Let's not forget: the Spirit of God is in us, and His purposes are outside of us. Let's prioritize loving people well, protecting friendships, harmony, and unity within the church, before we even think about being effective in the great wide open. That means committing to all Paul urges us to do in Philippians 2: doing nothing out of selfish ambition or vain conceit; in humility considering others better than ourselves; refusing to gossip; and being quick to forgive.

FREE TO LOVE

Love like oil

'If you love Me, obey My commandments. And I will
ask the Father, and He will give you another Advocate,
who will never leave you. He is the Holy Spirit, who leads
into all truth. The world cannot receive Him, because it isn't
looking for Him and doesn't recognize Him. But you know Him,
because He lives with you now and later will be in you.'
John 14:15-17, NLT

Perhaps too often we take for granted this incredible gift of God Himself in the Holy Spirit: our lawyer, truth guide, constant confidante, consoler, and transformer. And yet our abiding access to His power, comfort and companionship is our hope of victory in this life. The Holy Spirit is described as fire (Acts 2:3-4), wind (Acts 2:2), a dove (Luke 3:22), water (Isaiah 44:3), and oil (Isaiah 61:1, Acts 10:38). Fire purifies. Wind blows away chaff. Doves represent peace. Water refreshes. The anointing of oil was always directly associated with the presence and power of the Spirit.

This last metaphor – oil – is particularly meaningful and powerful when it comes to our relationships. As Spirit-filled believers, we can ask Him to flow freely over us, and through us, so that we glide past other believers without causing harm. The Holy Spirit lubes us, for want of a better image, so that any rough, sharp edges are smoothed, and easily passed over. Even in our dealings with non-believers who don't have the Holy Spirit, His anointing on us should give them a soft, kind, merciful and gracious interpersonal experience.

May God's Spirit fill you today with fervor to love with effortless, oiled ease.

Free to ask yourself:

These questions are drawn from themes covered over the past five days.

- Is God convicting you about reordering your priorities, particularly in your home? If you're married with kids, what might it look like, even today, to put your husband's needs above those of your kids?

- Who are you choosing to love in this season of your life? Are you seeing the fruit of your selfless decision? If you never see the fruit, are you ok to keep loving that person anyway?

- What might 'friends before function' look like for you, in your current church involvement?

- Read Romans 12:10. It's about real *agape* love – delighting in another's soul and wanting to see them blessed, even if it costs you. What does the Holy Spirit's refreshing, peace, purification, and anointing mean to you today, as you commit to loving someone?

Free to write it out:

It's possible, in a family or friendship group or organizational team, to wear the uniform of a servant, without having the heart of a servant. Spend some time journaling, asking God to show you where and how you need Him to change your heart so you can love others freely (without pretense, bitterness, or self-pity, and without expecting anything in return).

_____

_____

_____

_____

_____

_____

_____

_____

_____

_____

FREE TO LOVE

Do hard things for love

Mordecai sent this reply to Esther: 'Don't think for a moment that because you're in the palace you will escape when all other Jews are killed. If you keep quiet at a time like this, deliverance and relief for the Jews will arise from some other place, but you and your relatives will die. Who knows if perhaps you were made queen for just such a time as this?'
Esther 4:13-14, NLT

Esther's a beautiful Jewish girl. King Xerxes picks her to be super-sub, replacement queen. She now has the inside track on the foreign culture in which she finds herself. The man, Haman gets promoted over all Xerxes' nobles and officials. He commands everyone to bow down to him. Mordecai, Esther's family guardian and a God-fearing man, refuses. Haman takes this personally and manipulates the king into agreeing to have all Jews in the empire slaughtered. Mordecai is devastated and sends a message asking Esther to plead with the king on behalf of her people. Except, everyone knew you didn't just approach the king with a question. In Esther's day, you waited to be summoned, or you got killed, so she is *not* keen to do what Mordecai asks.

In Mordecai's reply we see a loving leader. He doesn't pull rank; he lends strength and courage. He reminds her who she is, and how she's been uniquely positioned to influence, not just adapt. She agrees to the plan, saying, 'If I die, I die.' (Esther 4:16)

Sometimes love will require hard things of us, and that's ok. We have in us the strengthening Spirit of the God who did for us the hardest, most loving thing of all.

Here goes everything

On the third day of the fast, Esther put on her royal robes
and entered the inner court of the palace, just across from
the king's hall. The king was sitting on his royal throne,
facing the entrance. When he saw Queen Esther standing there
in the inner court, he welcomed her and held out the gold scepter
to her. So Esther approached and touched the end of the scepter.
Esther 5:1-2, NLT

Esther must have felt alone and afraid. Walking towards the throne of King Xerxes – uninvited – she must surely have wondered, 'Is this my biggest mistake, or my bravest move?' But she was abiding in God. She knew where her real life lay and so she could say, 'If I die, I die.'

Maybe you've felt alone and afraid over this past season. Doubt has crept in, and you've asked that same question: biggest mistake, or bravest move? You've gone back to all the things you believed God said (all the confirmations and prayers and wise decision-making routes) but you've still wondered. Hear again Mordecai's words to Esther: 'Who knows if perhaps you were put here for just such a time as this?'

Perhaps you're feeling vulnerable – like you're walking around without skin, and you just can't muster up any more brave. Take courage from Esther who pushed herself into the uncomfortable space of risking her life before the king, and Jesus who pushed Himself into the most uncomfortable space imaginable for us. You've got His strength in you to reach out one more time and take just one step towards another human who needs the grace and truth of a loving God.

FREE TO LOVE

Unmissable, unstoppable

> So on March 7 the two decrees of the king were put into
> effect. On that day, the enemies of the Jews had hoped
> to overpower them, but quite the opposite happened.
> It was the Jews who overpowered their enemies.
> Esther 9:1, NLT

God's name isn't mentioned once in the book of Esther. Yet, marvelously, He's there all the time. He's orchestrating events to save His people, and He's unstoppable.

Maybe you feel like God's name isn't coming up in your story right now either. You feel forgotten. You're out on a limb. You're wondering, as I imagine Esther may have wondered, *Am I insane to even be taking a chance on this thing? Is loving people worth the risk? What if God's not in this? What if I miss God?*

The fact that you're concerned about God's presence in your story is a good thing. It shows you haven't given in to apathy or rebellion. And Esther's story can put such wind in your sails, because though all the odds were stacked against her and her people, 'quite the opposite happened,' and God gave them victory.

Also, it's unfeasibly hard to miss God because He's a really big target. He's everywhere, and He wouldn't have invited you to follow Him if it were impossible to do so. You are not forgotten. You were born for such a time as this. Jesus has set you free to bring His love, grace, and truth to the attention of a waiting, watching world. And the same God who gave Esther favor before the king will grant you favor as you follow Him into His purposes for you.

FREE TO LOVE

The beginning of giving

'For God so loved the world that He gave His one and only Son,
that whoever believes in Him shall not perish but have eternal life.'
John 3:16, NIV

Generosity is the seedbed of salvation. 'For God so loved the world that He *gave* ...' It's God's inordinate generosity towards human-kind – His willingness to love and serve and give sacrificially despite an unthinkable cost – that gives us life, hope, identity, and an eternal future. He calls us to be like Him – to love and serve and *give* like Him. His Spirit in us empowers us to do so. When we get up close and per-sonal to God, His generosity is contagious, and when others bump up against our generous lives, they'll catch it too.

Oxytocin is a peptide hormone and neuropeptide normally produced in the hypothalamus and released by the posterior pituitary. It plays a role in social bonding, reproduction, childbirth, and the period af-ter childbirth. Bottom line: it's a hormone that makes you happy and brave. It fights insecurities, anger, and the darkness of depression. (It even helps with IBS.) And research shows oxytocin is released when we're *generous*.

Our hormones are not a mistake; it's utterly wondrous how God built our bodies with such wisdom and intentionality. Oxytocin brings on labor, so it's no surprise that when God is birthing something new in us or our communities, generosity will always be a part of the story. When we live openhandedly, the light of heaven flows through us, de-feating the darkness of greed, increasing creativity and satisfied self-lessness, and creating win-win situations wherever we find ourselves. Freely we've been given. Let's freely give.

FREE TO GIVE

Kingdom economy

For God is the one who provides seed for the farmer
and then bread to eat. In the same way, He will provide
and increase your resources and then produce a great harvest
of generosity in you. Yes, you will be enriched in every way
so that you can always be generous. And when we take
your gifts to those who need them, they will thank God.
2 Corinthians 9:10-11, NLT

Where the world operates on buying and selling, the Kingdom grows on sowing and reaping. Where money makes the world go round, love expands God's Kingdom. And if you've been trusting God with your budget and your bottom line, you will doubtless have experienced the splendid mystery of how He makes a way where there seems to be no way. We are free to economize our lives on Kingdom currency because God hasn't got us contracted out for a fee. We're not working for wages. He has forged an eternal covenant with us. He knows our needs. And He will never forsake us.

God calls us to responsible, wise living. We're to save (Proverbs 21:20) and invest (Ecclesiastes 11:1), but we can always afford to be generous. When we truly believe He owns everything in the world anyway and whatever we have is on loan from Him (Psalm 50:10), and when we truly believe He's our loving Heavenly Father who promises to provide (Philippians 4:19), then it's far easier to be less hung up on our cravings and necessities, and to give generously whenever and wherever we see a need.

FREE TO GIVE

Free to ask yourself:

**These questions are drawn from themes
covered over the past five days.**

- What's the biggest risk you've ever taken? Was love involved?

- Esther 10:3 reads, 'Mordecai the Jew became the prime minister, with authority next to that of King Xerxes himself. He was very great among the Jews, who held him in high esteem, because he continued to work for the good of his people and to speak up for the welfare of all their descendants.' How did God turn things around in your life when, even though everything seemed to be against you, you faithfully loved people anyway?

- When there was too much month at the end of your money, how did God come through for you?

- Read 2 Corinthians 9. How is God challenging your thinking around generosity?

Free to ask God:

HEAVENLY FATHER,

You are the ultimate lover and giver. Help me take the daily risk of loving people well, regardless of how that turns out for me. Keep me from taking for granted Your wise, generous, loving provision. And open my eyes to needs that my resources – which are really just Your resources – can meet.

AMEN.

Hot potato

'Yours, O LORD, is the greatness, the power, the glory,
the victory, and the majesty. Everything in the heavens
and on earth is Yours, O LORD, and this is Your kingdom.
We adore You as the one who is over all things.'
1 Chronicles 29:11, NLT

Giving makes us feel good, because Jesus was right when He said, 'It is more blessed to give than to receive.' (Acts 20:35) But we need to be alert, and realistic about our weaknesses, because the good feeling of giving can tip us over into pride. We pat ourselves on the back for being so kind and holy, which completely defeats the God-glorifying purpose of our generosity.

So, there's a habit we could cultivate to keep us giving humbly, and to keep us focused on making life better for others, not ourselves: *quickly* pass on the hot potato of glory to God. All the glory to be had, in all the universe, is God's anyway (Revelation 5:13). It doesn't belong to us, and never will. We're to honor our fellow humans, sure. But only God gets glory. When you give, and some of that glory inadvertently lands on you, remind yourself it doesn't belong to you. Glory is so hot, so heavy, so holy, you can't bear it anyway. Pass it on quickly. Only God can bear the weight of glory.

And of course, let's not take selfies with orphans and Instagram the experience to within an inch of reality. The secret to giving is giving in secret. Andy Stanley so rightly says, 'The value of a life is always measured in terms of how much of it was given away.'

FREE TO GIVE

All that matters in the end

As the time drew near for Him to ascend to heaven,
Jesus resolutely set out for Jerusalem.
Luke 9:51, NLT

Luke's meticulous gospel details how Jesus calls His first disciples, and launches His ministry of love, healing, and restoration. He's all about the poor, the downtrodden, the marginalized. Jesus establishes His Kingdom as being upside down to the world's order of things – a reversal of common social values – because we tend to seek out the pretty and the popular, the rich, the educated, the connected. He establishes His Kingdom as being inside out. He's less concerned about external manners and more concerned about internal motives. And in Luke chapters 9 and 10, after Jesus has sent His disciples ahead of Him to preach and heal, His journey to Jerusalem begins. Luke records the final words of God on earth, in the months leading up to His death and resurrection.

If you were doing a road trip and it was your final journey because you had less than a year to live, what would you say to your spouse, parents, colleagues, or kids? I'm guessing you wouldn't waste time. You'd cut to the chase. Your words would most likely reveal your deepest values. What Luke archives for us in these chapters reveals the deepest values of our Savior as He heads intentionally towards His death. And here's what Jesus talks about: prayer, humility, trust, simplicity, justice, love, grace, faith, kindness, forgiveness, integrity, honesty, and *generosity* – to mention just some of His values.

Let's encourage one another to liberally season our words and ways with these things, the way Jesus did, no matter how much time we have left.

No more Mr. Nice Guy

> Then the Lord said to him, 'You Pharisees are so careful to
> clean the outside of the cup and the dish, but inside you
> are filthy – full of greed and wickedness! Fools! Didn't God
> make the inside as well as the outside? So clean the inside
> by giving gifts to the poor, and you will be clean all over.'
> Luke 11:39-41, NLT

Jesus sometimes turned His attention to the haters. He'd be talking to His disciples and mesmerized followers, then suddenly He'd address His enemies, and it was no more Mr. Nice Guy. Yet His words in these situations still revealed His upside-down, inside-out, Kingdom values. Luke records a detailed conversation between Jesus and some Pharisees and lawyers. He doesn't hold back. He isn't scared of offending them. And it's obvious His enemies aren't asking questions to learn from Him, but to sabotage and undermine Him.

It's staggering to think that, even though Jesus issues a harsh rebuke, He's the same Jesus who never once sinned. He was enduringly, abidingly loving every moment of His life. So even as He's scolding these guys, *He's loving on them*. He's going to die for them not long after this. He's reprimanding them because He wants to correct them with the truth. He's pointing out the tragedy of their pride and hypocrisy.

As twenty-first century Christians under grace, we may not think of ourselves as first-century Pharisees under law, and yet Jesus' warning is for us too. May we never impose made-up legalistic standards on others. May we rather turn falsehood upside down and inside out by preaching free entry into the Kingdom for anyone humble enough to repent.

FREE TO GIVE

Phari-me

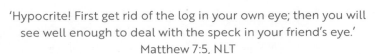

'Hypocrite! First get rid of the log in your own eye; then you will
see well enough to deal with the speck in your friend's eye.'
Matthew 7:5, NLT

The word *pharisee* means *separatist*. Pharisees would separate
themselves from others because they thought they were more
spiritual. If we're honest? We do the same. There are disturbing simi-
larities between the pharisees and religious experts of Jesus' day, and
us. Our human habit is to use boundary-markers to separate ourselves
from others, to establish identity. We assess people all the time, by
which side of a particular boundary line they fall, and we establish our
own identities that way too. (State school or a private school? Instant
coffee or freshly ground?) We have straight lines in our head and all
the time we're making inside-and-outside judgments: *This falls inside
my culture; that doesn't. You're inside my socio-economic bracket;
you're not. You're invited to my birthday party; you're not ...* We do
this with our spirituality as well. It's our habit as Christians to make up
external ways of differentiating ourselves from people who are not
Christians – or who are not *real* Christians, like us.

First-century rabbinic teachers were obsessed with the uncrossable
lines of circumcision, dietary laws, and Sabbath keeping. We're pre-
occupied with different things – styles of worship, or how people dress
for church. It's a beautiful thing to freely express our spirit-and-truth
worship within the diversity of our temperaments and cultures. But we
dare not think we're better than people who don't do things our way.
Let's never separate ourselves, allowing our partialities and predilec-
tions to keep us from giving freely, the way Jesus freely gave to us.

Stalk the lantern

> For what gives you the right to make such a judgment? What
> do you have that God hasn't given you? And if everything you
> have is from God, why boast as though it were not a gift?
> 1 Corinthians 4:7, NLT

Yesterday we read that what the pharisees and law experts practiced – and what we often practice – is *boundary-marker* spirituality. What Jesus practiced and taught was *true* spirituality, which focuses not on the boundaries, but on the center. It doesn't focus on who falls inside or outside the margins but on Who is in the middle: Jesus.

You might think of it this way: we tend to play games of Simon Says. If you imitate a move when no one else does – because *Simon Says Do THAT* – then you're out. You've crossed a line and you can no longer play the game. Jesus is inviting us instead to play Stalk the Lantern. It's as if He's saying, 'I'm in the middle. I'm the center – the light of the world. Everybody, come close. Come as close as you can and come as you are. Come low.' In that kind of game, everyone is welcome to participate, and everyone is focused on the same central goal. Also, that kind of game inspires humility. If you're keen to win, you must aim low.

When we forget the boundaries we've set up in our snobbery or self-righteousness and simply move towards the center, real transformation takes place. Instead of making sure we're falling on the right side of a limit, we'll be focused instead on becoming more like Jesus, and representing Him well to a fearful, fenced-in world.

FREE TO GIVE

Free to ask yourself:

These questions are drawn from themes covered over the past five days.

- Do you ever daydream about getting some sort of accolade, or about receiving the praise, admiration, and respect of a particular person or group of people? How could you rewrite the script of that fantasy, in which you ensure the glory bypasses you and goes straight to God?

- When you're at home in heaven, how do you hope the people you love will reminisce about your life?

- When last did you feel as if Jesus was rebuking or convicting you? How did you respond?

- Read Jeremiah 29:13, Colossians 3:1, and 1 Peter 2:1-25. How do the writers encourage you to focus on Jesus?

Free to write it out:

Everything Jesus talks about points to the upside-down and inside-out realities of the Kingdom. The world is impressed by showboating. Jesus turns that upside down and says, 'Go and pray in secret.' The world says, 'Look out for number one.' Jesus encourages us to self-forget, be radically generous, and join a mission much bigger than ourselves. The world is impressed by money and stuff. Jesus calls us to live simply. The world vies for power and position. Jesus says, 'Look out for the least of these.' Journal what comes to mind when you think of these opposing worldviews. Where do you feel this kind of tension in your life? Is the culture around you tugging you in one direction, while Jesus calls you in another?

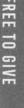

FREE TO GIVE

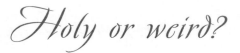

Holy or weird?

'I'm not asking You to take them out of the world,
but to keep them safe from the evil one. They do
not belong to this world any more than I do.'
John 17:15-16, NLT

FREE TO GIVE

Our Savior prayed we'd have a solid understanding that we're *in* the world but not *of* the world. This may justify us saying, 'Boundary-marker spirituality is important! We must come out and be separate (2 Corinthians 6:17)!' Absolutely. God says, 'Be holy, as I am holy.' (1 Peter 1:16) But Jesus taught us that what separates us from the world – making us different and marking our lives – is greater love for God, and greater love for people, who mean so much to Him. Of course, greater love for God also, always, inspires greater obedience to Him, which *will* make our lives look different from lives lived in rebellion to God.

John Ortberg tells the following story: 'Someone asked me whether I thought the church where I worked might be worldly. "What do you mean by 'worldly'?" I asked him. "Well, you use drama, and people are used to that in the world. And you play contemporary music just like they're used to hearing. So how will they know you're any different? Everybody knows that as Christians we're supposed to be different from people in the world by being more loving and more gentle, and everybody knows that we're not. So don't we have to do something to show that we're different?"' Ortberg goes on to say, tongue-in-cheek, 'In other words, "If we can't be holy, shouldn't we at least be weird?"'

Let's not be weird. Let's just love God, love people, and change the world.

Essential love

'Your love for one another will prove to
the world that you are My disciples.'
John 13:35, NLT

If you ever watched *The Simpsons* you'll know they live next door to Ned Flanders and his family, who are portrayed as Christians, unfortunately. In one episode the Flanders family has been away, and Homer says to Ned, 'Where've you been?' Ned replies, 'We've been away at Christian camp. We're learning how to be more judgmental.'

Newsflash: we don't have to be weird or judgmental to pointedly feel different from those outside the faith. Because the gospel insists that personal transformation – the inside-out, upside-down makeover of the human personality – is possible, and powerful.

When it comes to our styles, preferences, and cultural biases, what Augustine apparently said is so helpful: 'In essentials, unity. In non-essentials, liberty. In all things, love.'

We're saved by grace through faith in Jesus Christ the Son of the One True God who came to earth as a sinless man, was crucified, buried, and raised to life. He reigns in glory. He will come again. It's *essential* we agree on that. Can we wear shorts to church, or can't we? This is *non-essential*. Be free. Don't go against your conscience or purposefully spite someone. And in *all things*, love. Dallas Willard wrote, 'How many people are radically and permanently repelled from The Way by Christians who are unfeeling, stiff, unapproachable, boringly lifeless, obsessive, and dissatisfied? Yet such Christians are everywhere, and what they are missing is the wholesome liveliness springing from a balanced vitality with the freedom of God's loving rule ... Spirituality wrongly understood or pursued is a major source of human misery and rebellion against God.'

FREE TO GIVE

Older, better, freer

May God give you more and more grace and peace as
you grow in your knowledge of God and Jesus our Lord.
2 Peter 1:2, NLT

If we're keen to give of ourselves and our resources, more and more freely, and get going with Jesus on this journey of changing the world, let's ask ourselves:

Am I more joyful now than I was a year ago? (Not necessarily happier, richer, more successful. Just more joyful. It's an inside-out thing. It's also kind of upside down because you're a year older and life just gets tougher. It seems impossible that we should be getting *more* joyful. But it's not.) *Am I less sour and disapproving? Less judgmental, exclusive, and proud? Less likely to keep hurting people by pushing them against pseudo-spiritual electric fences of my own making? Am I more focused on the center – Jesus? When my unbelieving co-worker has a question about God, am I more approachable than I used to be? Where there's injustice or hypocrisy, is there fire in my eyes to bring heaven to earth? Am I more generous?*

Let's dream together for a moment. What if, with every passing year, our love for God and people poured from the inside of us, out onto the world? What if it was irresistible, bowling the world over – turning the world's expectations and order of things upside down – in such a way that the world concluded Jesus must be for real. Let's center our lives on a radical Savior who caught the attention of friends, strangers, and enemies, because He lived upside down and inside out, freely giving away His love, and ultimately His life.

Faithful

'If you are faithful in little things, you will be faithful in large ones.
But if you are dishonest in little things, you won't be honest
with greater responsibilities. And if you are untrustworthy
about worldly wealth, who will trust you with the true riches
of heaven? And if you are not faithful with other people's things,
why should you be trusted with things of your own?'
Luke 16:10-12, NLT

You may have heard people say things like, 'Show me your bank account and I'll show you your heart.' It's possible that's a little simplistic, but for sure, the truth is not far off. What I spend my money on reveals my values. Hoarding reveals my stinginess. Overspending reveals my lack of discipline and self-control. Both reveal my greed.

God, our Provider, uses finances to show us our hearts. He also uses our finances to draw us to Himself, because He's the source of all things and He meets all our needs.

As you consider what it means to be free to give, the challenge perhaps is to ask yourself if you're ok for your spouse or an accountability partner to take a look at your credit card statement, or if you'd be able to tell someone what you did with your annual bonus. If you're keeping these things a secret, why? What does that reveal to you about your motives? If you're married, you're one flesh in your finances too. If you're keeping financial secrets from your husband, know that he's probably keeping secrets from you too.

Come clean. Keep on being faithful with every cent you have to your name. God will meet your every need.

Give away

> Do not neglect the spiritual gift you received through the
> prophecy spoken over you when the elders of the church laid
> their hands on you. Give your complete attention to these matters.
> Throw yourself into your tasks so that everyone will see your progress.
> 1 Timothy 4:14-15, NLT

FREE TO GIVE

What spiritual gifts have you been given? How are you giving those gifts away – fully and freely – in the circumstances or community God has placed you? If you're not sure how to respond to these questions, would you be willing to ask God for the answers?

Don't believe the lie that your spiritual gifting is undiscoverable. You *have* been given a gift – possibly several gifts (1 Peter 4:10). In his letter to Timothy, Paul urges the younger leader not to neglect God's gift, but to give 'complete attention' to it. Paul's encouragement is for you and me too. We're to throw ourselves into using our gifts with energy, focus, joy, and charisma. We're to turn our gifts into verbs and *action* them to bless and serve others, because our gifts are *ours* but they're not *for* us. They're always for the benefit of others, and the glory of God. I'm always profoundly grateful when people choose to draw near to me and deploy their spiritual gifts to ease my burden, shed light on my path, alleviate my pain, show me something of God's character, or set me free in some other way.

A wondrous, win-win, supernatural thing happens when you step into the sweet spot of your gifting: you become a conduit of the presence, power, and purposes of God. Feel free to give away your gifts.

Free to ask yourself:

**These questions are drawn from themes
covered over the past five days.**

- How would you explain the essentials of your faith to an unbelieving friend or colleague?

- Are you more content now than you were five or ten years ago? What has changed in terms of your thinking, beliefs, faith, or circumstances?

- What small, unseen, seemingly insignificant habit or responsibility have you perhaps neglected lately? What would it look like for you be faithful in that small thing, today or in the week ahead?

- Read 1 Corinthians 12. Do you recognize yourself, or do you recognize opportunities to serve, in Paul's explanation of spiritual gifts? Does anything freak you out or confuse you? What are you excited to do for someone else, this week?

Free to ask God:

GOD,

I don't ever want to come across as weird, judgmental, or preachy. Teach me how to be humble and holy. Let love motivate my every interaction. I want to be trusted with big things. Show me where I'm cutting corners and strengthen me to be faithful in even the smallest things. And show me when, where and how I could be using my gifts even more effectively, to manifest Your presence, power, and purposes.

AMEN.

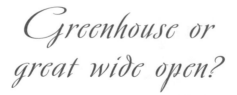

Greenhouse or great wide open?

'But you will receive power when the Holy Spirit comes upon you.
And you will be My witnesses, telling people about Me everywhere –
in Jerusalem, throughout Judea, in Samaria, and to the ends of the earth.'
Acts 1:8, NLT

That's where you are now: *the ends of the earth.* Thousands of generations of Christians have faithfully done exactly what Jesus told His first disciples to do. They've carried His message of hope from their homes to the big beyond, and somehow, somewhere, that message reached you. Now it's your turn to freely give what was freely given to you.

It's possible that up to now you've been more like a potted plant in a greenhouse. You've been thriving in the light, regular watering, and consistent temperature. You're beautiful, and comfortable. Greenhouses are necessary for plants to take root. But God created plants to thrive in the wild, and perhaps for you that time has come. He has seen fit to take you out of the greenhouse and plant you in the wild, to add to the atmosphere's oxygen. He's called you to thrive and flourish and plant more seeds in an environment that's probably more hostile to your growth. And yes, it's unthinkably hard some days, but you're being planted in soil your roots are designed for. Take heart. You'll be just fine. God runs the universe. The world is peripheral to His church, not the other way around. We can't stay in the greenhouse all our lives. It's good and right that we're planted in the world, so the world can see us bearing the kind of abundant fruit that is beyond rational explanation.

FREE TO GIVE

Don't pause the more

> But Israel violated the instructions about the things set apart
> for the LORD. A man named Achan had stolen some of these
> dedicated things, so the LORD was very angry with the Israelites.
> Joshua 7:1, NLT

The rest of Joshua 7 tells the story of what happened because of Achan's greed. The Israelites were 'soundly defeated' and 'paralyzed with fear' (Joshua 7:4-5) in the very next battle, and when Joshua cried out to God in consternation God told him to get up and get busy putting things right. God had more for His people, but it's as if He pushed pause on His blessings until they turned from their greed and honored Him with their money and their stuff, in attitude and action.

The results of greed might feel fun in the moment. Giving in to greed may give you a dopamine hit of pleasure. But it will never, ever, result in longtime happiness, and no matter how you justify your greedy choices, they will always have unsavory, life-sapping consequences.

It's hard to recognize greed in ourselves. 'Greedy' is such an ugly adjective that we hate to think it could ever be used on us. But to be truly free, and free to give, we need to be brave and vulnerable before God, risking the sting of conviction, and ask Him to show us where we are caving to gluttony, avarice, coveting or materialism.

Allow His kindness to lead you to repentance, and may you enjoy the plentiful harvest of blessing and peace released through your obedient, genuine, selfless generosity.

FREE TO GIVE

Building and blessing

Wisdom has built her house; she has set up its seven pillars.
Proverbs 9:1, NIV

Wisdom is personified in Proverbs 9. She's a woman who, firstly, has wisely created a strong home and, secondly, invited other people to an elaborate feast. We can use Lady Wisdom as an aspirational mirror because God calls each of us to build a life of wisdom, so that we can bless the world. It's a happy relief that God promises to give us wisdom if we ask for it (James 1:5). And Proverbs 9 gives us a beautiful picture of what that wisdom looks like and tastes like, and the repercussions of wisdom in our lives and the lives around us.

Wisdom's house is big and sturdy. Held up by seven pillars, it's a strong fortress not easily shaken. Some commentators suggest since the number seven often expresses completeness in Scripture, the passage perhaps indicates that the application of wisdom results in a complete, orderly, well-furnished house, one that lacks nothing. That's the dream, right? Imagine a complete, orderly, well-furnished house, lacking nothing ... But this is not about how we build our homes in the natural, *seen* world; it's about how we build our homes in the spiritual, *unseen* world.

It's nice to have nice things. Beauty, warmth, and a good coffee machine are important. They're part of God's blessings to us in the life He's created for us on this planet. But building our homes with wisdom – creating strong family culture – has everything to do with who we are, not what we have around us. When people enter your home, may they know without doubt it's a place of peace, where Christ is King.

FREE TO GIVE

Character trumps cutlery

She has prepared a great banquet, mixed the wines, and set
the table. Leave your simple ways behind, and begin to live;
learn to use good judgment ... Wisdom will multiply your days
and add years to your life. If you become wise, you will be the one
to benefit. If you scorn wisdom, you will be the one to suffer.
Proverbs 9:2, 6, 11-12, NLT

Wisdom has prepared a great banquet and set the table. She's
front-footed and habitual. She's created culture in her home,
like setting the table, to gather people.

What would it look like for you to build some home habits, to be a
blessing to others? Maybe you literally need to be more intentional
about setting the table to gather your people – not to be legalistic,
but just because God's Kingdom is built around dining room tables. Of
course, it's deeper and wider than that. It's a character thing, not just
a cutlery thing. What kind of culture are you creating in your home, to
welcome others?

Solomon's words in verse 6 are an incredible invitation: *begin to live!*
Real living starts with wisdom. Simple as that. And the truth that wisdom multiplies our days makes the invitation even more attractive.
Why would we *not* run hard after wisdom and grab hold of it with
everything we've got? It can only do us good, blessing us so we can be
a blessing to others.

Let's pray for wisdom and courage to invite people to feast from the
fruit our families are bearing, so our messy, ordinary, imperfect homes
would become microcosms of His home, the church – built to bless
the world.

Fake feeling or real deal?

Your promise revives me; it comforts me in all my troubles.
Psalm 119:50, NLT

It's no exaggeration to say billions of women worldwide are over-whelmed: soul-weary and in dire need of comfort.

Perhaps it's important to establish what comfort is *not*. In the toddler phase of parenting, I was so pleased whenever I saw another mom's kid having a tantrum, because *it wasn't* my *kid having a tantrum!* That would briefly make me feel better about myself. But that's not real comfort. That's just comparison that happened to land in my favor and led to pride. Just as often there was comparison that *didn't* land in my favor and made *me* look bad, which led to shame, hopelessness, or jealousy (which usually ends in us gossiping about people we should be learning from).

Also, don't expect to feel marvelously comforted the day your kid finally says, 'Mom, when I lived under your roof, you washed every pair of underwear I ever wore! I never really thanked you and I'm so sorry.' It's lovely to be thanked and appreciated. But even that won't fill your comfort tank for long.

If you're overwhelmed and you want real comfort? Go to God. The mysterious thing about real comfort is that, probably, no one else will ever witness the exchange that happens between you and the Father, when He pours His comfort into your heart. It happens in the secret places when you're not on duty or display. You're just you, before the throne of grace. And it's not a fake, fleeting feeling. It's the wondrous, satisfying real deal you'll want to share. You'll want to freely give the comfort freely given to you.

Free to ask yourself:

**These questions are drawn from themes
covered over the past five days.**

- Are you in the greenhouse or the wilderness?

- What might generosity – as opposed to greed – look like in your life today?

- What generally makes you feel better about yourself? Would you define it as comfort? Why or why not?

- Proverbs 9:1 (about Wisdom building her house) cross-references to Ephesians 2:20-22. How do these verses, as well as Matthew 16:18 and Colossians 2:3, add to your understanding of how God in His wisdom is building His house, the church?

Free to write it out:

Take time to journal about what kind of comfort you need right now. Be as detailed as possible. Only God will read your words. Pour out your heart to Him. He knows anyway.

FREE TO GIVE

Breathe strongly

'Comfort, comfort My people,' says your God.
Isaiah 40:1, NLT

Isaiah wrote his prophecy about 2,800 years ago. It wasn't written directly to us but to the kingdom of Judah in times of rebellion and revival. Yet the God-principles are unchanging, and they arrest our 21st century hearts in powerful ways, because *comfort* the way it's used in Isaiah is always to encourage and lend strength. The Hebrew word for comfort is *naham* and it can be translated to 'breathe strongly'. It can also be translated *give relief, cheer up, exhort,* and *fear not.* Comfort doesn't only console; it comes in time of calamity and gives help.

Our English word, 'comfort', is also meatier than we give it credit for. The prefix *com* means *with* and *fort* is from the Latin – *fortis* – meaning *strong.* So, if you say to someone, 'Can I comfort you?' You're saying, 'Can I with-strong you?' Comfort doesn't say, 'Poor you!' Comfort says, 'You can do it!'

I've realized however I *can't* do it, alone. I must go to the God of all comfort who made me, and say, 'If You've really called me to play this gig, I need Your strength.'

If you've walked with God for a bit, you'll know this: when you go to Him for comfort, He meets you where you're at, in your mess, but He doesn't sit with you there and go, 'Never mind, you're not so bad. Everybody's done that ...' He always draws our gaze upwards, away from ourselves and towards His magnitude, so that we get perspective on our struggles in light of His bigness. He gently, compassionately, always calls us to something higher. Better. Freer.

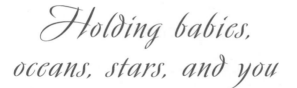

Holding babies, oceans, stars, and you

'He tends His flock like a shepherd: He gathers the lambs in His arms and carries them close to His heart; He gently leads those that have young. Who has measured the waters in the hollow of His hand, or with the breadth of His hand marked off the heavens?... Who is able to advise the Spirit of the LORD? Who knows enough to give Him advice or teach Him?'
Isaiah 40:11-13, NIV

Isaiah speaks to our shortcomings, fatigue, and insecurity in profound ways – as parents, professionals, friends, and general humans.

If you're a mom of tiny babies and you're numb with fatigue and no one told you it was going to be this hard: this affectionate Scripture is for you. He'll lead you gently.

In the next breath, Isaiah tells us God holds the oceans in His hand. He's enormous. He knows everything and has never needed anyone's advice. You can probably trust Him to show you which job to take, or which play therapist your daughter should see.

And if you're terrified because you and your kids face things that didn't exist fifty years ago, Isaiah has comfort for that too. In the very next chapter God says through the prophet, 'Who has done such mighty deeds, summoning each new generation from the beginning of time? It is I, the LORD, the First and the Last. I alone am He.' (Isaiah 41:4) Nothing about our culture has taken God by surprise. He'll equip us, and He'll equip our kids, reminding us, 'No one can snatch anyone out of My hand.' (Isaiah 43:13) Take comfort. You've got this because He's got you.

FREE TO GIVE

Facebook free

'I, yes I, am the one who comforts you. So why are you afraid
of mere humans, who wither like the grass and disappear?'
Isaiah 51:12, NLT

On insecure days – and fat days – when you don't measure up to the perfect people on Facebook or Instagram, God says to you through Isaiah, 'Why are you afraid of mere humans?' Like, why do you care so much? When we look to God for comfort – instead of trying to find comfort in a contrived image of ourselves we present to the world through our screens – operating in social media spaces becomes so much easier, and we're free to use those platforms to spread love, courage, and hope for the future. It also helps to remember what Anne Lamott famously said: 'A hundred years from now? All new people.'

We can't understand exactly how it works – because God's ways are higher than our ways and His thoughts are higher than our thoughts (Isaiah 55:9) – but there's a direct correlation between time spent with God and how much comfort spills over from our lives. If you've found comfort in God's presence, it'll be easy and obvious for you to give away comfort to others. If you're in a good place with God, you're going to be a comforting presence to those around you. (Of course, the opposite is true too. Let's not avoid intimacy with God, which renders us offensive, unsettling, and *dis*comforting.)

May God set you free from ridiculous digital expectations. May He put comfort, courage, and faith in your heart, so you can enjoy effortlessly comforting others.

FREE TO GIVE

Grace or grit?

'So give Your servant a discerning heart to govern
Your people and to distinguish between right and wrong ...'
1 Kings 3:9, NIV

Stewarding relationships and authority hinges largely on discernment in the moment. We walk a tightrope of grit and grace. Do I hang back to build resilience? Do I lean in and rescue?

Like, your teenager forgets his sports kit at home. If he's not at practice this afternoon in the right kit, he doesn't play the match on Saturday. Do you show grace and drive back to school to drop it off – or do you let consequences teach him to pack his stuff? There's no right or wrong answer. Pray for wisdom and lean into the prompting of the Holy Spirit. A thought will rise: *He'll survive this; let him learn while the stakes are low.* Or perhaps: *He needs to know today that you see him, and you'll go to the ends of the earth for him, the way I would.* Those are both beautiful responses. What's God saying to you? What kind of comfort is required? Is it a grit moment, or a grace moment?

We learn grace and grit in community. We watch others, and others watch us, loving, forgiving, extending grace to the undeserving. As we follow Jesus, freely giving as He gave, a watching world will catch the rhythm of our footfalls and follow us, following Him. And thank God, He didn't leave us to try and get anything right on our own. We can lean as heavily as we like on the Holy Spirit – the *Comforter* – to show us what kind of comfort we need to give to those around us.

FREE TO GIVE

249

DAY 243

Rise up

The LORD is the everlasting God, the Creator of the ends of
the earth. He will not grow tired or weary, and His understanding
no one can fathom. He gives strength to the weary and increases
the power of the weak. Even youths grow tired and weary,
and young men stumble and fall; but those who hope in the LORD
will renew their strength. They will soar on wings like eagles;
they will run and not grow weary, they will walk and not be faint.
Isaiah 40:28-31, NIV

If we're honest? We seldom think of ourselves as soaring on wings like eagles. We just make sure there's always milk. And mostly we're exhausted. There aren't many shiny prizes, earth-side, for the sacrifices we make for others. Most of what we do to love others is hidden. And yet, we have no idea what hangs in the balance of our ordinary stories and our ordinary homes. It's possible we're shaping destinies, every day.

And if you're reading this thinking, 'It's too late!' Because your kids are grown and gone, or your career is over, or you've resigned yourself to never marrying, or you're just too tired to keep giving, hear this: it's never too late to freely give what's been freely given to you. It's never too late to comfort someone. It's not too late for an awkward phone call to ask forgiveness.

It's never too late to make peace, or encourage the downcast, or unstick someone who is stuck, even if that someone is you. It might be the hardest thing you'll ever do, but God is your strength. You may just find yourself soaring on wings like eagles.

Free to ask yourself:

**These questions are drawn from themes
covered over the past five days.**

- Who is God asking you to comfort today? What will you say, or do?

- To whom do you compare yourself most? What triggers the comparison? What comfort does God offer you in that vulnerable space?

- If you're exhausted or disillusioned, what will it look like for you, today, to soar on wings like eagles?

- Read Philippians 1:9-10 and Hebrews 4:12. How do we develop discernment, to distinguish grace moments from grit moments? What is the result of discernment in our lives?

Free to ask God:

ALMIGHTY GOD,

As I read Your Word, looking for comfort for me and comfort for others, help me, most of all, to see You. As Your Word washes my mind, help me remember to SOAP: Scripture – Observation – Application – Prayer. I want to know You more, so I can comfort the distressed and the disheartened.

AMEN.

Cry out

> Tune your ears to wisdom, and concentrate on understanding. Cry out for insight, and ask for understanding. Search for them as you would for silver; seek them like hidden treasures. Then you will understand what it means to fear the LORD, and you will gain knowledge of God.
> Proverbs 2:2-5, NLT

The Hebrew word *binah*, translated *insight* in verse 3, conveys the idea of evaluating and understanding the times you live in and knowing the best course of action to take. It means inhabiting the present moment with prophetic eyes. And we should be desperate for *binah*. We're to *cry out* to God for that kind of wisdom, discernment, discretion, and insight.

It's not a stretch to say we're living through confusing, disconcerting days. The world is being shaken by frightening political, ideological, philosophical, cultural, environmental, and economic cataclysms. And did I mention we've all just lived through a global pandemic? Some people didn't get to live through it.

We've all experienced a measure of suffering, and if not full-blown suffering, at least unsettling inconvenience. All this has left us reeling, and so now more than ever we need to cry out to the God in whom lie hidden all the treasures of wisdom and knowledge (Colossians 2:3). We need acumen, clarity, understanding, encouragement, and incredible insight, because these lead us to the fear of the Lord. And when we fear God, all our other fears dissipate, and are eradicated. When we fear God, we're set free to learn and to live wisely and well. Let's cry out for insight.

FREE TO LEARN

Fertilizing faith

But grow in the grace and knowledge of our
Lord Jesus Christ. To Him be glory both now and forever.
2 Peter 3:18, NIV

FREE TO LEARN

If you're new to faith in Jesus, the whole concept of 'growing in your faith' might sound weird. Like, *what even is that*? Andy Stanley pinpoints five fertilizers that cause our faith to flourish. The first is private disciplines. These are the small but significant habits we practice that open our souls to God's deep work in us – things like prayer, reading Scripture, fasting, worship, rest, silence, and solitude. The word 'discipline' has connotations of harshness and strictness. But really, our private faith disciplines are just about us copying Jesus' lifestyle – incorporating the practices He modeled, to form our faith.

The second thing that grows our faith is practical teaching. Paul tells the Romans that faith comes from hearing the Word of God (Romans 10:17). You can probably think back to preachers you heard or conferences you attended that changed your life irrevocably, growing in you a more stalwart and resilient faith.

Third on the faith-building list is providential relationships – your connections to people whose influence has forever impacted your walk with God. Fourthly, personal ministry will grow your faith: serving others by using your resources and getting your hands dirty for a cause bigger than you. Lastly, our faith grows because of the impact of pivotal circumstances we live through – seasons during which the roots of our faith spread deeper and wider beneath the hard ground of wintery seasons.

Let's freely welcome these heaven-sent teachers, for our growth and goodness and the glory of God.

One and all

So eat your meals heartily, not worrying about what others
say about you – you're eating to God's glory, after all, not to
please them ... do everything that way, heartily and freely to
God's glory. At the same time, don't be callous in your exercise
of freedom, thoughtlessly stepping on the toes of those who
aren't as free as you are. I try my best to be considerate of
everyone's feelings in all these matters; I hope you will be, too.
1 Corinthians 10:31-33, MSG

Living for the audience of One – God alone – is a great way to learn, because it brings tremendous clarity. Whatever we're eating, drinking, thinking, planning, performing, or preparing for, it's to be done as an act of worship. For every little thing we do – replying to emails, online shopping, taking out the trash, brushing up on language learning or brushing teeth – it's only God's opinion and pleasure over us that really matters. And bringing that truth to mind clarifies our motives and methods. When we picture ourselves doing our thing before the King, it lifts our game.

At the same time, reminding ourselves to be considerate to others also teaches us to think more clearly. We learn about ourselves (our preferences, priorities, and pet peeves) and we learn about others, when we go about our eating, drinking, working, socializing, Netflixing, or vacationing, cognizant of how those things affect the people around us.

May the Holy Spirit sharpen your sensitivity towards those scripted into your story. What can you learn about them, and from them? May God deepen your desire to honor Him as the audience of your every seen and unseen moment.

FREE TO LEARN

Ask it

'Call to Me and I will answer you and tell you great
and unsearchable things you do not know.'
Jeremiah 33:3, NIV

Being free to learn means being free to ask for information, directions, clarification, and help. That takes humility. Solomon tells us the beginning of wisdom is fear of the Lord (Proverbs 9:10). It makes sense that we'll never grow in knowledge and understanding unless we fear God, because fearing Him means honestly, unguardedly, and in absolute unpretentiousness saying, 'You are God; I am not.' It's acknowledging our brains are too tiny to contain an expanding universe of knowledge. It's hard to teach an arrogant person, and fearing God takes all the wind out of our puffed-up selves.

All this means we need to swallow our pride, which will free us to ask others. Insecurity often has us pretending to know stuff we don't. Someone throws an acronym into conversation, and we nod as if we *totally* know *exactly* what they're talking about. Except, do we? Or someone says, 'You know (*fill in the blank – it could be a book title, movie, restaurant, or famous person we've actually never heard of*)?' And we lie, 'Sure!'. We do this because we don't want to look unsophisticated or uneducated. We pretend because we're insecure. Let's humble ourselves today.

Let's admit we still have so much to learn, and let's cultivate the habit of simply asking for explanations or admitting we're not as *au fait* as our friends or colleagues, when it comes to certain subjects. Just ask. People love to talk about what they know. Look for every opportunity to give others a chance to teach you and enjoy the learning curve.

FREE TO LEARN

Learn to long

I thirst for God, the living God.
When can I go and stand before Him?
Psalm 42:2, NLT

I've learned a lot from the golden retrievers we've loved as a family over the years. Our current dog, Joni, has separation anxiety. It's as if she just loves us a little too much. We have to perform all kinds of soothing techniques if we're leaving her alone at home for any length of time. We leave snacks and various other distractions. We leave the radio playing. If we don't, she suffers. And the neighbors suffer. She cries, barks, wines, scratches at the door – until we come home.

It's made me ask myself, 'Do I long for the presence of God, the way Joni longs for the presence of me?' The truth is, I don't seek out God's presence – the comfort of His nearness, His voice over me – nearly as much as I should. I tend to get distracted by the demands of my day, quite happy to go it alone until I hit a snag. Then I'd rather like God to weigh in on the situation. The truth is, I shouldn't take a single step into a day without His presence going before me and His presence hemming me in from behind.

And unlike Joni, I'm never left alone at home, wondering when someone will show up to love me again because God's banner over me is love, every moment. I have His presence with me constantly, and I'm free to lean into it. What might it look like for you today, to learn to long for God?

Free to ask yourself:

**These questions are drawn from themes
covered over the past five days.**

- How has God mixed one (or all) of these faith-growing fertilizers into your life's soil: private disciplines, practical teaching, providential relationships, personal ministry, or pivotal circumstances?

- Open your calendar for the week and pick one event. How can you mindfully live that occasion for the audience of One, and also with loving consideration of others?

- Who makes you feel particularly insecure? With whom do you feel you can be your unedited self, freely admitting your ignorance in some areas? What could you do to free yourself up to learn more around absolutely anyone?

- Read Psalm 16:11, Exodus 33:14 and Genesis 3:8 for some perspectives on God's presence. On a scale of one to desperate, how would you rate your desire to spend time with God? Don't let your answer condemn you or make you proud. Offer your honesty to God. He simply longs for you to long for Him.

FREE TO LEARN

Free to write it out:

Take a few deep breaths to slow your heartrate and let the obligations, worries, and wonderings of the week swirl and settle and become still. Try some stream of consciousness writing. It's nothing weird. Maybe start with, 'God, I want to come into Your presence and tell You about ...' and then just keep writing.

Strong swimmers

Let us think of ways to motivate one another to acts of
love and good works. And let us not neglect our meeting
together, as some people do, but encourage one another,
especially now that the day of His return is drawing near.
Hebrews 10:24-25, NLT

The world's cultural current is flowing more swiftly than ever, and we need tremendous spiritual strength and acuity to swim upstream.

We can start turning the tide by celebrating that God's grace is sufficient for whatever we face (2 Corinthians 12:9). No matter the cultural opposition you're up against, there is grace enough to bolster you for a beautiful resistance. There's grace for your kids too, no matter how afraid or out of control you feel when it comes to what they are dealing with in a secular, post-truth culture.

Next, we can remember that the purpose of family and community is to build wisdom and courage. That should galvanize us to tackle the waves of cultural hostility head on, because that's the only way we'll engender these attributes, and inspire others to do the same. We know life is difficult. We know we and our people will come across difficult things (John 16:33).

Hence, it's a no-brainer that we'll need both wisdom and courage. Part of our job as parents is to teach our kids to be strong swimmers, instead of just giving them flotation devices. Without trivializing hardship, it's a bracing privilege to equip our kids and others in our spheres of influence with the wisdom and courage they'll need to go against the flow.

FREE TO LEARN

Free to be honest

Don't lie to one another. You're done with that old life.
Colossians 3:9, MSG

To build a culture of wisdom and courage, we must lay our foundations on the bedrock of honesty. Jesus said, 'And you will know the truth, and the truth will set you free.' (John 8:32) That means, when it comes to our kids and others we're shepherding, don't ever lie. Our eldest son is visually impaired. Once when he was tiny, he asked if he could have some more chips. I said, 'No, the chips are finished,' because I knew he couldn't see the (still full) packet on the counter. I realized with horror I'd just told my son a blatant lie and vowed then and there never to do so again. So, when my husband didn't draw a salary during the Covid-19 pandemic, we felt it was a teachable moment, and told our kids. Not to freak them out, but to create an opportunity for God to grow their wisdom, courage, and faith – which He did, every time someone showed up at our door with food or put money in our bank account.

Furthermore, be honest about your kids' strengths and limitations. Don't tell them they're the best on the team when they're not. Rather say, 'Have fun! Do your best! I love watching you play!' because you can say all of that truthfully. Equally, let them dream, and keep praying with them and for them as they give those dreams to Jesus.

We can always justify to ourselves why it's safer to withhold truth, and yet to build a world-changing culture of wisdom and courage, we must be known for our indefatigable integrity.

Free to question

'And you shall remember the whole way that the
Lord your God has led you these forty years in the wilderness,
that He might humble you, testing you to know what was in
your heart, whether you would keep His commandments or not.'
Deuteronomy 8:2, ESV

FREE TO LEARN

If you're a parent, you've probably found your kids use bedtime and car time for all their questions. Use that time to question them too. *Anything bugging you? Do you need to forgive someone? Apologize? Are you jealous of anyone?* That kind of habitual questioning teaches them to be honest with themselves, and it might challenge you to be honest with yourself too.

There's a difference between innocence and naivety and encouraging our kids to question equips them to know the difference. Innocent children climb trees and look forward to teatime, but they don't follow the guy who says he'll give them a puppy. Naïve children get into his car. Innocence maintains purity. Naivety leads to danger.

All this of course also means we're to be ready for the questions our kids and others have. God doesn't expect us to know all the answers. How could we ever? But we can get into the habit of paying attention to the Holy Spirit's whispers. If He raises a red flag in your thoughts, pray into that situation. Pray for wisdom. You're free to answer with, 'I don't know the answer but I'm ok to hold onto this question, because God definitely knows the answer. One day He'll tell us, in this life or the next. In the meantime, we can trust Him.' May God be with you in your questioning and your answering.

Unafraid of unknowns

Great is our Lord and mighty in power; His understanding has no limit.
Psalm 147:5, NIV

God has set us free to learn, because we have unlimited access to His throne of grace, and we can approach anytime to ask for wisdom. We can also trust God completely in seasons of uncertainty. The psalmist says, 'For the Lord God is our sun and our shield. He gives us grace and glory. The Lord will withhold no good thing from those who do what is right.' (Psalm 84:11) If it's good for us to know something, God won't withhold the information. Where our kids are concerned, we get to pray, not only for wisdom to answer their questions, but even when to pre-empt their questions and equip them with information before they even know they need it.

We also needn't fear the cynical questions of others. God is big enough to handle the biggest of human doubts. He can handle the railings of the angriest critic. He's running towards humanity. He longs for people to turn to Him, even more than we long for them to turn to Him. We can trust their salvation to the Savior Himself. We can keep running towards people too, casting a vision of hope and offering unsolicited comfort and reassurance.

May you create space in your home and in the arena of your relationships for people to rest and wrestle with God. May you pray that every hidden, horrid thing would come into the light: all the frustration, anger, and doubt that someone you love is harboring in their heart. And all the time, may you stay humble and teachable, unafraid of the unknowns.

FREE TO LEARN

Proof of life

When he arrived and saw this evidence of God's blessing, he was filled
with joy, and he encouraged the believers to stay true to the Lord.
Acts 11:23, NLT

The church in Jerusalem sends Barnabas to check out what's happening in the church at Antioch. They've heard stories of crowds of
Gentiles coming to faith in Jesus. Barnabas arrives and sees evidence
of God's saving grace and lifegiving power at work in that community,
and he's elated.

What was happening at Antioch seemed weird to the predominantly
Jewish church in Jerusalem. But they learned the truth that the gospel
is free to every ethnicity. And we need to keep this truth front of mind
too when we encounter different expressions of worship. A particular
style of ministry might not be your favorite. *But is there evidence of
God's grace?* Is there every indication that God is using the work of His
people to reach the world with His love?

Os Guinness wrote, 'For Jesus, spirituality is clearly not a life of con-
templation divorced from a life of action. There is nothing of the
super spiritual or secular distortion we so often encounter in the
church. There is only a rhythm of engagement and withdrawal, work
and rest, release and recharge, crowds and solitude, in the midst of
the most effective public life ever lived.' Perhaps we need to learn to
monitor or define spirituality more in these terms, and less according to the straight lines of our own making. Wherever you find your
feet, learn to look for evidence of God at work through His unforced
rhythms of grace.

Free to ask yourself:

**These questions are drawn from themes
covered over the past five days.**

- If you look back over the last year, can you trace how you've grown in wisdom and courage?

- Do you feel free to be honest? In what situations or with what kind of people are you tempted to cover up the truth?

- Do you ever feel threatened or panicky when people ask you questions you can't answer? Are there certain questions you consider to be taboo – questions you'd never ask and questions you hope no one ever asks you?

- Read Psalm 8:2 and Matthew 11:25. What have you learned from one of your kids or from a much younger believer – someone who you'd think should be learning from you?

Free to ask God:

GOD,

Keep me humble and teachable. No one likes a know-it-all. I don't ever want to be that person! Keep me curious and grounded. Help me to ask the right questions and trust You for wisdom. Lead me into Your truth.

AMEN.

FREE TO LEARN

Pass

'But He knows where I am going. And when
He tests me, I will come out as pure as gold.'
Job 23:10, NLT

Maybe you crushed every exam at school, college, or university. Maybe you break out in a cold sweat at the thought of taking a test. It doesn't matter where you find yourself on the academic spectrum. We all need to get comfortable with the truth that God tests us. Testing is part of the maturing process He puts us through, to make us more like Jesus.

We need to pass the test of silence. Matthew 15 gives the intriguing account of a Gentile woman who begs Jesus to deliver her demon-possessed daughter. Matthew 15:23 says, 'But Jesus gave her no reply, not even a word.' If you read on, you'll see He was testing the genuineness of her faith and the posture of her heart. Initially, Jesus is silent. But make no mistake: He heard the woman. If God seems silent? Don't for a moment think He hasn't heard you.

God also calls us to pass the test of timing (because we need to learn that delays are not denials, and we need to learn not to sulk when it seems our gifts haven't been recognized), the test of rejection (because offence may precede the miracle), and the test of perseverance (because James 1:12 reminds us, 'Blessed is the one who perseveres under trial because, having stood the test, that person will receive the crown of life that the Lord has promised to those who love Him.'). May you pass every one of the Father's tests with flying colors, for your good and His glory.

Jesus plus nothing

*Yet we know that a person is made right with God
by faith in Jesus Christ, not by obeying the law.*
Galatians 2:16, NLT

God launches His rescue operation through the Jews, but by the time Paul writes his letter to the Galatian church there are as many non-Jewish followers of Jesus as there are Jewish followers of Jesus. The Jewish Christians are a bit irritated by this. They feel the non-Jewish Christians should also obey the Jewish Torah – the law – which means no bacon, no changing light bulbs on the Sabbath, and the biggest deal of all, get circumcised! They're saying to the Gentile Christians, 'Forget what Paul says! Obey the law! Get circumcised.' So, in chapters 1 and 2, Paul reminds the Galatians of the Jesus-plus-nothing gospel, and he challenges them, asking why on earth they would embrace a different gospel.

Initially, the Jewish believers had accepted the message about Christ crucified. But then they'd twisted the gospel to fit their preferences and biases, and we're not above doing the same thing. We know we're saved by faith (Ephesians 2:8) and blessed by obedience (Deuteronomy 11:27, Luke 11:28) – blessed, that is, with the biproducts of peace and comfort that come from doing life the way it's designed to be lived, even when it's difficult. But we mix this up, sometimes, and we consciously or subconsciously start thinking we're saved by obedience (works righteousness) and blessed by faith (the prosperity gospel, which is little more than saying, 'If you rub the genie lamp three times ...'). This is the un-truth Paul dismantles in Galatians, and we're free to learn from him that the gospel is wondrously simple, straightforward, and free.

Good works don't cut it

But we who live by the Spirit eagerly wait to receive
by faith the righteousness God has promised to us.
Galatians 5:5, NLT

In Galatians 3 and 4, Paul talks about how Abraham, like us, was saved by faith, not by doing a bunch of good things. The Galatians would've responded: 'Wait! If salvation has always been by faith, then why did God give the law?' Paul explains that the law was intended to be temporary, and its purpose was twofold. Firstly, it showed up Israel's sin. It said, 'This is how high you're supposed to jump. You can hardly get off the ground. You need help.' So, the law is good – but it makes us look bad. Secondly, the law kept Israel in line – like a bouncer at a night club, or a strict teacher. It kept them safe, until the promised Messiah came. Jesus was the faithful Israelite who *never* broke the law. But He died to take onto Himself the consequence of Israel's failure, and to set Israel – and us – free from sin.

And then in Galatians 5 Paul describes and defends this freedom that's ours for the taking. He explains how the only thing that truly transforms us is the power of the indwelling Holy Spirit. There are some violent verses in this chapter. Circumcision was a tangible (and painful) manifestation of strict obedience to the Torah – the ultimate sign that you were embracing the letter of the law and scoring points with God by doing stuff.

Paul is desperate for believers to understand that good works can't buy our freedom, earn God's favor, or produce faith. These are all His unmerited gift to us.

Culture shock

'For just as the heavens are higher than the earth, so My ways
are higher than your ways and My thoughts higher than your thoughts.'
Isaiah 55:9, NLT

The definition of culture shock is, 'the feeling of disorientation experienced by someone when they are suddenly subjected to an unfamiliar culture, way of life, or set of attitudes.' Maybe you felt like that when you moved countries, or went from school to university, or started a new job. Maybe the first months of marriage or parenthood felt like a culture shock to you. It felt like you were constantly trying to push doors open because you hadn't read the sign that said 'Pull'. You felt disoriented. You didn't quite know what to do with this new way of life you'd been thrust into.

In the gospels, Jesus shows us another kind of culture shock. He flips the social script completely, and it's nothing like what the crowds, the Jewish leaders, or His closest friends expect. He confronts them with a dizzying, new culture they don't quite know what to do with: the Kingdom culture He came to birth. Everything Jesus says and does and predicts is not what the people presume it should be. They're *pushing*... And He says, 'I want you to pull,' because the Kingdom always moves in an opposite spirit to the world. It pulls when the world pushes. It's always upside down to the world's way of seeing things and doing things. God's ways are always different, higher, and better than anything we can come up with, and if we immerse and orientate ourselves in Kingdom culture it will only ever do us good.

Coup de grace

As He talked about this openly with His disciples, Peter took
Him aside and began to reprimand Him for saying such things.
Mark 8:32, NLT

Jesus' disciples needed to adjust to the culturally shocking truth that
He came to bring, not a *coup d'état* which the Jews were hoping for,
but a *coup de grace*. In this first-century Jewish world, the idea of a
Messiah – what the Jews, including the disciples, had their hopes set
on – was a victorious military leader who would triumphantly rescue
them from Roman tyranny. Understandably, they could totally get behind the vision of a rebellion or a coup.

And yet Jesus didn't stage a *coup d'état*. He staged a *coup de grace*.
A *coup de grace* is the final blow or shot given to a wounded person
or animal. It's the merciful death blow for the sake of setting the person free from pain. Except, Jesus surrendered Himself to the *coup de
grace*. God administered the death blow, but the mercy was poured
out on us. That decisive, shocking act of grace was for our benefit, to
set us free from the pain of our pasts. We see here in Mark 8 that Peter
is happy to proclaim Jesus as the Messiah, but then he reprimands
Jesus for predicting His own death, effectively saying, 'That's not the
plan! You're not supposed to die. You're supposed to move into the
government buildings, overthrow the oppressors, and wave a new
flag.' Thankfully, Jesus – gentle and strong – holds to the better, higher
plan. He builds a new culture, laying the foundations with His own life,
which He gave away, for us.

FREE TO LEARN

Free to ask yourself:

**These questions are drawn from themes
covered over the past five days.**

- How might you explain in your own words, to a friend who doesn't yet know Jesus, that you're saved by faith and blessed by obedience, rather than saved by obedience and blessed by faith?

- Can you think of a time when you experienced culture shock? How is the culture of your church community radically different from the culture of secular society around you?

- Why was the *coup de grace* staged by Jesus so shocking, in the face of both Roman and Jewish culture?

- Read Galatians 6:9 and Romans 5:3-5, about passing the test of endurance and perseverance. Where is God pressing you, to press on?

Free to write it out:

Write down the names of people whom you'd love to see putting their faith in Jesus. Spend time praying they'd come to a full understanding of the truth that no amount of good works can ever put them in the good books of God, but that God Himself freely offers absolute absolution.

_____

_____

_____

_____

_____

_____

_____

_____

_____

_____

Me first!

'What is your request?' He asked. They replied, 'When You
sit on Your glorious throne, we want to sit in places of honor
next to You, one on Your right and the other on Your left.'
Mark 10:36-37, NLT

In the second part of the gospel of Mark, Jesus predicts His death three times, and every time He does, the disciples follow it up with, 'Cool. Ok! Can I sit next to You in heaven?' Or they argue with each other: 'I'm the greatest in the Kingdom of heaven.' 'No! *I'm* the greatest in the Kingdom of heaven. And you're not invited to my birthday party!'

Jesus is trying to explain to them the customs and conventions of the shocking, upside-down Kingdom culture He is creating, and they just don't get it. They don't understand selflessness and aiming low. They can't seem to fathom what it means to leverage one's time and potential for the furthering of others.

We're quick to criticize the disciples. We roll our eyes and say, 'Wow, they were *so* immature in their faith.' Yet we do this very thing. We're so easily caught up in the world's ways, which promise us that rubbing shoulders with the leader – the man or the woman of the moment – will bring status and fame and invitations to all the right events.

Kingdom culture says that rubbing shoulders with the leader – Jesus – will result in dying to yourself, to the extent you'd be happy to let someone else blow out all your birthday candles and open your presents. May we forget ourselves, and in that, learn to move into the incredible freedom of going second.

After versus Before

He took the seven loaves, thanked God for them, and broke
them into pieces. He gave them to His disciples, who distributed
the bread to the crowd. A few small fish were found, too, so
Jesus also blessed these and told the disciples to distribute
them. They ate as much as they wanted. Afterward, the
disciples picked up seven large baskets of leftover food.
Mark 8:6-8, NLT

If the world's culture had a gift shop selling souvenirs there'd be t-shirts and key rings saying, 'Entitled' and 'What's in it for me?' We all feel the tug of Western culture. We *expect* great things to happen for us because we *deserve* them. (*Afterwards*, if it occurs to us, we may or may not say thank you.)

In the Kingdom culture Jesus demonstrates, He turns that upside down. He gives thanks *before* something amazing happens. His thanksgiving precedes the miracle. In Mark 8, Jesus is about to supernaturally feed thousands of people, like He did in Mark 6. It's another moment for Him to delight in miracles. Not enough food? Fantastic! Let's pray, then feed loads of people.

What Jesus is teaching His disciples here is not a kind of name-it-and-claim-it, make-a-wish theology. He simply thanked His Father for the seven loaves they had in their hands. But it's as if His gratitude ushers in the miracle. So instead of waiting for God to tick a bunch of things off our lists before we thank Him, Jesus is inviting us to draw near and begin to offer sacrifices of thanks for what He *has* put in our hands – then rest in the truth that He knows what we need.

FREE TO LEARN

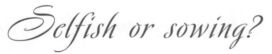

Selfish or sowing?

The generous will prosper; those who
refresh others will themselves be refreshed.
Proverbs 11:25, NLT

In the story of the feeding of the multitudes we looked at yesterday, Jesus shows us the difference between selfishness and sowing. The crowd is hungry. The disciples are surely whining: 'We're *also* famished and exhausted. Please don't make their problem ours. Where are we supposed to find food for everyone?' But Jesus shows them, and us, a better way. He says, 'Well, what *have* you got there? Ok, just bring it. I'm God.' Instead of closing His fists in selfishness or self-preservation, He opens His hands, and He begins to sow.

In Proverbs 11:25 Solomon explains the extraordinary, upside-down, Kingdom principle that when you feel you have nothing to give – when you badly need some refreshing yourself – you offer it to someone else and God turns that into nourishment for your soul. I'm guessing Jesus, like the crowd and His disciples, is also tired and hungry, after three straight days of preaching. His response? He feeds and refreshes and meets the needs of *others*.

Imagine the wells of refreshing that might spring up across our cities and communities if we all committed to doing this, for a month, or forever. If you'd love to get a text from a friend? Pick up your phone and go first. No matter how much you may need someone to hand you a tall glass of ice-cold water, ask God to give you gentle, encouraging, lifegiving words to water the souls of people you'll encounter today. And as you pour yourself out unselfishly, may you enjoy floods of refreshing.

Sowing in times of famine

Those who plant in tears will harvest with shouts of joy.
They weep as they go to plant their seed,
but they sing as they return with the harvest.
Psalm 126:5-6, NLT

In Genesis 26 we read that a severe famine strikes the land. God gives Isaac some instructions. He plants seeds and harvests a hundred times more grain than he planted. There's some conflict with the people around him because jealousy makes you nasty and they fill up his wells with dirt and all sorts of things go down. Ultimately, he digs another well and calls it *Rehoboth*, which means 'open space'. It doesn't make sense to sow in a time of famine. It doesn't make sense to then reap a hundredfold, or to be brought into a spacious place. But that's Kingdom culture.

Maybe global goings-on are indicating to you it's the worst time ever to start a business, or have a baby, or plant a church. And yet we're living by the rhythms of a different culture. We're not buying and selling. We're sowing and reaping. God is your provider. He will not be mocked. If He is who He says He is, then you will reap (financially or in some other way), and you'll be led into a spacious place.

Don't be afraid. When you come to the end of yourself and all your resources, you'll find Jesus is still there, and He is enough. He invites you into the freedom of selflessness where you'll discover that it's in giving yourself away, like He did, that you'll reap a harvest of refreshing.

Free from idols

Son of man, these men have set up idols in their hearts
and put wicked stumbling blocks before their faces ...
speak to them and tell them, 'This is what the Sovereign
LORD says: When any of the Israelites set up idols in their hearts
and put a wicked stumbling block before their faces and then
go to a prophet, I the LORD will answer them Myself in keeping
with their great idolatry. I will do this to recapture the hearts
of the people of Israel, who have all deserted Me for their idols.'
Ezekiel 14:3-5, NIV

To learn to lead people into freedom, we must recognize the signs of idolatry. Every human, after all, worships something or someone. If a person isn't worshiping Jesus, there'll be something else taking His place.

Pray for insight, discernment, and discretion as you spend time with people. *Listen.* What do they talk about most? What do they typically spend their time and money on? These are often indications of what people worship. (Let's never stop asking ourselves these same questions!) Ask God to show you the idol: food, sex, drugs, money, alcohol, a person's kids, the approval of a boss or a parent, Amazon, the idea of getting married? Idols show up in countless shapes and forms, and we all fall into the trap of being distracted and lured by their shiny-happy promises of satisfaction.

Once we understand someone's belief – or what they hope for from their chosen idol – we can gently and respectfully talk them down from the ledge of false assurances by uncovering the truth of the matchless gospel of Jesus, the hope who never disappoints.

Free to ask yourself:

**These questions are drawn from themes
covered over the past five days.**

- What situation will you likely find yourself in today, in which you can choose to go second, instead of jostling for prime position?

- What are you trusting God for? What kind of a miracle do you need? What will it look like for you to give thanks, in these circumstances?

- Right now, do you feel you're in a time of famine or feasting? Either way, what might it mean for you to sow the seeds you have in your hands?

- Read Exodus 20:3-6, Colossians 3:5, Jonah 2:8 and 1 John 5:21. In which areas of your life do you tend to set up idols – health, career, family, or other?

FREE TO LEARN

Free to ask God:

JESUS,

You came as a King to wash the feet of those who would betray and deny You. Make me like You, putting others' needs above mine. Fill me with relentless gratitude even as I wait for You to make a way through the Red Sea of my circumstances. Help me to keep sowing, even in times of famine. Show me where I've set up idols in my heart. The throne of my life is for You and You alone!

AMEN.

Free to keep learning

An intelligent heart acquires knowledge,
and the ear of the wise seeks knowledge.
Proverbs 18:15, ESV

If you've picked up this book, I'm quite certain you long to learn and grow freely in your awareness and appreciation of God, others, yourself, and life in general. Me too. And of course, you and I both know we'll never know it all. That shouldn't discourage us. It should give us greater eagerness to learn, because there's still so much wisdom that we can look forward to absorbing and assimilating.

However, making continuous, critical judgments closes off our minds to understanding and creativity. The solution is to move judgment into the space of learning, by asking the right questions instead of jumping to conclusions. Questions bring clarity and can alleviate negative emotions. For example, we can keep learning about God, others, life, and ourselves, by asking people how best we can serve them. Learn to say, 'How can I position myself so I'm not adding to your stress?' or 'I'd love to understand how you've experienced this situation.'

And then, ensure you have a reflective space of your own, to filter out the noise and listen for signals from God. I've no doubt, friend, you have a high SQ, EQ and IQ, and you're a gift to the world. Make time to be quiet, so your decisions, ideas and judgment calls aren't just accurate, but also lifegiving. And if you live a life of high exposure – if you're known in your community and if you interact with numbers of people – seek out hidden spaces of servanthood where there's nothing in it for you. There's learning there, and freedom.

Interfering God

> About that time David's son Adonijah, whose mother was Haggith, began boasting, 'I will make myself king.' So he provided himself with chariots and charioteers and recruited fifty men to run in front of him. Now his father, King David, had never disciplined him at any time, even by asking, 'Why are you doing that?'
> 1 Kings 1:5-6, NLT

FREE TO FAIL

David's failure to discipline his son very nearly cost him his throne. If Nathan, Bathsheba, and others hadn't stepped in, resulting in David hurriedly appointing Solomon as the rightful heir to rule over Israel and Judah, history would've told a very different story.

Perhaps you resented your mom or dad for interfering in your life, growing up. And yet, far worse than an interfering parent is a parent who never interferes. Thankfully, your Heavenly Father interferes! He loves you enough to fight for you, and to fight for the best possible outcomes for you. How tragic and lonely a place would the universe be if God didn't care what we did with our lives, or what became of us?

Let's welcome God's interference in our stories because Jesus stops us on the path of shame – He interrupts our self-flagellation and self-pity – and He sets us on the path of life. Let's ask God to interfere in our lives and the lives of our kids, because none of us is ever in a non-aligned environment.

C. S. Lewis wrote, 'There is no neutral ground in the universe. Every square inch, every split second is claimed by God, and counterclaimed by Satan.' Praise God that He has dealt with your past and He will interfere with your present, for your future.

Using losers

Jesus replied, 'I tell you the truth, Peter – this very night,
before the rooster crows, you will deny Me three times.'
Matthew 26:34, NLT

In His final months on earth – on the road to Jerusalem, and death – Jesus maximized His ministry of preaching and healing, manifesting His perfect wisdom and knowledge, His perfect power and patience, and His perfect love. Tension is building as His death draws near, and He cuts to the chase, saying things like: 'I love you guys! One of you is going to betray Me.'

Just after that, He says to Peter, the rock upon whom He will build His church: 'But I have pleaded in prayer for you, Simon, that your faith should not fail. So when you have repented and turned to Me again, strengthen your brothers.' (Luke 22:32). We know that Peter did just that. He's been strengthening us, the church, for some two millennia, through his writings which have been preserved.

The beautiful truth we glean from watching Jesus' friendship with Peter play out is that He doesn't give up on Peter. He sustains Peter's faith, and He fulfils His plans in and through Peter. His mercy, kindness, grace, and favor don't dissipate because of Peter's rebellion or fear or flakiness. And all of that is true for you and me too. We're all failures in some shape or form. But how unthinkable and incredible that God uses losers like us. More than that, as we seek to know God and make Him known, He transforms us, turning our downfalls and defeats into Kingdom victories.

FREE TO FAIL

Sleep, stress, slash

Judas walked over to Jesus to greet Him with a kiss. But Jesus said,
'Judas, would you betray the Son of Man with a kiss?' When the
other disciples saw what was about to happen, they exclaimed,
'Lord, should we fight? We brought the swords!' And one of
them struck at the high priest's slave, slashing off his right ear.
Luke 22:47-50, NLT

For context, here's what's happening: Jesus and His disciples leave the upstairs room where they've just had supper together, and head for the Mount of Olives. Jesus asks His disciples to stay alert and pray, because human history hinges upon what will go down on this night. Jesus walks on, a stone's throw from His friends, and asks His Father to take from Him the terrible suffering He's about to endure, 'Yet I want Your will to be done, not Mine.' (Luke 22:42) An angel appears to strengthen Him. He keeps on praying, in a state of utter anguish. He finds His disciples fast asleep, probably exhausted by grief. He's just told them He's going to die. They must be so afraid, so overwhelmed. He asks them again to pray. And then the betrayal happens. Now they're awake! And offering to fight!

The disciples go from one extreme to the next. First they sleep – then they slash. Stress is always revealing, isn't it? Just like Peter, we go into the extremes of our personalities – reacting from our raw temperaments – when we're uptight or anxious. Let's be brave enough to ask those closest to us about our natural bents and tendencies when life is pressured, so we can surrender the weaker elements of our personalities to God.

I Am

Jesus fully realized all that was going to happen to Him,
so He stepped forward to meet them. 'Who are you looking for?'
He asked. 'Jesus the Nazarene,' they replied. 'I AM He,' Jesus said.
(Judas, who betrayed Him, was standing with them.) As Jesus said
'I AM He,' they all drew back and fell to the ground! Once more
He asked them, 'Who are you looking for?' And again they replied,
'Jesus the Nazarene.' 'I told you that I AM He,' Jesus said.
John 18:4-8, NLT

Jesus has just been confronted by His betrayers. Astonishingly, He's not shocked or afraid or angry. He's fully in control. His life isn't being taken from Him. He is relinquishing it. His reference to Himself as 'I AM' is a throwback to Exodus 3 when Moses says to God, 'What if I go back to the Israelites and tell them, "The God of your fathers has sent me," and they say, "What's His name?" What should I tell them?' And God says, 'Tell them I AM who I AM. Tell them I AM sent you.' On the Mount of Olives, God in flesh says, 'I AM ...'

So, to be clear, Jesus *actually* called this meeting, in the garden. Everyone is in this garden, on this night, because of Him. His disciples are there to 'pray for Him' (or not) and 'fight for Him' (which they do haphazardly, unwisely). Judas and his crew think they've orchestrated the meeting, to arrest Him and have Him killed. They all think they're in control – but they're not. Even when things go horribly wrong, we all sometimes think we're in control. Mercifully, we're not, and Jesus is.

Free to ask yourself:

These questions are drawn from themes covered over the past five days.

- How has God interfered in your life, over the past year? How did you respond?

- Can you trace how God has used you for His Kingdom, even though you've gone through seasons of doubt or distraction that you would term as failure?

- When you squeeze a tube of toothpaste, toothpaste comes out. When you're squeezed by the pressures of life, what comes out of you? What are your typical knee-jerk reactions in times of stress?

- Flip through Genesis and Exodus, to read the stories of Abraham, Joseph, and Moses. How did they fail? How did God use them?

Free to write it out:

**Ask God to highlight the failures you've been carrying
with a sense of shame or disqualification. Write them out
and surrender them to Him. Write out the truth that
He causes all things to work for your good, even your
mess-ups. Praise Him that He'll weave your botches
and fiascos into a story that ultimately glorifies Him.**

FREE TO FAIL

At a loss for words?

*In the beginning the Word already existed. The Word was with God,
and the Word was God. He existed in the beginning with God.
God created everything through Him, and nothing was created
except through Him ... So the Word became human and made
His home among us. He was full of unfailing love and faithfulness.
And we have seen His glory, the glory of the Father's one and only Son.*
John 1:1-3, 14, NLT

As the One who really called the meeting in the garden on the night He was betrayed, there are a couple of things to remember about Jesus, the great I AM.

Firstly, when Jesus was here on earth, He was 100% man and 100% God, which completely short-circuits our brains if we try to wrap our heads around it. Secondly, John calls Jesus 'the Word'. Jesus created language, truth, and communication. He spoke out the universe. And Jesus, the Word, was confined to the silence of a woman's womb. For nine months, He didn't speak. The Word couldn't say a word. He also didn't exit the womb speaking in full sentences. He was fully human.

But Jesus the fully-human was also fully-God. He choreographed the meeting in the garden with His enemies and friends, and it was all about Him. Because He's fully God, He is all-knowing, all-powerful, all-loving. If you like big words, Jesus is omniscient, omnipotent, and omnibenevolent.

So next time something or someone leaves you speechless, know that Jesus chose to be rendered speechless too, for your sake. He was fully human, and He understands. He's also fully God, and you can lean on the power of His wisdom and His words.

Omni-everything

You know me inside and out, You know every bone in my body;
You know exactly how I was made, bit by bit, how I was sculpted from
nothing into something ... You watched me grow from conception
to birth; all the stages of my life were spread out before You,
the days of my life all prepared before I'd even lived one day.
Psalm 139:15-16, MSG

At twenty-six weeks of pregnancy, a baby's eyelids are fully formed. Even though there isn't much to see *in utero*, a baby will start to keep his eyes open and blink them when he's awake. When our omnipotent, omniscient, omnibenevolent, and omnipresent God was forming His disciples' eyelids, He knew then that they'd close those eyelids, and sleep, in the hour He'd need them most. At eight weeks of pregnancy a baby's upper lip and nose have formed. In week fourteen, the roof of a baby's mouth is fully formed, and his constant sucking reflexes strengthen his cheeks. When our everywhere-always God made Judas in the womb, He knew those little lips would one day kiss His cheek in betrayal. He made him and loved him, anyway.

You, too, were formed in a womb. When you were there, only Jesus could see you. He saw you in ways no scan ever could. He already saw the stories you'd live. The good, the bad, the embarrassing, the painful. Jesus set your fetal heart beating, and He will decide when your heart will beat for the last time. He has seen you and known you deeper, wider, higher, and longer than anyone else. And still, He loves you completely, in your failures and greatest feats.

FREE TO FAIL

Stopping for the slave

But Jesus said, 'No more of this.' And He
touched the man's ear and healed him.
Luke 22:51, NLT

It's awe-inspiring to think Jesus called a meeting in a dark garden to arrange to relinquish His life for the very people who would arrive to arrest Him. It's even more incredible to note that Jesus doesn't actually stop this meeting in the garden for Peter or His other disciples, or His betrayer, or His attackers. There's someone else – a nobody – embedded in this story. Jesus stops the proceedings of the meeting for the slave. And everything that goes down in these few minutes – the brief pause in the efforts to get Jesus arrested and killed – reflects what Jesus is about to do for all of humanity.

Peter realizes his Master is about to be arrested. He lashes out in fierce loyalty and de-ears the high priest's slave. He's an act-now-apologize-later kind of guy. Jesus is the Prince of Peace, and He stops what's going on and says, 'No more of this.' The slave isn't even named in Luke 22. He's an extra. And yet Jesus performs His last healing miracle, before His death, on this slave. Here in the darkness of the garden as His darkest hours unfold, He makes for His beloved enemy, the slave, another ear for the one He knew He would heal one day even as He was whispering to those first cells to split and multiply, to form an ear in the womb. There's no surprise in His eyes.

He forms His enemy. Then He stops everything, to fix His enemy.

On the cross, He stopped – split history in half – to fix you too.

Slave made king

> None of your offspring throughout their generations who has
> a blemish may approach to offer the food of his God. For no one who
> has a blemish shall draw near, one who is blind or lame, or one who
> has a mutilated face or a limb too long, or one who has a broken
> foot or a broken hand, or a hunchback, or a dwarf, or a man with a
> blemish in his eyes or an itching disease or scabs or crushed testicles.
> Leviticus 21:17-20, ESV

Yesterday we saw Peter slash off the ear of the high priest's slave, whom Jesus then heals. The renowned first-century historian, Josephus, also records a story about ears being sliced off. Antigonus cut off Hyrcanus' ears to disqualify him from becoming high priest. And we now know from Leviticus that you couldn't become a priest if you were in any way disfigured. Peter, in chopping off the ear of the high priest's slave, is disqualifying the slave from ever becoming high priest himself.

The slave's name is only mentioned in John's account. It's Malchus, meaning *king*. Except, he's a slave, not a king. He's a slave, not a priest – and he'll never be a priest because he's lost an ear. He's the lowest of the low, and he's just been made lower.

But Jesus, King of kings, knows the slave's name, and doesn't treat him like a slave or an enemy. He restores to him, not just his missing ear, but the love and dignity of which he's been stripped, and which his name suggests he deserves. Mercifully, Jesus does this for us: loving us like the royal priests we're destined to become.

Fix you

'For You were slaughtered, and Your blood has ransomed
people for God from every tribe and language and people
and nation. And You have caused them to become a Kingdom
of priests for our God. And they will reign on the earth.'
Revelation 5:9-10, NLT

What happened in the Garden of Gethsemane is a picture of God's plan for humanity. We were God's enemies, and slaves to sin, but He restored us to rule and reign with Him. Jesus was mutilated on the cross, to mend us. And that's why Peter, who swung his sword in the garden, could later say of the slave Malchus, and of us: '... for you are a chosen people. You are royal priests, a holy nation, God's very own possession. As a result, you can show others the goodness of God ...' (1 Peter 2:9) This is what the heavenly chorus is singing about, in Revelation 5.

Perhaps you're in a weird season of disconnectedness, or disconcertedness. Maybe you don't feel royal, free, or included in a bigger story. It's possible you've felt particularly unseen. Perhaps you've dropped off the edges of your church community. You long for someone to stop what they're doing and notice you.

Friend, if no one ever stops an actual meeting for you, know this: Jesus stopped breathing for you. He notices you. He knows you. He loves you. Where once you were His enemy, He's made peace with you. Where once you were a slave, He's set you free. He forms you, and He stops everything to fix you, so you can say, like Malchus, 'I was deaf but now I hear. And that's amazing grace.'

Free to ask yourself:

**These questions are drawn from themes
covered over the past five days.**

- Are you in a financial position or a work relationship or a family dynamic which has unfairly silenced you in some way? How can you bring that to God? What truth does He speak over your silence?

- What gives you greatest comfort today: God's omniscience, omnipresence, omnipotence or omnibenevolence?

- Can you trace how God has moved you from slavery to royalty?

- Read 2 Corinthians 3:18. How does this truth encourage you, where you feel scarred by sin in some way?

Free to ask God:

LORD,

Thank You for loving me so much that You'd be willing to stop everything to fix me. Thank You for willingly going to the cross, where You were disfigured for my deformities and depravities. Thank You for restoring me, so I can live into my full potential and glorify You. Thank You for clothing me with righteousness and calling me royalty and saving me a seat at Your table. Don't let me forget I'm no longer a slave.

AMEN.

Social media fail

We do not dare to classify or compare ourselves with some who commend themselves. When they measure themselves by themselves and compare themselves with themselves, they are not wise.
2 Corinthians 10:12, NIV

We set ourselves up for certain failure when we compare ourselves to others, and social media – that giant generator of envy – is the worst place to spend our time if we're keen to avoid comparison.

It's fair to say our culture's relationship with technology, which might be termed an unconsciously conscious addiction, isn't sustainable. Technology makes us far busier, and far unhappier. We spend hours of our lives online – time we'll never get back once it's gone – comparing ourselves, our kids, our homes, our holidays. When last did you come off Instagram feeling happier, more content, more grateful? Mostly, our doom scrolling through newsfeeds, or the echo chambers of social media platforms, leaves us disgruntled, frustrated, afraid, disappointed, and most often, jealous. And when it comes to Twitter, it's easy to nurture negativity as the anger of people all over the world washes over us in tweets and retweets.

We're just human like everyone else, but as Jesus' followers we *do* know better than to seek the instant gratification of likes, attaching our identity to the number of hearts on a post. When you get the urge to check social media, why are you actually craving it? Is God nudging you to unfollow some unhelpful accounts? Let's shoot for more warm-bodied conversations, checking in with folks by asking honest, out-loud questions and offering honest, from-the-heart answers. It's not a fail-proof idea, but you could try taking a weekend-long digital sabbath. Be drastic, and intentional, and free.

FREE TO FAIL

Healthy or harmful?

'For from the heart come evil thoughts, murder, adultery,
all sexual immorality, theft, lying, and slander.'
Matthew 15:19, NLT

As we bring our failures before the throne of grace – knowing we'll find mercy, grace, and freedom – it's helpful to understand where our words, thoughts and mindsets come from. We know our thinking affects our feeling which affects our doing. Our words – nasty or nice – are born within our brains, so if we're harboring toxic mindsets, we'll end up contaminating everything and everyone we touch.

Ask God to show you if any of these harmful mindsets are making up your mental landscape:

A mindset of *entitlement* has you thinking in terms of contracts, not covenants. *Perfectionism* is rooted in fear of rejection, and a deep need to seek approval. It can lead to dishonesty as you cover up your *imperfections*. *Pride* has you thinking you know everything, hungry to be right and to feel superior. *Craving comfort and independence* keeps you from relying on others. *Criticism* destroys the safe place you ought to find in your marriage and other close friendships and relationships, making those closest to you feel unsafe in your presence. Lastly, a need to *control* just displays an absence of faith in God.

Healthy mindsets are formed when we're willing to yield to truth, unafraid to peer into the dark corners of the soul. Let's pray for soft, teachable hearts, quick to confess to God and each other. Let's humble ourselves. Let's never allow a critical thought to wander free in our minds. And when we hear God's voice prompting us to act for the good of the world, let's not delay. *Just do it.*

Holy fire

'And I Myself will be a wall of fire around it,' declares
the Lᴏʀᴅ, 'and I will be its glory within.'
Zechariah 2:5, NIV

This verse is about the city of Jerusalem. God was promising to be her protection and radiance. While we shouldn't take a verse like this out of context and apply it directly to ourselves, it does reveal the nature of our loving, powerful Heavenly Father. He promises to protect us too, as the psalmist proclaims: 'Those who live in the shelter of the Most High will find rest in the shadow of the Almighty. This I declare about the Lᴏʀᴅ: He alone is my refuge, my place of safety ...' (Psalm 91:1-2) And He promises to make us radiant with joy as we look to Him for help (Psalm 34:5).

Where failure has crumbled the walls of your life, trust God to rebuild and protect. Trust God that His truth will stand like stone, and that every lie and accusation of the enemy will be burned up and blown away. Trust God to fight for you. Ask Him to obliterate words spoken over you or about you that simply aren't true. God promises to use your mess-ups and the misfortunes of life for your good (Romans 8:28-29). Be intentional about asking Him to use what has caused you unthinkable hurt, for something beautiful that points to His Kingdom and glory. May God be a wall of holy-fire protection around you, and your glory within as He continues to transform you, lead you into all truth, and give you victory.

FREE TO FAIL

Christ in you

> But if Christ is in you, then even though your body is subject to death because of sin, the Spirit gives life because of righteousness.
> Romans 8:10, NIV

We've already looked at Paul's explanation of 'Christ in you, the hope of glory' (Colossians 1:27). We'll never wrap our heads around this vast truth, but maybe it's enough to accept that, if our enormous, eternal Jesus is so intimately involved in every detail of our lives – *living in us* – then surely there is definitely, *always*, hope.

'Christ in you, the hope of glory' means we have the hope of heaven and sharing in His glory there. It means here on earth we don't have to *hold* all the things, and *know* all the things, because Jesus holds all things together, and in Jesus is all wisdom and knowledge (Colossians 1:17, 2:3). We just get to press into Him to get to all that wisdom and knowledge, and so we don't get distracted or deceived. And as we lean closer to Him, praying for more wisdom, we begin to find answers, direction, discernment, and insight for our journeys.

'Christ in you, the hope of glory' also means we begin to find peace for the tough, unanswerable things we carry, knowing that every question *does* have an answer and Jesus knows them all even if we never do. So, if you don't have all the answers right now, what *has* God revealed to you (Deuteronomy 29:29)? Just do that, knowing that His life-giving, hope-generating Spirit is in you, working His will for your good and His glory.

Truth tension

The Sovereign Lord is my strength! He makes me as
surefooted as a deer, able to tread upon the heights.
Habakkuk 3:19, NLT

To better understand what Paul meant by 'Christ in you, the hope of glory' consider this: you don't have to carry the heavy tension of seemingly contradictory truths because your arms are already too tired. Like, maybe in one hand you're forced to hold the very heavy truth that you were raped. Or you haven't been healed. Or you're still not pregnant. You're still single. You're still unemployed. Your husband is still drinking too much. Your daughter is still addicted to TikTok. And in the other hand you're trying to cling to the truth that God is your protector, God can heal, He does provide and create life, He does break our chains and hear our prayers and He does love you and His plans for your life are perfect.

You're looking at all this going, 'But how's that possible? How can *both* be true? How can God's promises be just as true as my difficult reality? Has God even noticed that He seems to be contradicting Himself, in my life?'

In Jesus, all things hold together, and in Him lie hidden all the treasures of wisdom and knowledge (Colossians 1:17, 2:3). He understands how both truths can be true. He understands everything. It makes sense to Him. He's strong enough to hold all those difficult, contradictory, true things in your life. You can drop your arms. Let Jesus carry the tension. If we're in Him, and He's in us, and He holds all things – then we don't have to do the holding at all.

Free to ask yourself:

**These questions are drawn from themes
covered over the past five days.**

- When are you most tempted to lose track of time as you scroll through social media? What kind of guardrail could you put in place to prevent you from setting yourself up for failure in this area?

- Have you identified some harmful mindsets? What are the healthier, more helpful alternative thought patterns you could choose to adopt?

- You are *in Christ,* and Christ is also *in you* (Colossians 1:27-28). How does each part of this supernatural paradox comfort you?

- Read Matthew 11:28-29 and Philippians 4:6. If you can't see exactly how God will come through for you, what is God saying to you about the tension you're currently carrying?

Free to write it out:

Write down the hurtful words that have been spoken over you or about you, or the negative opinion someone seems to have of you. Write down a prayer of repentance if any of the accusations leveled against you are true. Now write down God's truth spoken over you and ask Him to fight for your reputation.

_____

_____

_____

_____

_____

_____

_____

_____

_____

_____

Three-word sermon

'I, the Lord, will make My home in Jerusalem with My people.'
Joel 3:21, NLT

Joel was one of the minor prophets. His name (and the name of the book he wrote) means *Yahweh is God*. That's a three-word sermon right there. But it's worth reading the whole book of Joel if you never have. Maybe you're thinking, 'What does a guy who wrote some poetic prophecies thousands of years ago have to say to us in the 21st century?' Remember, 2 Timothy 3:16 tells us *all* Scripture is God-breathed, and useful. I know you'd agree we desperately need the God-breathed Scriptures – His lifegiving wisdom – to help us not just survive, but as God's people, to thrive in these days, and Joel has something profound to say to us.

It's not clear exactly when Joel wrote this book, and it's an unusual book because Joel doesn't accuse Israel of a specific sin – like say, worshiping the golden calf. He uses big metaphors to communicate big themes, and that makes the truths he proclaims applicable to so many of the scenarios of human history.

Joel quotes from at least eight other Old Testament writers and prophets. His reflection on all these biblical texts helps him make sense of the tragedies of his day, and that gives him hope for the future. In the same way, as we reflect on biblical texts, the book of Joel included, we'll be able to make sense of the tragedies of our day too.

The very last verse of the book of Joel (Joel 3:21) contains another three-word sermon: *With My people*. Yahweh is God, and no matter what you're up against, He is with you.

FREE TO FAIL

Ruin

The fields are ruined, the land is stripped bare. The grain is
destroyed, the grapes have shriveled, and the olive oil is gone.
Joel 1:10, NLT

Joel begins his prophetic book by describing the ruin that's come
to his people. You've probably noticed: our world has seen some
ruin in recent years too. And Joel says we're to tell our children about
all this in decades to come (Joel 1:3) because it would be a shame to
waste the generational wisdom we'll gain from our experiences.

Joel then depicts the ruin caused by a recent locust plague. But unlike
the locust plague God sent against Egypt, back in Exodus, this time
the locusts are coming against Israel. The situation is dire. Our world
today, too, is experiencing economic devastation, because of wars,
refugee crises and a global pandemic from which we'll take decades
to recover. Scripture reminds us that economic devastation has happened before – but it's not the end of the story.

In chapter 2 Joel announces a future day of the Lord. Disaster is on its
way to Jerusalem – again, locusts. This time, however, he's describing
the locusts metaphorically. They're depicted as being God's army.

This coming day of the Lord is frightening, to say the least, because, as
C.S. Lewis said, 'Pain is God's megaphone to rouse a deaf world.' God is
getting the attention of His people; He loves them enough to do that.
He loves us that much too, and He will use our ruined crops – and any
other ruin that crops up in our lives – to draw us to Himself.

Repentance

... the LORD says, 'Turn to me now, while there is time.
Give me your hearts ... Don't tear your clothing in
your grief, but tear your hearts instead ...'
Joel 2:12-13, NLT

Joel's response to the ruin we read about yesterday is to call God's people to repentance. It's God's kindness that leads us to repentance (Romans 2:4), not His wrath. Joel knows this. In Joel 2:11-13 he reminds the people that repentance isn't a show we put on. God wants our sincere, heartfelt turning from selfishness and evil.

Then Joel offers the reason for repentance. The rest of Joel 2:13 reads, 'Return to the Lord your God, for He is merciful and compassionate, slow to get angry and filled with unfailing love. He is eager to relent and not punish.' As believers, looking back at the writings of Joel through the lens of the cross, we can pray God's kindness would lead the nations to repentance. When things go globally crazy, people on every continent sacrifice normal life and run out of scaffolding around which to build their lives. Let's pray the Holy Spirit would awaken them to the truth that all they ever have to hold onto is Jesus. We can also pray God's kindness would keep on leading *us* to repentance.

When G.K Chesterton was asked, 'What's wrong with the world?' He always answered, 'I am.' Pray you'd hear God's voice in fresh ways as He convicts you of sin – because sin ruins things. And where ruin has interrupted your plans or dreams, remind yourself it's God's mercy and love – not His wrath and judgment – that interrupts and delays us, because He wants to transform us.

FREE TO FAIL

Restoration

'Don't be afraid, my people. Be glad now and
rejoice, for the LORD has done great things.'
Joel 2:21, NLT

To recap our readings of the past couple days: ruin has led the people to repentance. Now, God answers with a promise of restoration.
He responds to the people's repentance with love and pity, and He
promises three things:

Firstly, God promises to defeat evil. He'll defeat the threatening invad-
ers (the locusts) and turn them to their own ruin. Take comfort from
this: in this life or the next, your enemies and your adverse circumstances will be defeated. David writes, 'Yet I am confident I will see the
Lord's goodness while I am here in the land of the living.' (Psalm 27:13)
That's *this* life.

Secondly, God promises to reverse the devastation. He'll restore the
desecrated land, making it abundant again. In Joel 2:25 God says, 'I will
give you back what you lost to the locusts …' Other versions use phras-
es like, *I will repay you, I will restore to you,* and *I will make up to you.* I
don't know what restoration will look like in your situation, but I know
God writes page-turners, with lives surrendered to Him.

Thirdly, God promises He will presence Himself with His people through
the real, accessible pouring out of His Spirit (Joel 3:28-32). Fantastically,
this has already happened. In Acts 2, on the day of Pentecost, Peter
quoted Joel's exact words because God had sent His Holy Spirit, the
Comforter. We're already living in this dispensation of grace and if we
turn to our merciful and compassionate God, He will pour out His Spirit
on us, again and again.

FREE TO FAIL

Pain to pearls

So be truly glad. There is wonderful joy ahead, even though you have to endure many trials for a little while. These trials will show that your faith is genuine. It is being tested as fire tests and purifies gold – though your faith is far more precious than mere gold. So when your faith remains strong through many trials, it will bring you much praise and glory and honor.
1 Peter 1:6-7, NLT

As you think about the pictures Joel paints in his prophecy – ruin, repentance, restoration – perhaps ask God how they apply to you.

What might it look like for you to take your ruins to Jesus? Maybe your peace of mind is in ruins. Maybe you're facing the very real possibility of financial ruin, or the ruined health of someone close to you. Joel 3:16 says, '... the Lord will be a refuge for His people, a strong fortress ...' During a particular season of ruined circumstances, I wore my pearl earrings every day. A pearl is formed when an irritant – usually a parasite, and not the proverbial grain of sand – works its way into an oyster. As a defense mechanism, layers of a fluid called nacre are deposited around the parasite until a beautiful, valuable pearl is formed. I wore my pearls to remind me to pray God would change me through the inconvenience and uncertainty, forming something beautiful and valuable.

Then, what might repentance look like for you? Are you clutching any idols? Do you need to bring your emotions under Jesus' lordship? Your anger, disappointment, fear?

Lastly, can you rejoice in God's promised restoration? Let's be expectant for how God will turn our pain to pearls.

Free to ask yourself:

**These questions are drawn from themes
covered over the past five days.**

- We noted that *Yahweh is God* and *With My people* might be considered three-word sermons. Can you come up with a three-word sermon of your own, which is lending you courage or peace or perseverance in your current circumstances?

- Where do you see ruin in your country or community?

- Where have you seen repentance leading directly to restoration, in your own life or the life of someone close to you?

- Where have you seen pain (or parasites) turned to pearls? Do you know someone who has gone through an agonizing trial or trauma, only for God to ultimately transform the experience into something splendid?

FREE TO FAIL

Free to ask God:

ALMIGHTY GOD,

I'm so grateful for Your kindness, compassion, mercy, and love, all of which draw me to repentance, so my relationship with You and others can be restored. Please keep my heart soft towards Your nudging and prompting. You see the wreckage of my life. Please flood me with Your light, so Your glory might radiate from my roofless buildings and broken walls.

AMEN.

You're being watched

Then Jacob prayed, 'O God of my grandfather Abraham, and God
of my father, Isaac – O Lord, You told me, 'Return to your own land
and to your relatives.' And You promised me, 'I will treat you kindly.'
Genesis 32:9, NLT

Jacob cheats his brother Esau out of his birthright – a *very* big deal –
and their mom, Rebekah, tells Jacob to run away and save himself.
He works for Laban and marries Leah and Rachel. Then God tells him
to return to his homeland and make right with Esau. Jacob is terrified.
He reckons Esau's going to kill him. He even sends gifts ahead of him
to placate Esau, whom he's convinced must be furious.

The day of reckoning arrives. The two brothers approach one another.
Jacob introduces his family, including his favorite son, Joseph. Joseph
is young, but he witnesses his uncle, Esau, running to meet his father,
Jacob. Esau flings his arms around Jacob and forgives him. I've never
thought of Esau as a hero. I've always just thought of him as the hairy
one, who gets tricked. But a hero he most certainly is. Decades later,
Joseph would be called upon to forgive *his* brothers too, the way he'd
seen his uncle forgiving his father.

No human life is without failure. But what sets us apart as God-
honoring people of integrity is our willingness – our *freedom* – to
admit our failings and to seek reconciliation with those who have
been affected by our sin or lack of good judgment. We never know
which future leaders and world-changers may be watching our lives,
learning humility in the face of their hurts and failures too.

Take the high road

'Please, come closer,' he said to them. So they came closer.
And he said again, 'I am Joseph, your brother, whom you
sold into slavery in Egypt. But don't be upset, and don't be
angry with yourselves for selling me to this place. It was God
who sent me here ahead of you to preserve your lives.'
Genesis 45:4-5, NLT

FREE TO FAIL

We read yesterday that Joseph witnesses his uncle forgiving his father. Years later, Joseph is all grown up. He's in Egypt because his brothers did a terrible thing to him. Famine strikes. His brothers arrive, hungry and desperate, and Joseph says, 'Guys, it's me.' They're shocked and afraid, but Joseph forgives them, saying, 'You intended to harm me, but God intended it all for good.' (Genesis 50:20) Perhaps he's able to do this because as a young boy he had a remarkable example of what repentance and forgiveness looked like.

And the rest is history. Joseph's brothers settle in Egypt and become a great nation – which becomes a threat to Egypt and so they're enslaved. God raises up Moses to lead them to the Promised Land, where the Messiah would one day be born.

Judah was a recipient of Joseph's forgiveness, that day in Egypt. As governor, Joseph could've had them killed, which would've put an end to Judah's line and meant no King David, and no King Jesus. Joseph might've chosen resentment – cancelled a nation and the Messianic line – if decades earlier Esau had said to Jacob, 'You're dead to me.' (Drop mic.) Neither Esau nor Joseph could've known that humanity's destiny hung in the balance when they chose the higher road. We're free to choose that road too.

Love never fails

Love is patient, love is kind. It does not envy, it does not boast, it is not proud. It does not dishonor others, it is not self-seeking, it is not easily angered, it keeps no record of wrongs. Love does not delight in evil but rejoices with the truth. It always protects, always trusts, always hopes, always perseveres. Love never fails. But where there are prophecies, they will cease; where there are tongues, they will be stilled; where there is knowledge, it will pass away ... And now these three remain: faith, hope and love. But the greatest of these is love.
1 Corinthians 13:4-8, 13, NIV

Paul assures us that *love never fails*. That means, *it always works*. We might fail. We *will* fail. But our love, when offered in purity and sincerity, hits the mark every time.

Love never fails, even if you can't see it working, even if it feels like your kindness or compassion has had zero effect, and even if it feels like trying to love someone actually *worsens* the vibe in a relationship. If God is to be believed – and He most certainly is – then we must take Him at His Word, which says, *love never fails.* Paul also tells us not to give up on doing good, because at just the right time we'll reap a harvest of blessing (Galatians 6:9). You don't know when your love will reach a tipping point that sends an avalanche of God's undeniable goodness into someone's heart, transforming their life.

Keep showing up to love. The power, presence and purposes of God are made manifest when we are His loving hands and feet at work in the world.

FREE TO FAIL

Mountain-moving God

*My health may fail, and my spirit may grow weak,
but God remains the strength of my heart; He is mine forever.*
Psalm 73:26, NLT

Ann Voskamp said, 'When your world feels rocked, it's because God's moving your mountain.' Perhaps your failure in a particular arena of life has left you shaken. You don't feel like you can trust yourself, or the ground beneath your feet. Perhaps you've been shaken by the earth tremors caused by the failure of someone close to you. Those are real experiences – the result of lives lived in a broken world. We let ourselves down. We let others down. Others let us down.

But don't lose heart. God is guarding your faith. He's strong enough to hold your failures and disappointments, and those of others. Paul owns this truth, telling us, 'So now I am glad to boast about my weaknesses, so that the power of Christ can work through me.' (2 Corinthians 12:9) Also, our failure sometimes exposes the parts of our lives we need to surrender more intentionally to God. He shows up our weaknesses to show us our desperate need for Him and His intervention. Sometimes, there's a mountain to move and nothing short of an earthquake will do it.

Praise God for the times when He sees fit to put the wind at your back, giving you temporary, earthly success. Praise God for the times when things don't go your way, giving you temporary, earthly failure or setback. He uses both to chisel away at your character until the resemblance between you and Jesus is remarkable.

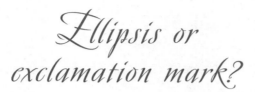

Ellipsis or exclamation mark?

*I have fought the good fight, I have finished
the race, and I have remained faithful.*
2 Timothy 4:7, NLT

Paul is referring to the end of his life and ministry, in this verse, and not just the end of a year. An yet it's a helpful principle to apply as we head towards another full, frenetic turn around the sun, as we resolve to finish strong.

Typically, at this time of the year, we all start winding down... We embody the slow fade of an ellipsis. *Dot-dot-dot* ... We find ourselves attending farewells and end-of-year functions and early Christmas parties and there are still dozens of life's loose strings to tie up but we're tired, so we're tempted to say, 'Oh well, let's just finish already ...' *Dot-dot-dot*. The end.

Let's trust God to give us a different kind of year-end this year. Let's trust Him for renewed strength – the kind of energy and tenacity you see in the last ten minutes of every football movie you've ever seen, when the underdogs decide to leave it all on the pitch, and they come off the field bruised, battered, exhausted, and dirty – but grateful and victorious. No matter how this year has been for you, God can redeem anything – even this late in the year. With the end of the year on the horizon, let's look to Jesus, and finish strong. Because if we head into the final month of the year, and Christmas, seeing Jesus clearly, we can finish the year less like the vague, petering out of an ellipsis... And more like exclamation marks! Brave, enthusiastic, happy, uncomplicated – and free to rest.

Free to ask yourself:

**These questions are drawn from themes
covered over the past five days.**

- Is there a person in your life who has shown you undeserved mercy, grace, and forgiveness? Does he or she know how grateful you are?

- If you've failed at something this year, what did you learn from that failure?

- What has shaken the ground beneath your feet, this year? Can you trace how God is moving your mountain?

- Read Philippians 3:13. Is there one thing you could start doing today, that would influence how you finish this year?

Free to write it out:

Reflect on the year so far. What has disappointed you?
What are you grateful for? What worked out
differently from what you'd pictured? Write down
your hopes for how you'd like to finish this year.

_____

_____

_____

_____

_____

_____

_____

_____

_____

_____

_____

I can see clearly now

For the law was given through Moses,
but grace and truth came through Jesus Christ.
John 1:17, NKJV

My husband, Murray, is an optometrist. A patient stormed into his practice once complaining aggressively about her contact lenses. They'd 'stopped working'. Murray tried to calm her and ushered her into his room, thinking something must've gone horribly wrong with one of her eyes because contact lenses don't suddenly stop working – when you were seeing just fine with them, yesterday.

Turns out, the patient was wearing two lenses in one eye and no lens in the other. She wasn't lying when she said she really couldn't see much. (The craziest thing? She had *driven* herself to the practice.)

As humans, we do this. We focus too much on one thing, and it skews everything else. Like, we should be wearing a truth lens in one eye and a grace lens in the other. Instead, we wear two grace lenses in one eye with no truth whatsoever which blurs the lines, distorting our view of a Holy God. Or we wear two truth lenses with zero prescription for grace and that makes us see everything in the straight lines of law and religion. Frighteningly, though our vision is shocking and we're a danger to everyone around us, we still think we can drive our businesses, ministries, families, and friendships.

When our vision is clouded, we take hold of the wrong things. Let's choose to do for our spiritual vision what many choose to do for their physical vision, come the end of a year. Let's gear up towards a strong, eyes-wide-open year-end. Let's choose to see Jesus clearly and accurately, to finish strong.

End-of-year reality check

Some were jeered at, and their backs were cut open
with whips. Others were chained in prisons. Some died
by stoning, some were sawed in half, and others were killed
with the sword. Some went about wearing skins of sheep
and goats, destitute and oppressed and mistreated.
Hebrews 11:36-37, NLT

In Hebrews 11, the writer gives us a kind of executive summary of Old Testament faith heroes (Abel, Enoch, Noah, Abraham, Isaac, Jacob, Sarah, Joseph, Moses' parents, Moses himself, Rahab, and on it goes), recounting how some faith-filled folks were gruesomely tortured.

Imagine time warps were really a thing and you got to have a conversation with one of these heroes. Imagine she says to you, 'So, how's your week been?' You say, 'Insane! We're in the middle of work appraisals. I'm hosting Thanksgiving for the *entire* family in a couple weeks. Plus, I was late for work this morning because the barista spilt my coffee and I had to wait for a refill. I mean, can I just catch a break somewhere?' The faith hero replies, 'Wow, I'm sorry. That's rough. My husband was sawn in half last week for professing Jesus.'

I'm not making light of martyrdom. It's just that it's time for a reality check. All these Hebrews 11 heroes pleased God because of their focused, unwavering faith. And they were looking *ahead* – putting their faith in the Messiah still to come. Mercifully, we're on the other side of that moment in history when Jesus broke into the darkness with blazing light. We're free to *know* that Messiah, and the abundant life He came to bring. Let's end this year with less complaining. More perspective.

Take a look. Get a grip.

Therefore, since we are surrounded by such a huge crowd of witnesses to the life of faith, let us strip off every weight that slows us down, especially the sin that so easily trips us up. And let us run with endurance the race God has set before us. We do this by keeping our eyes on Jesus, the champion who initiates and perfects our faith.

Hebrews 12:1-2, NLT

Hebrews 12 gives us straightforward advice on how to finish strong – whether we're finishing a year, or a life.

Firstly, verse 2 tells us we're to keep our eyes on Jesus. We can draw courage and inspiration from the truth that, 'Because of the joy awaiting Him, He endured the cross, disregarding its shame. Now He is seated in the place of honor beside God's throne.' (Hebrews 12:2) The writer of Hebrews reminds us we haven't endured anything close to the pain and hostility Jesus went through (Hebrews 12:3-4). He goes on to encourage us that God disciplines us only because He's an unimaginably loving Father. What an honor, to have captured God's attention. What a privilege that He sees fit to treat us like His children (Hebrews 12:5-11).

The writer's second appeal for us to finish strong comes in Hebrews 12:12-13: 'So take a new grip with your tired hands and strengthen your weak knees. Mark out a straight path for your feet so that those who are weak and lame will not fall but become strong.' As we look to Jesus, we're to get a grip, remembering who we are, whose we are, and how much we've been blessed and equipped to live the life we're called to.

Light and balance

Jesus spoke to the people once more and said, 'I am the
light of the world. If you follow Me, you won't have to walk in
darkness, because you will have the light that leads to life.'
John 8:12, NLT

We saw in Hebrews 12:2 that we're to keep our eyes on Jesus. This begs the question: *What happens when we do?*

If you get dressed in the dark, it generally doesn't go well. But flick a light switch and suddenly you can *see* you've put your shirt on inside out. With the lights on, you make better decisions. In John 8:12, Jesus calls Himself the light of the world. He says, 'If you follow Me? You won't have to walk in darkness because you'll have the light that leads to life.' If we keep our eyes on Jesus – the light of the world – we see ourselves more accurately. We see what we're doing more honestly. We see our sin for what it really is, and it's revolting. We also see ourselves as our Heavenly Father sees us, forgiven and free.

Our strength to stand is also directly related to our vision. Try this at home. Stand on one leg. If you focus on a particular spot in front of you, you'll be able to balance on one leg for a long time, probably, flamingo-style. Then close your eyes and stand on one leg. You might be able to do it, but it's harder.

Keeping our eyes open, and on Jesus, strengthens our knees and we can balance. Our aim is accurate. There's less chance of being blindsided by enemy-hurled missiles. We finish strong.

The big three

Do not love this world nor the things it offers you,
for when you love the world, you do not have the love of the Father
in you. For the world offers only a craving for physical pleasure, a
craving for everything we see, and pride in our achievements and
possessions. These are not from the Father, but are from this world.
1 John 2:15-16, NLT

We read yesterday that looking to Jesus results in us recognizing our own sinfulness – which feels like bad news, doesn't it? But again, the writer of Hebrews urges us: '...let us strip off every weight that slows us down, especially the sin that so easily trips us up. And let us run with endurance the race God has set before us. We do this by keeping our eyes on Jesus, the champion who initiates and perfects our faith.' (Hebrews 12:1-2)

It's lousy to see our own sin, but for our greater growth and good it's so necessary to recognize that most of our sin can be sorted into these three big categories: pleasure, possessions, and prestige. Another translation of 1 John 2:15-16 talks about 'the lust of the flesh (pleasure), the lust of the eyes (possessions), and the boastful pride of life (prestige).'

Would you be willing to ask Jesus to open your eyes, so that by His light you can see your sin for what it really is? Would you be willing to be honest with yourself? What's tripping you up? What's blinding you? What's making you lose your balance? Let's rest in God's grace, which isn't just pardon for our transgressions, but power for our transformation.

FREE TO REST

Free to ask yourself:

**These questions are drawn from themes
covered over the past five days.**

- Do you find yourself leaning more into grace at the expense of truth, or truth at the expense of grace? How would balancing these two elements of God's character – His holiness (truth) and His love (grace) – correct your perspective?

- Have you been feeling sorry for yourself lately, because of the stress you've endured? Does your situation look different when you view it in the light of Hebrews 11?

- What causes you to (metaphorically) lose your balance in life? How might walking in Jesus' light change your stability in that situation?

- Read 1 Timothy 6:9-11. How is Paul's warning to Timothy similar to the sentiments expressed by John in 1 John 2:15-16?

Free to ask God:

JESUS,

It's the end of the year and I'm tired, but I want to finish well, glorifying You! Give me clarity as I look to You. Strengthen my weak knees and help me to get a grip. Thank You that Your powerful mercy is free to me, and available fresh every day.

AMEN.

Free to be disciplined

And have you forgotten the encouraging words God
spoke to you as His children? He said, 'My child,
don't make light of the LORD's discipline, and don't give up
when He corrects you. For the LORD disciplines those
He loves, and He punishes each one He accepts as His child.'
Hebrews 12:5-6, NLT

We need never be scared to confess our sin to our Heavenly Father. We needn't be afraid of His discipline. We're His kids. I'm relieved and grateful – more than I am angry or surprised – when one of my boys comes to me to own up to some or other misdemeanor, because it means he wants to make right with me. When your kids step forward, knowing they will receive your parental discipline, they're leaning in – they're drawing closer to you. They wouldn't do that if they didn't love you and trust you and feel safe within your discipline.

We're safe within God's discipline. It's not God against us. It's God siding with us, against our sin. It's God going, 'I hate your sin. It breaks My heart because it separates Me from you. So, I'll pay for your sin. I'll put it on My account so that you won't be charged for it. Let Me come along side you. Let Me show you a better way to live.'

I'm praying we'd look to Jesus, to rightfully understand our sinfulness. I'm praying we'd look to Jesus, to rightfully understand how He sees us – which is, cleansed, and transformed from orphans and outsiders to children in His house.

Dark days

As for me, I look to the LORD for help. I wait confidently for God
to save me, and my God will certainly hear me. Do not gloat over me,
my enemies! For though I fall, I will rise again. Though I sit in darkness,
the LORD will be my light. I will be patient as the LORD punishes me,
for I have sinned against Him. But after that, He will take up
my case and give me justice for all I have suffered from my enemies.
The LORD will bring me into the light, and I will see His righteousness.
Micah 7:7-9, NLT

When the prophet Micah wrote these words, I think he may have been exhausted. A lot of people hated him. They hated his big, important, unpopular message about God. But although he's tired and disappointed, and he has good reason to be miserable, he's determined to look to God, get a grip, and finish strong.

It's possible, at this late stage in the year, that you're angry with God, or just exhausted and disappointed. You feel let down in some way. You're not interested in looking to Jesus. You're definitely not interested in seeing your sin. You're not even interested in seeing yourself the way God sees you.

If you close your eyes and turn from God? He still sees you. So, if you're mad at Him, please look at Him, and fight with Him. Wrestle with God. He knows you're mad, anyway. Also, wrestling requires grappling: close contact. You have to hang on to the person with whom you are wrestling. Get a grip on Jesus, even as you try to get a grip on life.

Free to wonder

Oh, how great are God's riches and wisdom
and knowledge! How impossible it is for us to understand
His decisions and His ways! For who can know the
Lord's thoughts? Who knows enough to give Him advice?
Romans 11:33-34, NLT

A kid I know was asked on a Geography test, 'What is a meteorologist?' She wrote, 'Someone who guesses the weather.' She wasn't too far off. Even the best weather prediction apps and instruments can't foretell the future. We don't know exactly which days in the next year the wind will blow or when it will rain or snow.

Only God is privy to that information in all its fullness because He creates and unleashes the weather, all over the world. God designed conception and pregnancy to keep the gender of a baby hidden in darkness until the big reveal of birth. I *totally* found out I was having boys, and there's nothing at all wrong with sonars and scans that give us a heads up on these things. But our desire to know things in advance really just reveals our need to think of ourselves as somehow in control. We equate being in the know, with being in charge.

Perhaps you're coming to the end of this year with more questions than answers. That's ok. God has designed life around unknowns, and He reveals the certainties we long for as and when He sees fit, for His glory and our good. It's ok to rest, today, in the truth that God knows the answer to every question you carry. He doesn't just predict your future. He's already present there.

Pleasure and purpose in the pause

So I say, let the Holy Spirit guide your lives. Then you won't be doing
what your sinful nature craves ... Since we are living by the Spirit,
let us follow the Spirit's leading in every part of our lives.
Galatians 5:16, 25, NLT

If you're someone who tends to *make* things happen (as opposed to someone who generally *lets* things happen), you've probably spent most of your life waiting. Waiting for God to answer prayer. Waiting for Mr. Right. Waiting for a friend to show up. Waiting for a job. Waiting for a baby. Waiting for a reply to that email. Waiting for an opportunity, or a dream to come true. Waiting for someone else to hurry up and get ready already because you were born ready. If that's *not* you? I'm pretty sure you know someone like this – your husband, sister, roommate?

It's agonizing to hear this when you're enduring the frustration of the wait, but maybe this time of the year can be the season of laying down your dreams once again. Slowing down. Keeping in step with the Holy Spirit and allowing Him to guide and direct every part of your life – in His way and in His time.

Far too often, I've overshot the mark, overplayed my hand, gotten ahead of myself, and made a fool of myself – instead of keeping pace with the presence of God. Put post-it notes on your fridge, your sink, your soul: *God is never late*. He takes pleasure over the pause because He's accomplishing His perfect purposes, in His perfect time, in you and through you.

Bird in the hand

'Are not two sparrows sold for a penny? Yet not one
of them will fall to the ground outside your Father's care.'
Matthew 10:29, NIV

If you're anxious or overwhelmed because you feel unseen or lost in
the crowd, please let this magnificent fact wash over you: there are
at least 50 billion individual wild birds in the world, and 1.6 billion of
them are sparrows. God knows about it every single time one of those
sparrows flaps its wings for the last time. You don't have to get into a
flap yourself about where you are right now. You needn't doubt for
a second that God knows about your problems, or your pain, or the
unspeakable complexity of your circumstances. He holds you in the
palm of His hand and you are so much more valuable than a sparrow
worth half a penny. God paid for you with His life, which makes you
priceless. Considering the cosmic lengths God went to, to win you to
Himself, He's not about to forget you, or overlook you, or lose track of
your life.

Not only does God know when birds fall from the sky, He also knows
their migratory patterns. He designed them with the phenomenal
instincts that carry them across oceans and lead them to roost in
the same eaves or trees every year. They find their way home across
continents and time zones. You can trust their wing-maker.

As this year winds down, and you look past Christmas to the horizon
of a new year, rest in God's care and in His knowledge of every detail
of your life.

Free to ask yourself:

**These questions are drawn from themes
covered over the past five days.**

- Has God disciplined you over the last few weeks? What was your response?

- What unknowns and uncertainties are you carrying? Do you believe God knows, and is certain about, your future?

- Do you tend to make things happen, or let things happen? What would it look like for you to trust God in the waiting, in the season you're in?

- Read Philippians 4:19. Are you lacking anything you need to survive today?

Free to write it out:

If you're angry with God – or disappointed or dissatisfied or confused – write out your specific gripes and longings. He's big enough to handle whatever you throw at Him. Use your words to grapple with the frustration you're harboring. Trust God to lead you to a place of surrender and peace.

Soul paralysis

And the Lord's healing power was strongly with Jesus.
Some men came carrying a paralyzed man on a sleeping mat.
They tried to take him inside to Jesus, but they couldn't reach
Him because of the crowd. So they went up to the roof and
took off some tiles. Then they lowered the sick man on his mat
down into the crowd, right in front of Jesus. Seeing their faith,
Jesus said to the man, 'Young man, your sins are forgiven.'
Luke 5:17-20, NLT

We looked at this passage back on Day 57, focusing on the faith of the paralyzed man's friends. But this story is also about how Jesus is more intent on healing your soul than your sickness. The paralyzed guy is desperate for physical healing. His mates go to great lengths to get him to Jesus, the Healer. But Jesus first says, 'I see your faith. You're forgiven.' He's far more concerned about setting the guy free from spiritual paralysis than physical paralysis. Like any good doctor, He's doing triage – determining the priority of the patient's treatments based on the severity of his condition, so He saves his soul before fixing his legs.

Jesus *physically* heals the paralyzed man, too, before His critics, the Pharisees. He heals him to prove His identity and authority – to prove He's powerful and loving enough to forgive, redeem, and save. He doesn't just heal to give the guy an easier life, although I'm sure his life got easier after this. He heals to make the reverberations of His glory tangible: the crowd is awestruck. May you, too, give awestruck thanks for God's work on the insides and the outsides of beautiful you.

Dinner with the Doctor

Later, as Jesus left the town, He saw a tax collector
named Levi sitting at his tax collector's booth. 'Follow Me
and be My disciple,' Jesus said to him. So Levi got up,
left everything, and followed Him. Later, Levi held a banquet in
his home with Jesus as the guest of honor. Many of Levi's fellow
tax collectors and other guests also ate with them. But the Pharisees
and their teachers of religious law complained bitterly to
Jesus' disciples, 'Why do you eat and drink with such scum?'
Jesus answered them, 'Healthy people don't need a doctor –
sick people do. I have come to call not those who think they are
righteous, but those who know they are sinners and need to repent.'
Luke 5:27-32, NLT

Straight after healing the paralyzed man who came in via the roof, Jesus leaves town, and meets Levi the tax collector (the guy who will later be called Matthew and will write one of the gospels). Jesus calls him. Levi calls his friends, and throws a party at his house, with Jesus as guest of honor. The Pharisees are back like a bad rash, and they've got a new accusation: 'Why do you eat and drink with such scum?' Jesus says, 'I didn't come for those who think they've got it all together. I came for those who know they're falling apart.'

At this dinner party of ill-repute, Jesus literally fleshes out the gospel the way Scott Sauls describes it: 'The gospel creates the environment for us to freely own that we are a) worse off than we ever dared to think, and simultaneously b) more loved than we ever dared to hope...'

Wrestle until you rest

... spitting on the man's eyes, He laid His hands on him
and asked, 'Can you see anything now?' The man looked around.
'Yes,' he said, 'I see people, but I can't see them very clearly.
They look like trees walking around.' Then Jesus placed His hands
on the man's eyes again, and his eyes were opened. His sight was
completely restored, and he could see everything clearly.

Mark 8:23-25, NLT

It's ok to ask, 'Who does God heal, and how?' Because maybe you've begged God for healing and there's been no healing. I get it. I'm the mom of a visually impaired kid who needs healing. Healing hasn't happened. So why are some people healed and others not?

On a particular day recorded in Luke 6, Jesus healed everyone (Luke 6:19). On another day, he healed just one man amongst many sick men (John 5:1-9). In John 9, Jesus meets a blind man. He's the same God who said, 'Let there be light!' He could've just said, 'See!' Instead, He spits on the ground – makes mud – tells the guy to wash in a particular pool – and he sees. In Mark 8, Jesus meets another blind guy whose friends beg Jesus to heal him. Again, Jesus makes mud, but the healing turns out to be a process that takes time. There's no mention of this blind man having any faith at all, and it's a relief to know that our faith doesn't give God His power. He heals to *bolster* our faith, more than *because* of it.

It's ok to wrestle, until you can rest, in the mysteries of our great Healer whose ways are beyond tracing out (Romans 11:33).

Live – and rest – by faith

For we live by faith, not by sight.
2 Corinthians 5:7, NIV

By faith, rest in this: when Jesus was on earth, sometimes He healed everyone. Sometimes He healed one man, or one woman. Sometimes He healed immediately. Sometimes it was a process. Sometimes part of the healing was sending someone on a journey. He healed by breaking bread. He healed from a distance. He healed with a touch. He healed when people touched Him – or even just touched the hem of His clothes.

Since His death and resurrection, Jesus continues to heal. He even heals people who don't believe in Him. He heals centerstage and He heals when no one's looking. And sometimes – oftentimes? – He lets brokenness run its course.

And because God invented decision-making, He doesn't owe us an explanation for His perfect decisions regarding when, who and how He heals. However, and whoever, God chooses to heal, we don't give Him His power. We dare not force God into our healing formulas. He will not fit. But take courage from the truth that you can keep knocking on the door of heaven, bringing before the throne of grace your every plea (Hebrews 4:16).

Take courage from the truth that God is your loving and generous and infinitely resourced Father. Take courage from the truth that He is at work all the time, whether you see it and feel it, or not. Take courage from the truth that He is the guardian of your faith and His right hand upholds you (Psalm 63:8). Take courage from the truth that you will be healed, if not in this life, then certainly in the next.

Subtle, sensational healing

When God's people are in need, be ready to help them.
Always be eager to practice hospitality.
Romans 12:13, NLT

Sometimes the faith-bolstering healing work of God is more subtle than the deaf hearing or the lame walking. Sometimes miracles happen in ways as powerful and as underrated as dropping off a meal for the overwhelmed parents of a colicky baby. You just don't know how God might use that gesture to bring not just practical help, but healing.

In Luke 5, when the Pharisees ask the disciples, 'Why are you eating and drinking with these people?' Jesus answers, 'Because they need a doctor.' He's eating with them because they need spiritual healing. The role of community and hospitality in healing can't be overstated. Jesus loved people in their homes around meals and we can imitate Him and love our cities and communities from around our dining room tables too. Also, there's so often a correlation between spiritual and physical health. Research shows that 95% of your serotonin is produced in your gastrointestinal tract. So, your digestive system doesn't just process food; it guides your emotions and there's some science to the idea that you are what you eat.

Let's take note: God created good food, to do us good. Jesus spent time healing people and eating with people. So much subtle but sublime healing happens at your kitchen table when you're in your slippers, people pitch up, and you pour tea. Maybe one thing you say, or one witnessed interaction with your family, shifts the trajectory of their thoughts just a couple degrees and they're never the same again. Make no mistake. That's a healing miracle.

Free to ask yourself:

**These questions are drawn from themes
covered over the past five days.**

- How have you experienced spiritual or emotional healing in your life?

- Has God ever healed you physically? How did the experience bolster your faith?

- Have you experienced healing or restoration on occasions when people have invited you into their home and loved on you?

- Read Hebrews 11:6 and Romans 1:17. How would you paraphrase these verses, to explain to someone what it means to live by faith?

Free to ask God:

LORD,

You're the ultimate Healer. I know nothing is too hard for You. I know Your power and love are both infinite. I bring You my desperate need for healing. Please don't withhold healing from me if healing will bring You glory. Strengthen my faith to trust that if You choose not to heal me right now, or ever, it's because You're writing an even better glory story with my life. Pour out Your sustaining grace on me.

AMEN.

House calls

The LORD nurses them when they are sick and restores them to health.
Psalm 41:3, NLT

Countless diseases and conditions can be treated effectively if caught early and prevented entirely through regular screening. Same-same spiritually. Jesus calls Himself our doctor, because He heals us, sick with sin. See your doctor. Early detection of sin in your life will save you so much pain. Prevention through regular screening will save you even more. Allow God's Word to x-ray your life.

Our son Cameron needs to see his optometrist regularly, to check that the pressure in his eyes isn't rising to a level that will damage the optic nerve. Wonderfully, his optometrist makes house calls – because his optometrist is also his dad. So, not only does he bring his optometric instruments to our house at night to test Cam's pressures, he lives with us. He sleeps over! And he tests the pressures again in the morning because sometimes the reading can be different, at different times of the day. Cameron eats supper with his optometrist every night. Plays soccer in the garden with him. Calls him dad and tells him all the stories from his day and the secrets of his heart.

I think my boy is so lucky because there have got to be very few visually impaired children on the planet who live with their primary eye care specialist. It's a picture of the gospel. Because Jesus our great Physician wants to make house calls. He wants to move in with us, where we can be at rest with Him. He wants to be the unseen guest at every meal, healing our homes with His presence and His peace.

Serve and spread the news

> After leaving the synagogue that day, Jesus went to Simon's home, where He found Simon's mother-in-law very sick with a high fever. 'Please heal her,' everyone begged. Standing at her bedside, He rebuked the fever, and it left her. And she got up at once and prepared a meal for them.
> Luke 4:38-39, NLT

Another way we might rest and revel in the healing power of Jesus is to internalize the truth that we're healed to serve God and others, and to spread the news of His grace.

In Luke 4, Jesus goes to Simon's house. Simon's mom-in-law is seriously ill, and those around her are distraught. Jesus heals her, and immediately she gets up and cooks for Him and the others in the house. Talk about *not* milking the moment and wallowing in a bit of attention and self-pity. She wastes no time. She reckons, 'I am good to go! Let me be useful.'

We see a similar thing in Levi (who becomes Matthew), in Luke 5. Jesus calls him, accepts him, and forgives him. And Levi responds to that mercy and love – that *spiritual* healing – by paying it forward to his friends. He hosts a dinner party. He serves. He doesn't just sit on his good fortune saying, 'Wow! Lucky me!' He intentionally spreads the news and spreads the love.

If God has seen fit to heal you – physically, emotionally, or spiritually – how are you channeling your gratitude and your energy? Whom can you encourage with the story of God's goodness to you? Who needs your practical help, or prayer? Don't delay. Serve and spread the news.

Victory

The righteous will see it and be amazed. They will laugh
and say, 'Look what happens to mighty warriors who do not trust
in God. They trust their wealth instead and grow more and more
bold in their wickedness.' But I am like an olive tree, thriving in
the house of God. I will always trust in God's unfailing love. I will
praise You forever, O God, for what You have done. I will trust
in Your good name in the presence of Your faithful people.
Psalm 52:6-9, NLT

Take a moment today to rest in the wondrous reality that one day, your rest will be uninterrupted. Evil will be defeated. Good will triumph. Peace will reign. Joy will be unending. Love will flood every dry valley. Paul said it this way: 'Yet what we suffer now is nothing compared to the glory He will reveal to us later.' (Romans 8:18)

In Psalm 53, David points out how evil people grow bolder in their acts of destruction and their love of wickedness. And yet despite the gross malevolence of their intent, God's people flourish under His protection and provision. Global unrest may have you downright terrified. The newsfeeds on your phone would suggest that evil is stronger than good. *But God.* Take a deep breath right now. Allow the Holy Spirit to fill you and comfort you as you stop your anxious wonderings and take hold of the truth that though the battle rages on, it's just the enemy's final, frustrated thrashing and lashing because victory already belongs to the Lord.

FREE TO REST

Rehearsing rest

*Before daybreak the next morning, Jesus got up
and went out to an isolated place to pray.*
Mark 1:35, NLT

The Greek word translated *isolated* in this verse wasn't a desolate wilderness where Jesus would feel weak and alone. It was a place of strength: a space where He could engage with God and be free from what John Mark Comer calls the 'heavy tyranny of others' opinions.'

Being free to rest – and stepping into the strength that results from rest – requires some ruthless intentionality around the spiritual practices of silence, solitude, simplicity, slowing down, and the sabbath. These habits can feel unachievable in our frenetic world, but it *is* possible to begin to practice them. You don't have to launch into a four-day silent retreat as your first foray into the world of these disciplines. Start small. That's why they're called *practices*. You'll get better and the practices will become easier, over time.

Starting small might look like trying just three deep breaths, once a day. Clear out one drawer. Go for a walk and sit on a park bench, alone, for five minutes. Switch off your phone for a couple of hours on the weekend. Even just these small incremental habits will begin to change the rhythm of your days as you practice being present to God, other people, your own soul, and all that a moment has to offer. As if you've been cast by God as Director, keep rehearsing the part of being a more rested person, bringing a more restful presence, to each moment you act out or inhabit.

Central Park

The Jesus said, 'Let's go off by ourselves to a quiet place and rest awhile.' He said this because there were so many people coming and going that Jesus and His apostles didn't even have time to eat.
Mark 6:31, NLT

Jon Acuff explains how, if you fly over New York City, you'll be struck by the expansive, tranquil green space that is Central Park – and by the high-density, concrete, urban squeeze all around it. You may be tempted to say, 'What don't they *build* on all that land? So many high-rise apartment blocks could fit there! New York could be home to thousands more people! What a waste of space in a tightly-packed city where real estate is so pricey!' But Jon explains that if you lose Central Park, *you lose New York.* You lose the life and soul and breathing space and sanity of one of the biggest, busiest cities on the planet. Leaving that green space just as it is, is what makes the rest of the city work. It's what makes the rest of the city a great place to live.

You need a Central Park of your own, in your life. Don't for a moment think you need to *build* on every free space, every extra hour in your schedule. Rather, you need to schedule the nothingness of rest and re-calibration. It's what puts the life and soul and space and sanity in your tightly packed life. Don't feel guilty. Your Central Park is what makes your life work, and worth living. It's what makes your life beautiful.

Free to ask yourself:

**These questions are drawn from themes
covered over the past five days.**

- If Jesus made a house call to you, tonight, what kind of healing would you ask Him for?

- Do you know someone who received physical healing, and turned that blessing into actively serving others? How have you been inspired to use your health to be useful to your community?

- What one five-minute activity (or lack of activity) could you institute this week, with the intention of building it into a habit, to practice resting?

- What's your Central Park? How are you fencing it in to make sure the urban sprawl of your life doesn't creep into it?

Free to write it out:

Our final few weeks' devotions are about being free to dream. Write down the dreams you're laying before God. What small hopes do you hold for Christmas? What goals and plans are forming for the new year or even the next ten years?

_____

_____

_____

_____

_____

_____

_____

_____

_____

_____

FREE TO DREAM

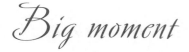

Big moment

Early the next morning Joshua and all the Israelites
left Acacia Grove and arrived at the banks of
the Jordan River, where they camped before crossing.
Joshua 3:1, NLT

I'm not sure where you find yourself right now, but the end of one year and the start of a new one can signify a big moment in our lives. Mostly, big moments are big because we'll only live them once, and because they can alter the trajectory of our lives.

The first few chapters of the book of Joshua detail a big moment for God's people. They cross over into the Promised Land and there's so much we can learn from how they lived that experience. To recap preceding events: Israel is enslaved in Egypt. God sends Moses to liberate them. God makes a covenant with Moses and His people at Mount Sinai. The people behave badly. Moses leads them through the wilderness. He dies. Joshua takes over. Israel is finally ready to enter the Promised Land. First, Joshua sends spies to check things out around Jericho. Rahab is an enemy of Israel, but she believes that God is God. She helps the spies. They promise to help her. The spies return saying, 'It's a go.' And Joshua reckons it's time to cross the Jordan.

In chapters 3 through 6 of Joshua, we see how God leads Joshua to five decisions as he takes the nation into the Promised Land. We'll look at each decision over the next five days, as we ready our hearts to dream. In the meantime, if you're on the cusp of a big moment? Begin to pray.

Consecrate

Joshua told the people, 'Consecrate yourselves,
for tomorrow the LORD will do amazing things among you.'
Joshua 3:5, NIV

The Israelites arrive on the banks of the Jordan. Three days later word is sent out that, when the time comes, the priests are going to carry the Ark of the Covenant across the river and the people are to follow them at a respectable distance. It's at this point that Joshua tells them to purify or consecrate themselves because God is going to do great wonders among them.

To consecrate something is to make it sacred, holy, or pure – to set something apart for a higher purpose. Here, it's the people themselves who need to be purified and set apart for a higher purpose. The reason? God is going to do amazing things among them. He's saying to them, 'Get ready. I'm up to something big.'

Even though Jesus has already consecrated you – declaring you to be blameless, pure, and set apart for a higher purpose – if you're on the brink of a big moment and you hope for God to do great wonders in your midst? *Come before Him and consecrate yourself.* Allow God to deal with your dirt. Too often we want to change the world, but we're unwilling for God to change us. Consecration is asking ourselves, 'Who do I need to forgive? What do I need to repent of?' Consecration means recognizing what Jesus has done for us and leaning into the higher purposes for which He has set us apart, understanding fully that His *higher* purposes for us mean we aim *lower*, because humility is always an invitation for God to do extraordinary things.

FREE TO DREAM

Cross

Today you will know that the living God is among you ...
The priests will carry the Ark of the LORD, the Lord of all the
earth. As soon as their feet touch the water, the flow of water
will be cut off upstream, and the river will stand up like a wall ...
Then all the people crossed over near the town of Jericho.
Joshua 3:10, 13, 16, NLT

The Israelites consecrate themselves, and God does great wonders. They miraculously cross the Jordan the same way they crossed the Red Sea. This is Joshua's second act.

I've crossed the (actual) Jordan, on a bridge, on a bicycle, as a tourist. And when I'm on the edge of big moments, I ask myself: 'Am I crossing *this* Jordan as a tourist, because I want to say I was there, and I took the selfies for Instagram? Or am I crossing as a traveler? On my own two feet, fully present to the moment, and willing to get the blisters of perseverance, commitment, sacrifice?' There wasn't a bridge or a bicycle in sight, for the Israelites. They walked across themselves, every one of them (Joshua 3:17).

In the same way, your relationship with God is *yours*. Your decision to 'cross over' by committing to God's purposes, is *yours* alone. And you're called to be so much more than a tourist. Right at the end of his life, Joshua addresses the Israelites for the last time, saying, 'But if you refuse to serve the Lord, then choose today whom you will serve. Would you prefer the gods your ancestors served ...? But as for me and my family, we will serve the LORD.' (Joshua 24:15)

FREE TO DREAM

Carry the story

In the future your children will ask, 'What do these stones mean?' Then you can tell them, 'This is where the Israelites crossed the Jordan on dry ground.' For the LORD your God dried up the river right before your eyes, and He kept it dry until you were all across, just as He did at the Red Sea ...
Joshua 4:21-23, NLT

Joshua's third decision is to instruct God's people to carry the story of how He came through for them. One man from each of Israel's twelve tribes takes a stone from the Jordan riverbed and they build a memorial, for generations to come.

If God has delivered you, don't miss the opportunity to convey the story into the future. We're culture carriers, for our children, and their children. We're culture carriers for the Kingdom. We're building culture all the time through our words and habits. We're creating culture in our families, churches, workplaces. And in big cultural moments we need to ask ourselves intentionally: 'What story do I want to tell my kids, my grandkids, about the choices I made and why I made them? What story do I want *them* to start telling? How can I live this story so that those coming after me will hear about how God took His glory?'

The psalmist writes, 'We will not hide these truths from our children; we will tell the next generation about the glorious deeds of the LORD, about His power and His mighty wonders ... So each generation should set its hope anew on God, not forgetting His glorious miracles and obeying His commands.' (Psalm 78:4, 7)

FREE TO DREAM

Covenant

At that time the LORD told Joshua, 'Make flint knives
and circumcise this second generation of Israelites.'
Joshua 5:2, NLT

J oshua's fourth decision was around the concept of covenant. All the men get circumcised, and the people celebrate the first Passover in the Promised Land.

Physical circumcision may not apply to us, but circumcision is a *cutting away*, right? Ask God to show you what you need to cut away from your life – what you need to sacrifice, to move into this next season and possess all He has for you. Maybe it's entitlement, or apathy, or addiction. Maybe it's fear of commitment, fear of loosening your grip and being generous. Maybe it's just sugar, or Netflix. You have an opportunity now to cut some things away – to leave behind things you don't need to take with you, going forward.

And then the people celebrate the Passover, to remember how God passed over the homes of the Hebrew slaves, rescued them from Egypt, and made a covenant with them. All that was a shadow of Jesus – a picture of the body and blood of the Lamb of God sacrificed for us, so we might be rescued from death and set free from slavery to sin. So, for us today, on the brink of big moments, re-establishing covenant feasts might look like us filling ourselves with Jesus – deciding we're all about the good news of His body broken for us, His blood shed for us. We're all about giving Jesus His rightful place in our lives and communities so He'll do things in us we can't do ourselves, and He'll take us places we can't take ourselves.

FREE TO DREAM

Free to ask yourself:

**These questions are drawn from themes
covered over the past five days.**

- John Eldridge defines consecration as, 'the fresh act of dedicating yourself – or your home, a relationship, a job, your sexuality, whatever needs God's grace – deliberately and intentionally to Jesus, bringing it fully into His kingdom and under His rule.' How is God challenging you to consecrate yourself in your current season?

- What's your Jordan? What would it take, to cross it?

- If you look back on this past year, what's the story of God's faithfulness you'd love to carry over to the next generation? Or, how might you start living a different story, from tomorrow, and into next week and next year, so that it's a Kingdom story you'd be excited to tell your kids, and grandkids, one day?

- Read 1 John 1:8-10 and Ephesians 4:22. What is God asking you to cut out of your life?

Free to ask God:

COVENANT-KEEPING GOD,

You held back the waters of the Jordan so Your people could cross over into the inheritance You'd prepared for them. I know You can do it again. Please purify me for Your purposes. Make me brave to cross over into all You have for me, so I'll have glory stories to tell of Your goodness.

AMEN.

Courage

> Joshua went up to him and demanded, 'Are you friend
> or foe?' 'Neither one,' he replied. 'I am the commander of
> the Lord's army.' At this, Joshua fell with his face to the ground
> in reverence. 'I am at your command,' Joshua said. 'What do
> you want your servant to do?' The commander of the Lord's
> army replied, 'Take off your sandals, for the place where
> you are standing is holy.' And Joshua did as he was told.
> Joshua 5:13-15, NLT

Joshua encounters this intimidating man who turns out to be the commander of heaven's army. Joshua asks whose side the guy is on, and he says, 'God's side.' This is God's battle and God's plan. Israel will spectate from the side lines. Joshua's response is to worship God, and then to muster the courage to explain to the people God's very unconventional battle plan (six days of quiet laps around Jericho, and then some shouting on day seven). But Joshua's courage to obey inspires courage in the people. They take God's presence with them – up against an impenetrable, walled city – and they walk it out because God has revealed that they're going to win by obedience, prayer, perseverance, and worship. And you know the story: God gives them Jericho (Joshua 6).

Life in the Promised Land represented a massive shift in worldview for God's people, which is why Joshua's fifth charge to them is to be courageous. Similarly, for us, when we're called upon to change gears and embrace newness, courage might look like us arming ourselves with obedience, prayer, perseverance, and worship, trusting God's unconventional battle plan, and taking the next right step into our impenetrable circumstances.

FREE TO DREAM

Free to sing

Mary responded, 'Oh, how my soul praises the Lord.'
Luke 1:46, NLT

You're useful to God and His Kingdom when you embrace your purpose. To which you say, 'Awesome. What's my purpose?' Mary's purpose was simply this, and your purpose is the same: to know God and make Him known. Of course, the specifics of how purpose plays out in each of our lives will be fantastically different. How you make God known – through your context, your character – will be different from anyone else in the world. But if you whittle down to the essentials what you do as an advocate, a Starbucks barista, a teacher, a mom, or a landscape architect, your purpose and my purpose is to know God and make Him known.

Steve Jobs used to ask, when talking to people about purpose, 'What makes your heart sing?' Mary's heart sang when she visited Elizabeth because she was in her sweet spot – that place of embracing her purpose: knowing God and making Him known. Elizabeth's baby leapt in her womb at Mary's greeting, and one commentator writes, 'That's all the confirmation Mary needs. She sees clearly a most remarkable thing about God: He is about to change the course of all human history; the most important three decades in all of time are about to begin. And where is God? Occupying Himself with two obscure, humble women – one old and barren, one young and virginal. And Mary is so moved by this vision of God, the lover of the lowly, that she breaks out in song...' You're in no way obscure to God. He's called you to know Him and make Him known. You're free to sing.

Surrendering to Scripture

Mary responded, 'I am the Lord's servant.
May everything you have said about me come true.'
Luke 1:38, NLT

This is Mary's response when Gabriel tells her she's going to conceive the Messiah. Was she overwhelmed, terrified, excited, confused? Probably, and simultaneously. But she accepted what God was doing because she trusted Him. She trusted Him because she knew Him. She knew Him because she had spent time with Him. And the place where she spent all that time was Scripture.

For Mary (and for us today) knowing God is synonymous with knowing Scripture. She sings, 'For He made this promise to Abraham ...' (Luke 1:55). She knew about the Messianic prophecy in Genesis 12:3 where God says to Abraham, 'All the families on earth will be blessed through you.' Mary's song also mirrors Hannah's prayer in 1 Samuel 2 – a mom's grateful unleashing of praise. Mary is so steeped in Scripture it just flows from her.

In Luke 2, Mary goes into labor, angels sing, shepherds arrive, and Luke writes, 'Mary treasured up all these things and pondered them in her heart.' (Luke 2:19) It suggests that if Mary ever heard Mark Lowry's song *Mary, Did You Know?* in which he asks, 'Mary did you that your baby boy is Lord of all creation?' and other such questions, her answer may well have been, 'Actually, yes. I did know.' I'm not sure she fully grasped the cosmic, infinite realities playing out within the confines of her very finite life, because not one of us can wrap our heads around the mysteries of God. But perhaps it was enough that she simply knew and trusted God. It's enough for us too.

Dreaming despite desperation

Near the cross of Jesus stood His mother ...
John 19:25, NIV

An unmarried pregnant teenager, Mary inevitably faced tremendous scandal and humiliation. And think of Joseph's mates, hanging out and having a laugh: 'Hey guys, Joseph reckons he didn't sleep with his girlfriend. God got her pregnant! *Whatever*!' Mary and Joseph would have needed a robust theology of suffering to be able to withstand all that. And not just that. Ultimately, they would watch their son bleed out on a cross. Astoundingly, Mary's heart sang even though she probably understood that one day her heart would break. She chose to sing anyway because she knew God.

We saw yesterday that Mary knew God because she knew Scripture. And what her love of Scripture also gave her was strong spiritual muscle. I wonder if we aren't a bit flabby in this area because we live in a quick-fix, make-me-feel-good insta-culture. Perhaps, to let our lives sing – to prepare to embrace God's purpose for us in the world whatever that will look like – the most powerful and effective thing we can do is get to know God. Spend time with Him. When you come across attributes of God in your Bible, underline them. Use glitter pens if that's your thing. Make a list on your phone: *God is loving, wise, powerful, kind; He hates sin but He's completely merciful; He's infinite, just, unchanging* ... There are no shortcuts. Make an effort to develop what Tim Keller calls 'the hard-won habits of wisdom.' Get close to God – get to know Him more and more – so you can keep dreaming despite the desperation of your circumstances.

Down-to-earth dreaming

His mighty arm has done tremendous things! He has
scattered the proud and haughty ones. He has brought down
princes from their thrones and exalted the humble.
Luke 1:51-52, NLT

Mary's knowledge of and intimacy with God produced remarkable humility. Her humility didn't come from knowing all the facts about God or listening to all the podcasts about God. It came from knowing the person of God. Hopefully preaches, podcasts, Bible apps and devotionals like this one help us to get to know Jesus better. But it seems to me, as I watch the people I most admire, that it's knowing the *person* of Jesus Christ that humbles us. Because the more we discover of Him, the more our brains short circuit in their attempt to grasp His magnificence and we realize, more and more, how very small we are.

So, humility isn't looking down in self-deprecation. That's just another form of navel-gazing or narcissism. Humility always looks up and out: up to God, and out towards others. Mary didn't think too much of herself. She didn't think too little of herself. She just didn't think about herself much at all. She thought of God, and others. There's an energy and a cheerfulness about humility. Your humble friends are happy and uncomplicated, aren't they? The irony is that the people I most want to be like when I'm big are all very small because their lives constantly redirect people's attention to a massive God. They're content and grateful. They're just excited to do wonderful things for the Kingdom of God. And it's irresistible. It ushers in dream-come-true miracles.

FREE TO DREAM

Free to ask yourself:

**These questions are drawn from themes
covered over the past five days.**

- What makes your heart sing? Answer with the first thing that comes to mind.

- Are there a fistful of Bible passages that have brought you to a deeper, more real understanding of the person of Jesus?

- Is there a particular Scripture that saw you through the darkest night of your soul?

- Read Colossians 3:12, 1 Peter 5:5, and James 4:6-10. How does humility position you to step fully in God's purposes for you?

FREE TO DREAM

Free to write it out:

Mary's song of praise in Luke 1 is known as the Magnificat. Write out your own. Praise God for who you know Him to be. Write out your happy surrender to His ways of bringing you to know Him more and make Him known.

_____

_____

_____

_____

_____

_____

_____

_____

_____

_____

_____

Make Him known

Mary stayed with Elizabeth about three months
and then went back to her own home.
Luke 1:56, NLT

We've seen what it means for Mary to know God. But how does she make God known, and how do *we* make Him known?

Firstly, Mary speaks out about the greatness of God. People often say, 'Preach the gospel. If necessary, use words.' Our lives absolutely should speak loudly. But we do need to be ready, always, to explain our hope (1 Peter 3:15). You don't necessarily need to sing, like Mary does. It needn't be weird. Ask God to give you ways to weave His Name seamlessly and sincerely into conversations.

Secondly, Mary steps out. She stays with Elizabeth for the first trimester of her pregnancy. She's on the down low when no one can actually tell she's pregnant. And at the start of her second trimester, when pregnancy becomes more obvious, she heads back to her hometown where everyone knows her. She doesn't shy away from the stares and whispers, the disgrace and misunderstanding. Perhaps she's content in the truth that she's a daughter of a Heavenly Father who takes her shame and restores her dignity. And it seems that for Mary, to be known and understood by her Father is enough. She's unstuck, and ready to move confidently into God's plans. She knows God, and come what may, she's happy to make Him known.

Imagine the impact our lives would have on our families, communities, and cities if we more readily spoke out about the greatness of God, and if we more readily stepped out in fearless obedience.

Spirit in you

At the sound of Mary's greeting, Elizabeth's child leaped
within her, and Elizabeth was filled with the Holy Spirit.
Luke 1:41, NLT

When I was five months pregnant with my first child, I met Nelson Mandela. I was starstruck. I remember thinking, 'My unborn child is hearing the voice of this great man!' But I don't remember my baby jubilantly kicking my ribs.

Different story for John the Baptist, who is filled with the Holy Spirit even before his birth (Luke 1:15). A few days after Mary conceives Jesus, she hurries to see Elizabeth (Luke 1:39). Three days after conception, a baby is eight cells big. Unless you've had a visitation from the archangel, you don't even know you're pregnant. Mary walks into Elizabeth's house carrying the microscopic embryo of the hope of all the world. And at the sound of Mary's greeting, Elizabeth happily freaks out with, 'You're the Messiah's mom!' And baby John does an in-utero Karate kid maneuver of joy. He responds to the Spirit of Christ in Mary.

The truth is, no one's starstruck when they meet us, right? We're not Nelson Mandela. We're just our very real, very ordinary selves. And yet if we know Jesus, then there's something extraordinary inside us. He's given us His Holy Spirit and so we take His presence, His peace, and His power with us, wherever we go. Never underestimate that. Even if you're a new believer – even if Christ has only just been birthed in your heart – don't underestimate how God will use you to change the atmosphere of a room, an organization, a nation, the world. Be ready to make Him known.

FREE TO DREAM

O Christmas tree?

Accept other believers who are weak in faith, and don't
argue with them about what they think is right or wrong.
Romans 14:1, NLT

Part of what makes December a dreamy month for me is the spar-kling splendor of Christmas trees everywhere. Some people don't like Christmas trees, because they have their roots (ha ha) in pagan tradition. That said, there are plenty of things we talk about and sing about at Christmas that never really happened. Like, there was no drummer boy in Bethlehem. That's the gospel according to Boney M. Also, nowhere in Scripture are we told there were three wise men. They're simply referred to as 'magi from the East'. All we know for sure is that they brought three gifts, so over the centuries church tradition has cemented in our Christmas consciousness three kings. But there could have been two. There could have been eleven. Maybe they all just clubbed together for the gold, frankincense, and myrrh.

The essential Christmas truth is that Jesus Christ, the Son of God, came to earth wearing skin. He lived a sinless life, died a sinner's death, and was raised to life on the third day. He ascended into heaven. He reigns in glory. He will come again. We will be with Him forever.

Some non-essential Christmas ideas are that Christmas trees are twin-kling magnificence, or Christmas trees are pretentious paganism. No matter which camp you fall into, you won't lose your salvation over that difference of opinion. Let's get over ourselves and lovingly toler-ate and accept one another when it comes to neither-here-nor-there traditions because, thankfully, Christmas is not about us.

Unavoidable trees

A shoot will come up from the stump of Jesse;
from his roots a Branch will bear fruit.
Isaiah 11:1, NIV

Besides God and people, the Bible mentions trees more than any other living thing. There's a tree on the first page of Genesis, the Psalms, the New Testament, and on the last page of Revelation. Every significant event in the Bible is marked by a tree. One commentator writes: 'Whether it's the fall, the flood, or the overthrow of Pharoah, every major event in the Bible has a tree, branch, fruit, seed, or some part of a tree marking the spot.' And from the tree stump of Jesse's family, Isaiah tells us, would come Jesus, the true vine (John 15:1). God's wisdom is described as a tree of life, and apparently it's legit to be a tree-hugger because 'happy are those who hold her tightly.' (Proverbs 3:18) If we pursue the Bible's wisdom, we become like green-leafed, fruit-bearing trees planted by streams of water (Psalm 1 and Jeremiah 17).

You can't avoid Christmas trees at this time of year, because you have to buy your groceries somewhere. Even online, they will sparkle from your screen as you add items to your basket. But since all the trees of Scripture point to Jesus, and since the point of Christmas is Jesus too, then maybe, whether you love Christmas trees or not, you could let every lit-up tree you see remind you that God Almighty died on a tree because Adam and Eve ate from one. Let's allow the brilliant beauty of this special season to lift our grateful gaze to the Christ of Christmas.

FREE TO DREAM

Tree of life

Then the LORD God formed the man from the dust of the ground. He breathed the breath of life into the man's nostrils, and the man became a living person. Then the LORD God planted a garden in Eden in the east, and there He placed the man He had made. The LORD God made all sorts of trees grow up from the ground – trees that were beautiful and that produced delicious fruit. In the middle of the garden He placed the tree of life and the tree of the knowledge of good and evil.
Genesis 2:7-9, NLT

Matthew Sleeth writes, 'It's estimated that all the carbon, iron, calcium, and other elements necessary to make a human would cost $4.50 if ordered from a chemical supply house. The image of God forming Adam from the dust is not only poetic but also accurate: humans are dirt cheap. The value of a human, however, is not derived from the elements we're made of. We are jars of clay containing something priceless. It's the initial breath from God that makes the difference.'

A bronchogram of the human respiratory system is indistinguishable from the shape of a bare oak tree (Google it), almost as if we carry inside our dirt-cheap selves, by God's image in each of us, the tree of life. In Genesis 2, we're introduced to this tree of life, even as humanity is given moral agency through the tree of the knowledge of good and evil. Let's allow every Christmas tree to remind us of Jesus, our tree of life always present as an alternative to temptation. Let's find every excuse to celebrate our worth, forgiveness and freedom in Him.

FREE TO DREAM

Free to ask yourself:

These questions are drawn from themes covered over the past five days.

- What are your plans for the week ahead? Into which places and situations will you be taking God's Spirit?

- Do you love Christmas trees? Why or why not? Either way, could you channel your wonder or aversion into reminders to keep Christ at the crux of Christmas?

- Trees are planted all over the pages of Scripture. Which Bible story involving a tree, or trees, stands out most to you?

- Read Genesis 12:6, 18:1, 21:33 and 22:1-19, to trace some of the trees in Abraham's journey with God. (Interestingly, Abraham was the first human recorded to plant trees, and he did so as a declaration of faith.) How is God's faithfulness made manifest through these events?

FREE TO DREAM

Free to ask God:

CREATOR GOD,

You are the great gardener, growing trees and people for Your glory. Keep me mindful every day of Your glory in creation. Help me to live patiently, remembering that big trees grow slowly – but they give shade for generations to come.

AMEN.

FREE TO DREAM

Divine decoration

On each side of the river grew a tree of life,
bearing twelve crops of fruit, with a fresh crop each month.
The leaves were used for medicine to heal the nations.
Revelation 22:2, NLT

How stunning that a healing tree offers us hope in the last chapter of the Bible – and this hope echoes throughout Scripture. Matthew Sleeth writes, 'The reason so many people love trees is because we are created in God's image. God loves trees, and so should we. God put all these trees in the Bible for a reason. He had a world of symbols to choose from, but God decided to use trees to tell the gospel.' There's no space here to delve into every tree in Scripture but search up the trees involved in the lives of Noah, Moses, Isaac, Elijah, Zacchaeus, and others. Jesus said the Kingdom of heaven is like a tree. He spent His last moments of freedom before crucifixion in late-night prayer, in a garden of olive trees. At birth, Jesus was placed in a manger, made from a tree. He breathed His last on another tree. After His resurrection, Jesus was mistaken for a gardener except, it was no mistake. Adam was earth's original gardener, and Jesus is the new Adam who will redeem all of creation.

Paul describes Christians as branches grafted into Israel's tree trunk, with deep roots that help us stand when troubles come. And again, right at the end of Revelation, just before promising us He will come again soon, Jesus refers to Himself as the *root* and descendent of David. May every glittering, festive tree remind you of the hope we have in Christ.

FREE TO DREAM

The Christmas gospel

For a child is born to us, a son is given to us. The government
will rest on His shoulders. And He will be called: Wonderful
Counselor, Mighty God, Everlasting Father, Prince of Peace.
Isaiah 9:6, NLT

In this one verse, Isaiah gives us a beautiful theology of the Trinity. The Wonderful Counselor is with you right now – the Holy Spirit Jesus promised He would send to help and comfort you (John 14 and 16). Jesus called the Spirit the *parakletos*, meaning 'counselor'. And God's Son in human flesh – the Prince of Peace – was simultaneously Mighty God and Everlasting Father. God the baby was also God the Creator who makes trees grow. He knew which tree would be carved into His manger. He knew which tree would be fashioned into a boat He'd push away from the shore to preach to the crowds. He knew which tree He'd carry up that final hill.

The first verse in the Bible says, 'In the beginning God created the heavens and the earth.' (Genesis 1:1) The Hebrew for 'God created' is *Elohim bara. Elohim* is a plural noun. It's literally, 'Gods'. *Bara* is a singular verb. At first glance, then, the Bible opens with a grammar mistake. We see another such 'mistake' in Matthew 28:19. Jesus says, 'Go and make disciples of all nations, baptizing them in *the name* of the Father and of the Son and of the Holy Spirit.' All three persons in this verse share one name – Yahweh – because they are one being. It's the mystery of Christmas, echoed in the old hymn, 'Holy, holy, holy – Merciful and mighty – God in three persons, blessed Trinity.'

Festive prepositions

All right then, the Lord Himself will give you the sign.
Look! The virgin will conceive a child! She will give birth to a son
and will call Him Immanuel (which means 'God is with us').
Isaiah 7:14, NLT

A right understanding of our Everlasting Father rightly positions us to celebrate Jesus this Christmas Day. Just like we kiss *under* the mistletoe and put a star *on top* of the tree and so on, we'd do well to remember the prepositional truths of how we relate to God the Father. He's *for* us (Romans 8:31) and *with* us (Isaiah 7:14). He goes *ahead* of us (Deuteronomy 31:8). He hems us in *behind* and *before* (Psalm 139:5) and *underneath* us are the everlasting arms (Deuteronomy 33:27). That's not all. He's *in* us (2 Corinthians 4:7), and Zephaniah 3:17 reminds us He's *among* us, He sings *over* us, and He's right *beside* us (Psalm 16:8).

This Christmas, celebrate all the ways your Everlasting Father surrounds you, and positions you completely securely. You are carried and covered on every side. And actually, this is how we fight our battles, as the song goes. *It may look like I'm surrounded but I'm surrounded by You.* Your Everlasting Father stoops *down* to you. He lifts you *up*. And ultimately the message of Christmas is that He broke *through* darkness to bring His glorious light. And He did all this because, '... nothing can ever separate us from God's love. Neither death nor life, neither angels nor demons, neither our fears for today nor our worries about tomorrow – not even the powers of hell can separate us from God's love ...' (Romans 8:38-39)

Merry Christmas!

Do you want it?

One of the men lying there had been sick for thirty-eight years.
When Jesus saw him and knew he had been ill for a long time,
He asked him, 'Would you like to get well?'
John 5:5-6, NLT

You'll remember we met this guy in one of our earlier readings, when we looked at who and how Jesus heals. Amidst crowds of the sick and the dying, at the pool of Bethesda, Jesus healed just him. John notes that the man had been lame for thirty-eight years. Not thirty-two. Or forty-three. Or six. It's very random. Or is it? Because surely God is never, ever random, or capricious, even if His actions, from our narrow perspective, seem that way.

Incredibly, the Hebrew word for thirty-eight carries the idea of one's calling, life's work, or purpose. We see for example in Deuteronomy 2 that Israel finally entered into its calling after a delay of thirty-eight years.

It's also interesting that Jesus asks the lame man if he would *like* to get well. I wonder if perhaps He's asking him, 'Do you want to step into your calling – your life's work? Or do you want to keep on floundering about in sin?' Because in John 5:14 Jesus says to the man (who is now walking), 'Now you are well; so stop sinning, or something even worse may happen to you.' Jesus is definitely making a point. We can speculate, but perhaps the lesson we can take from this, if we're waiting for breakthrough or healing, is to search our hearts and ask ourselves if we'd like to get well: forgetting our selfish selves and stepping into all God has for us.

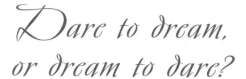

Dare to dream, or dream to dare?

And God is able to bless you abundantly,
so that in all things at all times, having all that
you need, you will abound in every good work.
2 Corinthians 9:8, NIV

The title of today's devotion sounds like the cheesy line of a motivational speaker. But cheese has its place. My prayer for you in these soft days between Christmas and New Year, when most of the world has briefly hit pause, is that God would awaken in your heart old dreams buried under cynicism, disappointment, or the pressures and busyness of life. May He also birth new dreams and a fresh vision of the possibilities ahead, so you'd walk into next year with expectation and energy. May you tie the loose strings of this past year into satisfying double-knots. And where live wires still spark and flash – exposed – may God insulate with forgiveness, peace, and goodwill to all. May you refuse to rehash your hurts, and instead rehearse God's promises. May He expand your capacity to hold heart-space for the things you'll never understand, even as you understand that He understands it all. If the locusts ate this past year? May God restore, refresh, renew, rejuvenate, regrow, and rework *all the things* for your good and His glory.

May you never postpone joy. May you celebrate even as you wait for the answers to come. May you be at peace with every person in your circle of influence, and at peace as far as it depends on you with every person in your circle of concern. May you be fully present – insightful and discerning – in every moment. May you dare to dream, and dream to dare.

Blessed are the intentional

I keep my eyes always on the LORD.
With Him at my right hand, I will not be shaken.
Psalm 16:8, NIV

We're all kept afloat by the favor of our powerful, merciful, loving God. On our own we're nothing and can do nothing. Still, in His mercy, He's given us agency and will to execute our gifting and our get-up-and-go. And so, my prayer for you in these new-year-preparation days is that you'd look after your body and your brain, make good choices, and form helpful habits.

May you remember, in every area of your life, that small change adds up. And when your head hits the pillow each night, may your rest be deep and untroubled, because all your days rest in the God who never does.

May your daily meeting with God be delight, not duty. May your early-morning alarm roll out a red carpet into His presence. May you wake up hungry for truth, the whole truth, and nothing but the truth. So help you God.

May you be fun to live with: an uncomplicated, creative, kind human to all your other humans. May chores be your choice: a practical expression of love and happy worship.

May you trust God to lead and provide. May you climb the mountains you've been trying to carry. May you borrow Jesus' feelings for people who are hard to love. May you borrow His courage when you can't even deal. May God grow in you a bona fide humility and generosity as you throw your energy and efforts into seeing others go further. May you leverage your influence to make life better for the bitter, to the glory of God.

Let it go, pick it up

My son, give me your heart
and let your eyes delight in my ways ...
Proverbs 23:26, NIV

These are the words of a father to his son, yet they mirror how our Heavenly Father longs for us to surrender our hearts to Him – to let go. And He longs for us to front-footedly step into all He has for us – to pick it up.

So, my prayer for you today is that Jesus would fill in the gaps of your ignorance or insecurity. May He eradicate your fears and stitch closed gaping soul-wounds with threads of faith and hope. Where God has pruned your life, may it be a reminder that you're so much more than the sum of your achievements, possessions, or prestige. May you see how the cutting back has been making space for greater growth and the resurrection of dormant dreams. When you floss and find fresh wrinkles, may you remember you're a masterpiece: a poem God is writing and reciting, for the first time in human history.

For every decision, invitation, or opportunity, may you ask yourself: 'What would an extraordinary person do?' And may God grant you clarity and calm. May you run at each day with the resurrection power of your Redeemer, who lives. May you celebrate that there is no condemnation for those who are in Christ. You are free indeed. May you keep it simple, and travel light. May you walk with the wise and become wiser still. May you see the goodness of the Lord in the land of the living. May you know your best years are ahead, and your future is bright because God is there.

FREE TO DREAM

Free to write it out:

New Year's resolutions are great. Set some goals! But the truth is, habits form your character, and your character shapes your destiny. On the cusp of this calendar flip, spend some time brainstorming how you might build some helpful habits into your life this New Year. Think about what you could do to make achieving your habits as easy and obvious as possible. Think about whom you might ask to check in on you, and cheer for you along the way.

_____

_____

_____

_____

_____

_____

_____

_____

_____

Free to look them up:

The freedom that's ours in Jesus Christ can be found on every page of God's Word. Here's a list of some Bible verses about freedom.

Exodus 6:2-7
Psalm 23:1-6
Psalm 34:19
Psalm 79:9
Psalm 91:14-15
Psalm 97:10
Psalm 118:5
Psalm 119:45
Proverbs 22:7
Isaiah 40:31
Isaiah 58:6-7
Isaiah 61:1-11
Jeremiah 34:8-17
Ezekiel 46:17
Matthew 23:4
Luke 4:18-19
John 3:16-17
John 8:31-36
John 10:10
John 14:6
John 15:1-8
Acts 13:38-39
Acts 15:10
Acts 17:10-11
Acts 24:23
Romans 6:7-22
Romans 7:6

Romans 8:1-21
Romans 13:8-10
Romans 14:1-23
1 Corinthians 6:12-20
1 Corinthians 7:21-22
1 Corinthians 8:1-13
1 Corinthians 9:19
1 Corinthians 10:23-33
1 Corinthians 16:13
2 Corinthians 3:1-18
Galatians 2:4-20
Galatians 3:1-29
Galatians 4:3-9
Galatians 5:1-26
Ephesians 2:8
Ephesians 3:12
Ephesians 4:1-6
Philippians 4:4
Colossians 1:1-29
2 Timothy 1:7
Hebrews 2:14-15
Hebrews 9:15
James 1:25
James 2:12
1 Peter 1:1-25
1 Peter 2:16
2 Peter 2:9-19

FREE TO DREAM

Bible reading plan

If you would like to read the Bible through in a year,
here is a daily reading plan to help you achieve your goal.

Day 1	Gen. 1-3	**Day 37**	Exod. 34-36	**Day 73**	John 1-3
Day 2	Gen. 4-6	**Day 38**	Exod. 37-40	**Day 74**	John 4-6
Day 3	Gen. 7-9	**Day 39**	Mark 1-3	**Day 75**	John 7-9
Day 4	Gen. 10-12	**Day 40**	Mark 4-6	**Day 76**	John 10-12
Day 5	Gen. 13-15	**Day 41**	Mark 7-9	**Day 77**	John 13-15
Day 6	Gen. 16-18	**Day 42**	Mark 10-12	**Day 78**	John 16-18
Day 7	Gen. 19-21	**Day 43**	Mark 13-16	**Day 79**	John 19-21
Day 8	Gen. 22-24	**Day 44**	Lev. 1-3	**Day 80**	Deut. 1-3
Day 9	Gen. 25-27	**Day 45**	Lev. 4-6	**Day 81**	Deut. 4-6
Day 10	Gen. 28-30	**Day 46**	Lev. 7-9	**Day 82**	Deut. 7-9
Day 11	Gen. 31-33	**Day 47**	Lev. 10-12	**Day 83**	Deut. 10-12
Day 12	Gen. 34-36	**Day 48**	Lev. 13-15	**Day 84**	Deut. 13-15
Day 13	Gen. 37-39	**Day 49**	Lev. 16-18	**Day 85**	Deut. 16-18
Day 14	Gen. 40-42	**Day 50**	Lev. 19-21	**Day 86**	Deut. 19-21
Day 15	Gen. 43-45	**Day 51**	Lev. 22-24	**Day 87**	Deut. 22-24
Day 16	Gen. 46-50	**Day 52**	Lev. 25-27	**Day 88**	Deut. 25-27
Day 17	Matt. 1-3	**Day 53**	Luke 1-3	**Day 89**	Deut. 28-30
Day 18	Matt. 4-6	**Day 54**	Luke 4-6	**Day 90**	Deut. 31-34
Day 19	Matt. 7-9	**Day 55**	Luke 7-9	**Day 91**	Acts 1-3
Day 20	Matt. 10-12	**Day 56**	Luke 10-12	**Day 92**	Acts 4-6
Day 21	Matt. 13-15	**Day 57**	Luke 13-15	**Day 93**	Acts 7-9
Day 22	Matt. 16-18	**Day 58**	Luke 16-18	**Day 94**	Acts 10-12
Day 23	Matt. 19-21	**Day 59**	Luke 19-21	**Day 95**	Acts 13-15
Day 24	Matt. 22-24	**Day 60**	Luke 22-24	**Day 96**	Acts 16-18
Day 25	Matt. 25-28	**Day 61**	Num. 1-3	**Day 97**	Acts 19-21
Day 26	Exod. 1-3	**Day 62**	Num. 4-6	**Day 98**	Acts 22-24
Day 27	Exod. 4-6	**Day 63**	Num. 7-9	**Day 99**	Acts 25-28
Day 28	Exod. 7-9	**Day 64**	Num. 10-12	**Day 100**	Josh. 1-3
Day 29	Exod. 10-12	**Day 65**	Num. 13-15	**Day 101**	Josh. 4-6
Day 30	Exod. 13-15	**Day 66**	Num. 16-18	**Day 102**	Josh. 7-9
Day 31	Exod. 16-18	**Day 67**	Num. 19-21	**Day 103**	Josh. 10-12
Day 32	Exod. 19-21	**Day 68**	Num. 22-24	**Day 104**	Josh. 13-15
Day 33	Exod. 22-24	**Day 69**	Num. 25-27	**Day 105**	Josh. 16-18
Day 34	Exod. 25-27	**Day 70**	Num. 28-30	**Day 106**	Josh. 19-21
Day 35	Exod. 28-30	**Day 71**	Num. 31-33	**Day 107**	Josh. 22-24
Day 36	Exod. 31-33	**Day 72**	Num. 34-36	**Day 108**	Rom. 1-3

About the Author

Dalene Reyburn is a well-loved speaker and best-selling author. She shares truth, courage and hope at www.dalenereyburn.com and contributes to various online magazines and devotionals. She has a master's degree in Applied Language Studies.

Dalene and her family are proudly South African, currently living in England.